Religious Minorities in Iran

Eliz Sanasarian's book explores the political and ideological relationship between non-Muslim religious minorities in Iran and the state during the formative years of the Islamic Republic to the present day. Her analysis is based on a detailed examination of the history and experiences of the Armenians, Assyrians, Chaldeans, Jews, Zoroastrians, Bahais, and Iranian Christian converts, and describes how these communities have responded to state policies regarding minorities. Many of her findings are derived from personal interviews with members of these communities as well as careful analysis of primary documents. While the book is essentially an empirical study, it also highlights more general questions associated with exclusion and marginalization and the role of the state in defining these boundaries. This is an important and original book which will make a significant contribution to the literature on minorities.

Eliz Sanasarian is Associate Professor of Political Science at the University of Southern California. Her previous publications include *The Women's Rights Movement in Iran: Mutiny, Appeasement, and Repression from 1900 to Khomeini* (1982).

T0371462

Cambridge Middle East Studies 13

Cambridge Middle East Studies has been established to publish books on the nineteenth- and twentieth-century Middle East and North Africa. The aim of the series is to provide new and original interpretations of aspects of Middle Eastern societies and their histories. To achieve disciplinary diversity, books will be solicited from authors writing in a wide range of fields including history, sociology, anthropology, political science and political economy. The emphasis will be on producing books offering an original approach along theoretical and empirical lines. The series is intended for students and academics, but the more accessible and wide-ranging studies will also appeal to the interested general reader.

A list of books in the series can be found after the index.

Religious Minorities in Iran

Eliz Sanasarian
University of Southern California

CAMBRIDGE UNIVERSITY PRESS
Cambridge, New York, Melbourne, Madrid, Cape Town, Singapore, São Paulo

Cambridge University Press
The Edinburgh Building, Cambridge CB2 2RU, UK

Published in the United States of America by Cambridge University Press, New York

www.cambridge.org
Information on this title: www.cambridge.org/9780521770736

First published 2000
Reprinted 2002
This digitally printed first paperback version 2006

A catalogue record for this publication is available from the British Library

Library of Congress Cataloguing in Publication data
Sanasarian, Eliz.
    Religious minorities in Iran / Eliz Sanasarian.
      p.   cm. – (Cambridge Middle East studies 13)
    Includes bibliographical references and index.
    ISBN 0 521 77073 4 (hb)
    1. Religious minorities – Iran.   2. Religion and state – Iran.
    3. Religious tolerance – Iran.   4. Iran – Politics and
    government – 1979–1997.   5. Religion – Iran.   I. Title.   II. Series.
    BL2270S26   2000
    305.6′0955–dc21   99-32293 CIP

ISBN-13 978-0-521-77073-6 hardback
ISBN-10 0-521-77073-4 hardback

ISBN-13 978-0-521-02974-2 paperback
ISBN-10 0-521-02974-0 paperback

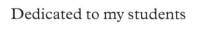

Dedicated to my students

It is not good to feel that one's own religion alone is true and all others are false. God is one only, and not two. Different people call on Him by different names: some as Allah, some as God, and others as Krishna, Siva, and Brahman . . . Opinions are but paths. Each religion is only a path leading to God, as rivers come from different directions and ultimately become one in the one ocean.

Sri Ramakrishna, *The Gospel of Sri Ramakrishna*, 8th edn. (1992), pp. 264–65.

Contents

Illustrations

Tables

Preface

The genesis of this book goes back to an incident at the University of California, Berkeley, in April 1986. I was lecturing on women's political participation in the Islamic Republic of Iran at the Center for Middle Eastern Studies when I noticed a young woman who was leaning against the door listening with great intensity. In the audience were three women in their fifties who were whispering uninterruptedly and were clearly disturbed by something. During the question-and-answer period, one of them expressed her displeasure with me. My comments had appeared to her as a defense of the Islamic government; she severely criticized the clerical regime and Ayatollah Khomeini. Seeing her difficulty in communicating in English, I asked her to speak in Persian; she refused. She was determined to prove to the audience that I was a backer of the Islamic forces in Iran. Her strong pro-monarchical sentiments were not lost on anyone; in those days facing this kind of misreading of one's talk was a common occurrence. I would have forgotten the incident except for what happened next.

When the lecture was over, the young woman who had been leaning against the door approached me. "Do you remember me?," she asked. I did not. "We entered Pahlavi [Shiraz] University together. We were classmates. Even then you were always with the Muslims. You never learn." I was intrigued. Later, surrounded by Iranian students, most with some leftist affiliation, we sat for coffee. Her anger burst out: "I read your book [referring to my first book on Iranian women]. What is this attraction you feel for these prejudiced people? Why should you as an Armenian write about them? Haven't they harmed and offended us enough?" Bewildered, I asked if she was an Armenian. "I am an Assyrian. For them, all of us are the same. We are those dirty Christians. I left Iran a long time ago determined to have no communication with Iranians. Then, today, I came to hear you, thinking perhaps things have changed. Maybe now that so many of the expatriates have experienced oppression at the hands of fundamentalists their biases have disappeared. Maybe those who have fled Khomeini are more civilized. But I was wrong; they will never change.

Never. Did you know what the three women said after your talk? They said it was all the fault of the good shah. He was so kind-hearted that he spoiled [rudad] our religious minorities. These Armenians, Jews, Zoroastrians, and Bahais conspired against him; they brought Khomeini to power. They destroyed our nation, and this one [referring to me] is a Khomeini agent. You see; they never change. Why aren't you as disgusted as I am?"

The brash young leftist idealists sitting around us were silent. I do not recall my response, but I do recall the feeling that she was not listening. I never saw or heard from her again but her words consumed me with curiosity. The ludicrous notion she attributed to the other women, that religious minorities were responsible for overthrowing the shah's regime and the founding of a Shii Muslim clerical-led state, raised many questions in my mind, eventually leading to the present work.

This book attempts to answer two questions: (1) what has been the overall policy of the theocratic Islamic state toward its non-Muslim religious minorities? And (2), how have the minorities dealt with state intrusion into their lives? Although there are small numbers of Hindus, Sikhs, Sabeans, and others in Iran, the focus of this investigation is on major non-Muslim religious minorities: Armenians, Assyrians, Chaldeans, Jews, Zoroastrians, Bahais, and Iranian Christian converts. Specifically, this study identifies the main ethnoreligious components, the history of official policy, possible variance in theocratic state policies, and the response of minorities.

The conceptual focus of the study is on the first decade of the Islamic Republic (1979–89); however, events and developments pertaining to 1989–98 are covered either in chapters or in the conclusion. The study focuses on 1979–89 for three main reasons: (1) state definition of Islamic ideology is the strongest during this time period and becomes more differentiated and obscured after Ayatollah Khomeini's death in 1989; (2) with some exceptions the legal, social, and political position of recognized non-Muslim minorities after going through a major upheaval in the early 1980s is routinized by the mid- to late 1980s; and (3) the fall of communism and the formation of post-Soviet states introduce new nuances which, along with domestic strife, further complicate the political scene. Of course, several developments in the 1990s are covered but only when they directly relate to the main points of the text.

It would have been easier but intellectually less challenging to focus only on one community and trace their trials and tribulations in greater detail. The designation "non-Muslim" had a special place in the belief structure of the Shii revolutionary ideologues, and no single community could shed light on the intensity and variance of the meaning and practice of state ideology. In addition, important differences in culture and history of the non-Muslim communities colored their varying reactions to state intrusion.

This study utilizes a variety of sources including personal interviews, primary sources, and documents obtained during a field trip to Iran in 1992, theological writings of religious leaders and various publications in Iran dealing with non-Muslim minority rights, thousands of pages of documents published by the government such as the proceedings of the Assembly of Experts and the Majlis, published interviews with leaders of religious minorities and Islamic authorities, and a myriad of media accounts of events verified in personal interviews by members and leaders of the non-Muslim communities. Periodicals published by non-Muslim minorities have also been used, albeit with caution, such as *Alik* (Wave) in Armenian, and *Cheesta* (Knowledge and Awareness) published by a Zoroastrian press in Persian. These publications have tried to introduce their communities' religion, tradition, and culture. They are message-givers to their communities and to the state, and also reflect the agenda preferences of editors or groups within religious minorities whom they represent.

The book first presents an overview of Iranian society and politics, explains the conceptual framework, and discusses the religious ideologues' views of non-Muslims. Chapter 1 introduces each main non-Muslim religious minority and explores the group's historical, social, and political segmentation from Muslim ethnic groups. Chapter 2 focuses on the drafting of the Islamic constitution and discussions held in the Assembly of Experts (Majlis-e Khebregan) in 1979. Accommodative and critical positions taken by deputies on the status of the non-Muslim population and the significance of the final outcome is analyzed. By focusing on four arenas of state–minority interaction – religion, education, communal life, and political representation – chapter 3 identifies several state policies vis-à-vis the Armenians, the Assyrians/Chaldeans, the Jews, and the Zoroastrians. Chapter 4 uses a psychological framework of ethnic conflict in order to explain the severity of the treatment of the Jews, the persecution of the Bahais, and the troubled Iranian converts to Christianity. Chapter 5 addresses minority responses to local governments and state policies. It distinguishes between similar and dissimilar responses, demonstrating that, in changing circumstances, marginal groups continue to act within the framework of a learned cultural tradition. In conclusion, this study takes on a larger issue: what are the perils of marginality in the Islamic Republic, and what is a fair assessment of marginality for an individual and a collectivity?

Acknowledgments

Completion of this book has been a lonely and painstaking process. The acute sensitivity of the subject, lack of sufficient resources, hesitancy and fear of the religious minorities, misinformation and false rumors emanating from Iranian officials and their opponents, my own personal affection for the religion of Islam (as distinct from outrageous acts which have been committed in its name throughout history), and a conscious effort to be fair to the country in which I was born contributed to a cautious and slow evolution of this work. Under these circumstances any assistance (major or minor) was deeply appreciated.

First, I would like to extend my gratitude to the countless members of religious minorities inside and outside Iran who confided in me, answered my questions, and provided me with documents and evidence. They cover a wide range of people and professions, from the poor wandering Bahai farmer who had lost all yet adamantly clung to his holy book, to children who recalled their experiences, to those leaders and community activists who welcomed me. All have asked to remain anonymous.

I am deeply grateful to Ervand Abrahamian, Shahrough Akhavi, and Houchang Chehabi for reading this manuscript in its entirety and offering helpful comments for improvement. Special thanks to Shahrough Akhavi for his meticulous conceptual and editorial work on this book. Thanks also to Lois Beck who read two chapters of the first draft. I appreciate the work of the anonymous reviewers for Cambridge University Press whose comments markedly enhanced the quality of the work. Marigold Acland, the Middle East Studies editor, deserves credit for patiently guiding this manuscript to its final destination. I would also like to thank Karen Anderson Howes for her inestimable help in editing this manuscript; her painstaking precision and care gave the book a new life.

I have benefited from the ideas and advice of the following people: Janet Afary, Aida Avanessian, George A. Bournoutian, Cosroe Chaqueri, Shirin Ebadi, Archbishop Yohannan Issayi, Edward Joseph, Mehrangiz

Kar, Firuz Kazemzadeh, Farhang Mehr, David Menashri, Eden Naby, Fariar Nikbakht, Floreeda Safiri, Nadera Shalhoub, and Sorour Soroudi. To all goes my whole-hearted gratitude. Of course, the perspectives and points of view expressed in this book are entirely my own.

Many individuals and institutions have aided my research: the National Spiritual Assembly of the Bahais of the United States; Iranian Christians International, Inc.; the California Zoroastrian Center; the Zoryan Institute for Contemporary Armenian Research and Documentation; Harvard University's Widener Library Middle East Collection, especially the librarians John Emerson, Alice Chucri Deyab, and their wonderful staff; Habib Ladjevardi for the use of the Iranian Oral History Collection; David Hirsch, Middle East bibliographer at the University of California, Los Angeles; and Janice Wood Hanks of the Von Kleinsmid Library at the University of Southern California (USC).

My research was funded by a small grant from USC's Faculty Research and Innovation Fund for 1988–89. I am indebted to former dean William Spitzer for his strong support and to former dean C. Sylvester Whitaker whose encouragement persuaded me not to give up on this project. Thanks to Michael Preston, a previous chair of my department, for granting me two administrative leaves to continue my work uninterrupted.

Most of the research on primary sources was undertaken as a visiting scholar at Harvard University Center for Middle Eastern Studies. The Ethnic Politics seminar organized by Karl W. Deutsch and Dov Ronen helped develop my ideas and the core framework for the book. My thanks to both of them, particularly Dov Ronen who offered me many fantastic ideas.

Although the bulk of the typing and technical work is my own, Jody Battles's typing of tables was invaluable. My students have been my true comrades-in-arms: Talin Der-Grigorian, Taline Ekmekjian, Andrea Kannike, Corinna Polk, Mikhael Reider, and Suren Stepanyan. I am deeply grateful for Avi Davidi's diligent and meticulous assistance and his dedication to this book; he was a godsend. My husband Sheldon Kamieniecki has read countless drafts of this book; I am indebted to his affectionate support. My sister Mary lovingly shared my trepidations on a daily basis and made this project her own. No words have yet been invented to express my indebtedness to the Yoga Center of California for teaching me that life flows from the innermost recesses of our soul. Without this knowledge I would have not survived the intense preten-tiousness, lack of principles, petty competition, and extreme hypocrisy permeating academic life.

During my visit to Iran in 1992, no one impressed me more than

Reverend Tateos Mikaelian. Courageously and openly he shared information with me, and I was convinced then that I had been on the right track all along. In the conclusion of our last meeting I invited him to visit me in United States; with a smile he replied: "I shall never leave this place." He was assassinated in 1994. Reverend, you live in my heart and this is for you.

Notes on transliteration and bibliography

All Persian, Armenian, and Arabic words have been translated parenthetically in the text. The transliteration adopted for Persian and Armenian words follows a simple system. All diacritical marks with a few exceptions have been omitted. The exceptions apply to quotations and published sources. After consultation of more than a dozen published works, it was clear that no unified system of transliteration for Persian words exists. Since this is a work in social sciences, therefore, every effort has been made to keep the transliteration clear and concise by preserving uniformity, applying the Persian pronunciation of words as often as possible, and maintaining the common usage of words. Discrepancies in transliteration may appear in cases such as the usage q or gh (q has been the norm here), or Abd-al-Baha instead of Abdol Baha, the version used for most such names. Translations are my own unless otherwise indicated.

The bibliography, as is customary, contains every work cited in the notes. However, since the articles from print and broadcast media sources are numerous and are fully cited in the notes, only a listing of the sources themselves appears in the bibliography.

Glossary

Ahl al-Dhimma	Protected People in Islamic communities
Ahl al-Ketab	People of the Book, referring to Jews, Christians, and Zoroastrians (in Iran)
ajam	non-Arab people
Dar al-Harb	the territory controlled by the non-Muslims where non-Islamic laws govern
Dar al-Islam	the territory where Muslim authorities are in charge and enforce Islamic laws
Ershad	guidance, direction; in this book, it refers to the Vezarat-e Farhang va Ershad-e Islami (the Ministry of Culture and Islamic Guidance)
faqih	an expert in fiqh, jurisprudent
ferqeh	sect
fiqh	Islamic jurisprudence
hadith	tradition, a saying attributed to the Prophet Mohammad
haram	religiously prohibited
hejab	Islamic headcover
jazieh	special tax paid by the non-Muslims to Muslim rulers
kafir	infidel, nonbeliever, non-Muslim
Majlis	Assembly or parliament; full form: Majlis-e Shoraye Islami, the Islamic Consultative Assembly
Majlis-e Khebregan	Assembly of Experts
Marja-e Taqlid	the highest rank among the Shii clergy, the Source of Emulation
millet	religious administration of the Ottoman Empire designed for the non-Muslim ethnoreligious communities giving them autonomy in religious affairs, certain administrative matters, and the judicial arena; this system predates Islam, but was

xviii

	given a religious coloring with the advent of Islam and the Ottomans designed it as an administrative model
najess	impure, unclean
nejasat	being impure, impurity
Pasdaran	Revolutionary Guards
qesas	retribution, law of retaliation, revenge for homicide
shariah	religious law of Islam
ulama	plural of alim, the learned men (clergy) of religious law of Islam
Velayat-e Faqih	"the government belongs to those who know Islamic jurisprudence," the rule of the supreme jurist or top theologian

Introduction: an overview of politics and society

Iranian modern history has exhibited constant fluctuation between extremes. Nationalism has turned into an intense anti-other diatribe and religious devotion has moved to bigotry. This study focuses on the relationship between the state and non-Muslim religious minorities (Armenians, Assyrians, Bahais, Chaldeans, Iranian Christian converts, Jews, and Zoroastrians) in order to explore the dynamics of this extremism and its impact. How far could an ideological state go in implementation? What form has this dogmatic impulse taken and to what end? And what has been the response of religious minorities?

This chapter explains the conceptual framework of the study, provides an introductory survey of Iranian politics in the twentieth century, offers a brief synopsis on the role of non-Muslims in Islam, presents the views of the non-Muslims held by the Shii revolutionary ideologues, and, finally, identifies several important issues in this research.

The study of ethnic groups (when relevant called minorities) reveals much theoretical unevenness. Researchers often entertain differing assumptions and conclusions. Case studies offer the most useful and elaborate frameworks, but they rarely seem to apply to other situations. And, as always, the nature of the case study has a direct bearing on its theoretical conclusions. Various dimensions of ethnicity appear too complicated and, at times, simply incomprehensible. Too many terminologies are used, frequently becoming mixed in an interlocking web of individual and disciplinary preferences. Yet this extensive literature remains intensely thought-provoking.

Defining groups

Most scholars have made a genuine attempt to be all-inclusive in identifying ethnic groups. Others have given up definitions and, instead, have moved on to the analysis of their behavior and actions.

Division of humanity was at the core of early definitions where people were separated along the lines of religion, race, language, culture, and nationality.[1] Many of these overlap, and gender and class divisions were not acknowledged. Schermerhorn's widely quoted definition of an ethnic group is a good example of an all-inclusive characterization:

a collectivity within a larger society having real or putative common ancestry, memories of a shared historical past, and a cultural focus on one or more symbolic elements defined as the epitome of their peoplehood. Examples of such symbolic elements are: kinship patterns, physical contiguity (as in localism or sectionalism), religious affiliation, language or dialect forms, tribal affiliation, nationality, phenotypical features, or any combination of these. A necessary accompaniment is some consciousness of kind among members of the group.[2]

Eight years later Richard Burkey made an addition to Schermerhorn's definition by differentiating between ethnicity and ethnic group. Ethnicity, he argued, was that diffuse sense of ancestry which formed the basis for membership in an ethnic group. Ethnicity, therefore, was a set of attitudes relative to individuals and, depending on circumstances, did not exclude religious differences or class conflict.[3]

This study does not indulge in definitions and differentiations between ethnicity, ethnic group, religious group, tribe, and nation. Any rigid distinction not only complicates the analysis, but also hampers understanding of the process of politicization in all these cases. Tribal, ethnic, racial, national, and religious entities can, for different reasons and under different circumstances, turn into unitary political actors. The only distinction relevant to this investigation is Muslim versus non-Muslim groups, each with further divisions. Details about their identity and relationship to the state are discussed in this chapter and the next. This study uses terms such as ethnonational, communal, ethnic, and tribal interchangeably. The term minority is reserved mainly for the non-Muslims since, in the contextual focus of this work, they are a clear numerical minority in Iran (barely 1 percent of the population). The word marginal is used mainly in reference to the non-Muslims, though the concluding chapter expands the meaning of marginality to the Muslims as well. For the purpose of this study, marginality is defined descriptively as being barely on the edge or border and existing "at the outer or lower limits."[4]

This inquiry concurs with Joseph Rothschild's assertion, influenced by Immanuel Wallerstein and Joseph Bram, that terms like ethnopolitics, ethnonationalism, ethnoregionalism, and ethnosecessionism are simply the analysis of "what happens when such entities bring their social, cultural, and economic interests, grievances, claims, anxieties, and aspirations into the political arena – the intrastate and/or the interstate arena."[5]

Conceptualizing this study

In the 1950s and 1960s political scientists began by emphasizing the formation of states, utilizing themes such as "nation building," "national integration," and "political development." Some were directly and consciously influenced by the historical developments in the West, while others were affected by the anti-colonial movements in the developing nations.[6] During the 1970s several scholars turned their attention solely to the study of ethnic conflict, aware perhaps of the presence of different realities in the Third World.[7] Often preoccupied with the search for an ideal polity, they devised specific themes to explain either the processes or the form of the polity.

The analytic sphere of "conflict regulation" or "conflict management" was one of the earlier developments in the field of ethnic politics. Instead of emphasizing the dynamics of the conflict, these studies explored recipes for regulating disputes. Often in a constructive spirit, they made prescriptions for the betterment of the political life of citizens.[8]

In most of these studies, the focal point was the "how to" technique of solving conflict.[9] At the heart of this perspective was the belief that ethnic uprisings can be stopped or controlled by measures carefully designed to achieve civil order in pluralist societies. Recipes included detailed discussions on structural changes, such as variations on federalism and regional autonomy. The scholarly mindset was deeply influenced by the American example – bargaining, compromise, and legal equality were revered. Crawford Young, for instance, suggested measures such as the recognition of the principle of equality for the individual and the collectivity, institutionalized access to authoritative allocation at the national level, and guaranteed security. But he warned against cultural oppression and coerced assimilation,[10] the most widely employed measures throughout the world.

The role and impact of modernization on ethnic politics was also of interest to specialists. It was discussed in combination with and in the context of conflict regulation, political development, assimilation, social mobility, and communication. Some argued that modernization could do away with separateness and bring about the merger of smaller groups into larger ones.[11] Others emphasized that modernization, in fact, has caused communal conflict. Samuel Huntington pointed to ethnic conflict in developed and developing nations and argued: "Modernization involves social mobilization; social mobilization generates communal identity and communal interaction; communal conflict and violence are the inevitable result."[12] Walker Connor dismissed the notion that modernization dissipates ethnic consciousness, and identified factors that had led to its increase.[13] Joseph Rothschild conceded that, while in some cases local loyalties may have been dissolved at the early stages of modernization, groups resist assimilation as modernization increases; they perceive it as a way to be absorbed by the dominant group.[14] In the early 1980s, Anthony Smith, a British sociologist, saw the emphasis on modernization as problematic, and argued that both sets of beliefs were in the "orbit of the liberal assumptions" and suggested merging culture and politics and viewing economics as a reinforcer of the two combined.[15]

Ethnic politics and Marxism have often crossed paths. Both Marx and Lenin recognized the potential of ethnic diversity as a force to sabotage class solidarity. Nationalist movements were scorned because they were perceived to be promoted by the middle class ultimately to serve their own needs, and those groups that fought mainly to retain their ethnic identity were viewed as socially and economically underdeveloped.[16] In fact, both perspectives suggested either a conspiracy or adherence to perpetual backwardness in the motivation of ethnic activists. In the Third World, socialism and nationalism were forced at times into coexistence; ideological rigidity was modified by political necessity. Scholars who clearly fall within the liberal paradigm have pointed to class without using the term with its dialectical and dogmatic connotation. References to economic inequality or scarcity, and uneven distribution of wealth are all in the province of class differences.

Class and politicized ethnicity have one important characteristic in common; both are identities that have been selected or interjected onto the individual or a collectivity. Dov Ronen saw both as manifestations of the quest for self-determination. He saw national, class, minority, non-European/racial, and ethnic self-determination as five manifestations of the individual's quest for her/his freedom. The activation of one or more of several identities resulted in a community of "us" versus "them." This, in turn, nurtured new perceptions of "them" and new identities were activated to confront others; therefore, successive quests for self-determination became an ongoing process.[17] He asserted that, whenever the government was perceived by individuals as an obstacle to the target of aspirations (freedom or goods), ethnic, national, or other identities were activated in order to bring about change.[18] This study relies upon Ronen's assertions in several places.

Numerous works do not embrace any one framework but combine several perspectives or are focused on one aspect of ethnic political dynamics.[19] What emerges from scholarship on ethnic politics is not so much faulty explanations, but simply a myriad of lenses, often colored by individualized assumptions and influenced by case studies. Most, however, are equipped with careful qualifiers. In combination, they provide a wide range of options (maybe too many options) and possibilities for future analysis.

The present volume deals with a unique case: a revolutionary self-declared Islamic theocracy and its dealings with very small but significant non-Muslim minorities. The subject defies the application of any one conceptual framework but combines several different approaches. The conceptual framework by necessity is eclectic; its focus is state–society relations where neither the state nor the society can be viewed as an organic whole. Two segments are identified: the overall state policy on religious minorities and the reaction of religious minorities to the state, which, in turn, may impact on policy prescription.

The state

Scholars are in agreement that the state plays a critical role in designing and implementing minority policy. In this study, the state is viewed as an administrative, legal, and coercive unit. Three levels of the state – state officials, state policies and institutions, and state ideology or definition of politics[20] – shape the outcome for the non-Muslim population.

State officials, agencies, and policies are placed in Milton Esman's framework by asking: what is it that the state elites want to achieve? What desired outcome is expected? In other words, what would they like to see? Goals determine policy design. Esman identified two distinct elite preferences. First, if the elite refused to accept or tolerate pluralism in society, they promoted homogenization or depluralization of society. The goal was to make everyone part of a collective whole and to do away with particularities. Assimilation either through coercion or "positive incentives" – by rewarding those who acculturate – was a method of enforcement of state policy. In extreme cases homogenization involved population transfers and killing (including genocide). Joining "the national mainstream" and abandoning the communal setting was an ongoing aim of the state elite.[21] This study suggests that the Pahlavi rulers' policy on ethnonationals and religious minorities was shaped by the goal to homogenize society and do away with diversity – to make everyone in an ethnic and religious minority into an "Iranian." Chapter 1 provides a historical introduction to the status of the non-Muslims during the pre-revolutionary era and demonstrates the contradictions inherent in desired outcomes for state elites.

If the state elites accept pluralism as an inevitable fact – "a permanent and legitimate reality" of society – Esman argues, their policy alters radically. In this second possible preference, they may coercively *exclude* certain minorities and "confer on one dominant ethnic segment a monopoly of political participation, economic opportunity, and cultural prestige." Or, as in most instances, the state officials may employ a policy of *subordination* where the state "generally offers the minority some rights, although they are inferior to the rights enjoyed by members of the dominant community."[22] Under the circumstances of subordination, a minority group may enjoy "freedom of enterprise" or even a higher per capita income than the majority, but it also experiences "significant state-sponsored discrimination" in other areas of life. The form and nature of discrimination may differ from one country and one minority to another.[23]

The Islamic Republic is embedded in this setting: from the beginning state officials were cognizant of ethnic and religious diversity in the country. In contrast to the Pahlavi state, the clerical-led regime has shown acceptance of the permanence of the pluralistic nature of society. It is an accepted practice for parliamentary deputies to introduce their provincial/ethnic identity during their speeches on the floor. (This would have been a betrayal of the "Iranianness" of the state under the previous regime.) Yet, as Esman's model suggests, acceptance does not preclude the use or the threat of use of coercion. The policy concerning constitutionally recognized non-Muslim minorities has differed from those non-Muslims not recognized in the constitution. Armenians, Assyrians, Jews, and Zoroastrians possess some valuable rights (e.g., voting for their own deputies, the right to assemble, and so forth), yet are excluded (overtly or covertly) from others and are, as will be shown, clearly a subordinated collectivity. The other two non-Muslim communities, the Bahais and the Christian converts, remain excluded. The state elites have been unanimously and venomously dismissive of both groups, targeting them for violence and persecution. In addition to coercion, the "effective control can be based on a wide range of political and economic mechanisms, institutional arrangements, legal frameworks, and sociocultural circumstances."[24] Chapters 2 and 3 explore the dynamics of policy and politics concerning religious minorities beginning with the debates on the Islamic constitution, then proceeding to the social, economic, and political mechanisms governing their lives.

In this study, the conceptualization of the role of the state is complicated by its revolutionary nature. The state is not settled and both the society and the state are experiencing rapid changes. The exhausting eight-year Iran–Iraq War (1980–88) and the refusal of autonomous and semi-autonomous actors to relinquish control additionally complicate the political and social scene. Further impacting on policy implementation has been the overall decentralized nature of the post-revolutionary state. If the state is disaggregated, as Joel Migdal suggests, into different parts from lower levels (including local and regional) to the commanding top leadership in the capital,[25] then the emerging differences in policy implementation can be easily understood. Disaggregation of the state shows that, despite a rigid ideology and some policy actions, implementation varies and the structure of society affects policy implementation.[26]

The third level of the state, state ideology, gives us a clearer picture of the dynamics behind state policy. The force of state ideology has caused the status of religious minorities to fluctuate between annihilation, exclusion, and perpetual submission. This study argues that contradictions have appeared more frequently at the first and second levels (state officials and state policy). Ideology (post-Khatami rhetoric notwithstanding) has been less conflictual and more consistent, and the main driving force of the state. The direct rule of the ulama (religious leaders) introduced a particular type of religio-cultural politics: the background of a significant number of the new revolutionaries was provincial; their defiance of the West and the Westernized elite was cloaked in "exotic mixtures of class rhetoric and religious scholasticism."[27] Ideology helps us understand the intensity of exclusion or submission of minorities. Through ideology the parameters of political action are defined, dominant and subordinate agendas set, and principles put into motion. State ideology tells us who is or is not entitled to membership in the polity and why. Esman refers to this aspect as "the image" that the state holds of a particular polity.[28] The beliefs and the mindset of the ulama are discussed here and their views reverberate throughout the book. To elaborate on the way in which "the image" of the minority polity translates into behavior, three components of perception, motivation, and action (from the psychology of ethnic conflict) inform the analysis of the role of prejudice, hate, and opportunism in the treatment of the Jews, Bahais, and Iranian Christian converts in chapter 4.

The response

Not all components of this study can be explained through the levels or the disaggregated parts of the state. Distinctions amongst minorities and their responses to the state are better examined through psychological and cultural dimensions of minority behavior. Fredrik Barth advances the concept of "ethnic boundary"; this boundary is social, cultural, and sometimes (but not in this case) territorial and always has a "continual expression and validation." It "canalizes social life – it entails a frequently quite complex organization of behaviour and social relations."[29] Changed circumstances impact on performance with the purpose of maintaining ethnic boundaries. The higher the level of insecurity and arbitrariness in the outside environment, the tighter the internal constraints become.[30]

Chapter 5 combines the unique cultural and religious "boundaries" of the recognized non-Muslim communities with a sociological typology on conformity to extrapolate similar and dissimilar reactions to state intrusion. In other words, the study addresses the questions of how the constitutionally recognized minorities have maintained their "boundaries," and how they have differed from each other in their responses based on internal social organization and cultural situation in society. Have the recognized non-Muslim minorities reacted as Esman's subordinated communities? Since they "possess some valuable rights, they are more inclined to express their discontents and aspirations by peaceful protest and political pressure."[31] The concluding chapter updates events and takes on a larger issue: what are the perils of marginality for the individual and the society, and, ultimately, what is the lesson?

Iran: an introduction

Pre-Islamic Persia was a multinational empire with Zoroastrianism as the dominant religion. The Arab invasion in the seventh century AD resulted in the spread of Islam. In the preceding centuries peoples of various Turkic and Mongol backgrounds settled in the area.

Contemporary Iran is a heterogeneous polity. The geographical setting and group characteristics have prompted a highly particularistic society where local loyalties and primordial ties remain strong. In a comparative study no *one* factor emerges as predominant in explaining the full nature of social diversity. The actual historical roots of ethnic, tribal, religious, communal, and national identities remain unexplored. Based on ethnic mythology, popular culture, and political exigency, there are different versions of the backgrounds of each group. One scholar suggests refraining from drawing boundaries around a single group, since tribal "identities are neither exclusive nor fixed." According to Lois Beck:

Tribal identity, as with ethnic and national identity, is an imagined identity based on continually revised conceptions of history and tradition in the context of contemporary circumstances. Identity is constructed. Tribal people in Iran invented and reinvented traditions according to changing sociopolitical conditions. Each tribal group was composed of people of diverse ethnolinguistic origins, yet each group forged its own customs and created legends of origins.[32]

Different titles have been used to identify these groups and their subdivisions. Communities have survived by mixing with others, by shifting loyalties, and by transforming themselves socially, culturally, and politically. Local particularism and settled or nomadic lifestyles affect the structure and the institutions of communities. As Richard Cottam observed: "There is only one safe generalization to be made about the tribes of Iran: that no generalization is valid."[33]

The total population of Iran in the mid-1980s was about 55 million, of which approximately 98 percent was Muslim (the Shii constituted about 93 percent, the Sunni 5 percent). The remaining population comprises Christians, Jews, Zoroastrians, Bahais, and others.[34] Although the population projection for the mid-1990s was 67 million, the total population was reported by government sources to be around 60 million.[35] The majority of the Sunni population resides in the Kurdestan, Sistan, and Baluchestan areas.[36]

Although the majority of the population is Shii, not all are ethnic Persians. In fact, if language is utilized as the main distinguishing feature of ethnicity, Persian, despite being the official language, is the mother tongue of barely half of the population of Iran. Other languages include Turkish, Kurdish, Baluchi, Luri, Arabic, Gilaki, Assyrian, and Armenian. Of the five dominant non-Muslim religious minorities, three, the Bahais, the Jews, and the Zoroastrians, have Persian as their mother tongue. Ethnically and linguistically, Turkic-speaking people (estimated at 14 million in the mid-1980s) are the largest minority in Iran.[37] But they are not a unified collectivity and are further divided along Shii–Sunni, subethnic, tribal, family, and local lines. Many Shii Turkic-speaking people (in particular the Azeris) have assimilated into the Persian milieu. In the 1990s the largest ethnic classifications are estimated as Persians (51 percent of the population), Azeris (24 percent), and Kurds (7 percent).[38] Table 1 provides a brief overview of politically significant ethnic/tribal/national groups in Iran: the Azeri, the Kurd, the Baluch, the Qashqai, the Bakhtiari, the Turkman, the Arab, the Shahsevan, and the Lur. Information about the population size of ethnic groups is scanty, unreliable, and difficult to obtain. Their cited population sizes are based on minimum and maximum numbers. It is safe to assume that, in line with a general increase in the overall population, there also has been an increase in the number of members of ethnonational groups.[39]

The ethnonational diversity of Iran raises the issue of the potential for secession. To clarify, in classifying potential ethnic groups with past claims to separatism, three groups stand out: the Kurds, the Baluch, and the Arabs. The first two are overwhelmingly Sunni, while the third has a majority of Shii.[40] Can one, therefore, conclude that the political threat of ethnic separatism is focused along Sunni–Shii lines? None deny that the Sunni minority has been well aware of its distinctiveness from the Shii. (This became clearer under the Islamic Republic.) History, however, shows that these three groups (along with other smaller ones) have never

Table 1. *Distinguishing features of Muslim ethnic groups*

Ethnic group	Estimated size	Religion	Language	Location	Extension across Iranian borders	Recorded major uprisings		Degree of assimilation
Arab	615,000– 2 million	Sunni and Shii	Arabic	Khuzestan province (southwestern part of Iran and near the Persian Gulf)	Iraq, Persian Gulf	1920–25:	united tribal uprising, separatist goals	degree of assimilation correlated with residence in Khuzestan; the more tribal the less assimilated; overall a mixed result
						1946:	a coalition of tribal chiefs asking for incorporation of Khuzestan into Iraq	
Azeri (Turks)	8.8–10 million	Shii	Turkic	Northwestern Iran, divided into two provinces of Western and Eastern Azerbaijan	Azerbaijan	1920:	the Khiabani Movement, nationalist-democratic and anti-imperialist	very high
						1945–46:	Democratic Republic of Azerbaijan established with Soviet help	
Bakhtiari	300,000– 1 million	Shii	Luri	Central-western region of Zagros mountains; spread mainly across four provinces of Khuzestan, Lurestan, Chaharmahal and Bakhtiari, Isfahan	None	1922, 1929:	both uprisings in response to Reza Shah's military and economic policies	very high
						1942–50:	no main demands, one leader's personal initiative	

	Population	Religion	Language	Location	Neighboring countries	Historical events	Mobilization
Baluch	500,000–1 million	Sunni	Baluchi	Province of Sistan and Baluchestan in eastern/southeastern part of Iran	Pakistan, southern Afghanistan, Persian Gulf, Turkmanestan	1928: Dost Mohammad's attempt to establish an independent principality; 1957–59: Dad Shah incident, began by killing of an American military aide and his wife, made up of a group of 24–50 individuals attacking government forces; 1969–73: Iraqi-assisted insurgency	low
Kurd	3–8 million	Majority are Sunni, significant number of Shii and adherents to the Sufi order	Kurdish (various dialects)	Province of Kurdestan and south of Western Azerbaijan; Shii concentrated in the Bakhtaran province	Iraq, Turkey, Syria, Armenia, Georgia, Azerbaijan	1919–22: the Simko Uprising attempted to establish an independent Kurdish republic; 1941–45: self-rule; 1945–46: the independent Mahabad Republic with Soviet help	low
Lur	300,000–580,000	Shii	Luri	Western province of Lurestan	None	Some Lurs have joined in with the Bakhtiari and Qashqai uprisings	high

Table 1 (*cont.*)

Ethnic group	Estimated size	Religion	Language	Location	Extension across Iranian borders	Recorded major uprisings	Degree of assimilation
Qashqai	800,000–1 million	Shii	Turkic	In southwestern province of Fars (in the Khuzestan province and the Persian Gulf coast), some in Isfahan province	None	1929, 1932: rebellions against Reza Shah's oppressive policies 1946: an uprising demanding reforms, trial of corrupt local officials, improvements in health, education, and roads, some local autonomy 1963: small-scale protests accompanied by non-Qashqais demanding reforms mid-1960s: small armed force led by two cousins raided police stations and in early 1970s joined the leftist forces in Kurdestan	moderate (limited assimilation with other ethnic/tribal groups such as Bakhtiari, Lur, and Boir Ahmad)

Shahsevan	310,000	Shii	Turkic	Northwestern Iran, spread from Eastern Azerbaijan province to districts between Zanjan and Tehran	None	1909: revolt against the Constitutionalist government (plundered the city of Ardabil) 1925: revolt against Reza Shah, chiefs defeated and executed by Reza Shah	highly settled and partially assimilated mainly within Azerbaijan
Turkman	1.1 million	Sunni	Turkic	Southeast section of the Caspian Sea in an area known as Turkman desert (Gorgan plains)	Turkmanestan and Afghanistan	1906–11: revolt against the Constitutionalists uprising against Reza Shah, carried out raids in the area 1925:	low (many have settled and become urbanized without becoming assimilated)

formed a united Sunni front against the Shii. To the contrary, each has been traditionally divided within itself.

Kurds, Baluch, and Arabs have another characteristic in common: they are border ethnic groups. All three have counterparts across the Iranian border; is this where the *potential* for ethnic separatism lies? But other crossborder groups, such as the Sunni Turkman (Turkmanestan Republic) and the Shii Azeris (Azerbaijan Republic), are not particularly separatist. Perhaps the only safe conclusion is that the border groups pose the strongest potential for separatism, which can be triggered by developments across the border. The readiness of an ethnic group to secede, however, is of vital importance. The Arabs have two options in their quest for separatism: to join with Iraq or to form an independent country. Will a large percentage of the Arab population of the south want to merge with a country led by Saddam Hossein? Will he allow an "independent" Arab state next door? The answers to both questions remain a firm negative considering that even Kuwait has had continuous problems with a host of successive Iraqi regimes. The Sunni–Shii division among the Arabs also militates against either option.

The Kurds and the Baluch demonstrate the highest potential for separatism. The fact that they are Sunni border ethnic groups is important, but other significant factors are also present: (1) their past history of political movements points to an unceasing quest for some type of independent statehood; (2) both ethnic groups, despite their intra-ethnic rivalry and their poverty, have shown strong crossborder connections and networks; (3) both groups possess large land areas and populations; and (4) their resistance to and lack of interest in Persianization has remained unchanged. All these issues are interconnected, making the Baluch and the Kurds, under the right circumstances, the two ethnic groups most likely to secede from Iran.

A brief survey of Iranian politics

The principal features of the relationship between the state and society and the non-Muslim minorities, each with its own unique characteristics, in the pre-1979 era are covered in the next chapter. Therefore, only a brief introductory survey is offered here.

Even in the eighteenth and the nineteenth centuries, the Iranian state had to cope with its hold over the provinces. The weakening of the center would easily lead to the weakening of the provincial authority.[41] In the twentieth century, the state's *intent* to alter the pluralistic milieu is easier to ascertain, however, than the nature of the state's *impact* in causing actual change.

Reza Shah is credited for strengthening and modernizing the Iranian state. During his reign (1925–41), widespread changes were militarily forced upon all segments of the population. New dress codes, mandatory teaching of the Persian language in schools, abolition of titles (such as mirza, amir, shaykh, khan), changes in place names (streets, towns, cities, provinces), and even the 1935 order to foreign governments to call the country Iran instead of Persia were all aimed at creating a unified (nation-) state.[42] These changes reflected the policy of linguistic de-ethnicizing of Iran by merging territorial entitlement with the Persianized monarchical center (e.g., Lurestan became Kermanshah, Arabestan became Khuzestan).[43] Tribal and rural communities were forced into compliance with the central government. To destroy ethnic cohesion, segments of ethnic groups were moved to other areas.[44] Sometimes the lands belonging to one family were given to another in the same ethnic grouping in order to weaken cohesion and to instigate intra-ethnic hostility.[45] Homogenization of society was the desired goal of the ruler. Collected taxes were channeled to the cities and used for building high-ways and for general improvements in transportation between the provinces and the center. Through a combined use of legislation and brute force, Reza Shah limited the authority of the ulama in social and political life, thereby increasing their antagonism to the monarchy.

Mohammad Reza Shah (r. 1941–79), like his father, emphasized Persian nationalism as state ideology and sought to modernize the country. His style was less forceful but more deliberate. During the early 1950s, the monarchy was seriously challenged by Prime Minister Mohammad Mossadeq. He objected to extensive foreign interests in Iran and eventually brought about the nationalization of the oil industry. The short period of Mossadeq's influence was accompanied by a weak central government and, in spite of him, it set in motion sporadic attacks against non-Muslims. The West was a target and so were non-Muslims. Mossadeq's removal restored the power of the central government. The shah combined modern state machinery to safeguard unity, control all segments of the population, and launch development. Oil profits allowed for a more deliberate minority policy. The affluence of the state empow-ered it to control and coopt those in the opposition, including ethnic and religious elites and many intellectuals (some of whom had once been pro-communist). Changes such as land reform and the nationalization of pas-tures further undercut the authority of tribal, ethnic, and religious segments.

Some have argued that, under Mohammad Reza Shah, the national educational system helped to undermine the citizens' diverse cultural values.[46] Teaching and publication in ethnic/national languages such as

Kurdish, Turkish, or Baluchi were forbidden. Although these groups continued to converse in their languages and dialects, it was hoped that the children would change their speech through their education in the public school system. All texts were in Persian and even in rural areas efforts toward literacy aimed at the youth followed a national uniform pattern. Learning Persian facilitated some change but did not result in widespread Persianization of youth. By the end of the Pahlavi reign, linguistic diversity had not vanished. In 1977 over half of all personnel of the armed forces were illiterate and many of the conscripts had come from areas dominated by non-Persian-speaking people.[47] The data coincide with the estimated illiteracy rate: by 1977 only 37 percent of the adult population was literate,[48] an apparent failure of the widely publicized literacy campaign. Despite changes brought by oil and a growing industrial sector and a middle class between 1965 and 1975, improvements in socioeconomic conditions such as literacy, life expectancy, and infant mortality were not impressive.[49]

The issue of integration of the non-Muslims in Iranian political life is discussed later. Educated Azeris, Kurds, and Qashqais backed Prime Minister Mossadeq, and some held prominent positions under his leadership.[50] Several Bakhtiari elite were close to the royal family and several Qashqais served as representatives in the Majlis. Some of the shah's leading commanders were of Kurdish (though mostly Shii) origin.[51] It is believed that the early promotion of one officer, General Rabii, by the shah was due to his Kurdish identity. As a Kurd, he was perceived by the shah as the least likely person to conspire with other officers against him.[52] Ethnic, national, and religious identities were meaningful to the rulers and were used to advance the state's cause.

The persuasive power of a wealthy authoritarian state, accompanied by an elaborate and much-feared intelligence network and financial rewards for those who cooperated, facilitated state control. The weaknesses and strengths of each ethnic and religious community were known to government authorities, information which was utilized in a shrewd process of attracting the elite while simultaneously using the threat of force to bring about compliance.

A great deal has been written about the specific events leading up to the 1979 Revolution. The overthrow of the monarchy has been traced to a myriad of causes ranging from successful mobilization of the opponents of the regime, to serious economic deficiencies of dependent capitalism, to conspiracy by the major oil companies and Western governments in order to maintain their influence over oil prices. Yet none of these possible explanations denies the dramatic overall role of the political system, which was riddled with waste, corruption, and political repression, in causing its own downfall. A diverse coalition of religious and secular men and women supported the overthrow of the monarchy.

The Islamic Republic

Ayatollah Ruhollah Khomeini had been in exile since 1964 due to his anti-government stance. His return to Iran in February 1979 marked the triumph of the Revolution. A Provisional Government headed by Mehdi Bazargan lasted from February to November 1979. During this time the constitution was written and ratified. Despite claims of Islam's universalism by theologians, scholars, and the Ayatollah Khomeini himself, the 1979 Iranian constitution in Article 12 identified Iran as a Twelver Shii Ithna'e Ashari state. The debate on this topic in the Assembly of Experts (Majlis-e Khebregan) was intense. Despite the objections of a minority of Sunni deputies, the overwhelming majority voted to declare Twelver Shiism as the state religion (fifty-two for, two against, and three abstentions).[53] In less than a week a select number of Tehran ulama submitted a letter of protest to Ayatollah Khomeini objecting to what they believed to be only a passing reference to Shiism and asked for a stricter wording. Their revision (not adopted by the Assembly) would have declared Twelver Shiism as the true Islam. The group was so adamant that the Assembly of Experts was forced to defend itself against the charge that it had slighted Shiism.[54]

The Provisional Government was challenged by all factions, particularly the militant clergy who embraced the concept of the rule of the top theologian (Velayat-e Faqih). The leadership of this group was organized around the Islamic Republican Party (IRP), an umbrella organization founded in February 1979 with Khomeini's approval. Foremost among its leaders were: Mohammad Beheshti, Abdol-Karim Musavi Ardebili, Ali Khamenei, Ali-Akbar Hashemi Rafsanjani, and Mohammad-Javad Bahonar. All were members of the Revolutionary Council (RC) and Beheshti was the head of both the party and the RC. While the party played a crucial role in executions, confiscation of property, the takeover of the American Embassy, and government purges, it was not the only actor on the scene. Not all pro-Khomeini clerics were associated with the IRP. Autonomous and semi-autonomous groups and individuals were acting on their own. During the first presidential election in January 1980, Abol-Hasan Bani Sadr, son of a cleric, who had studied in Tehran University and in Paris, won the election. His short presidency (officially ending in June 1981) was marred by the hostage crisis, clashes with

Islamic groups, the clergy, and the IRP, and the Iraqi attack on Iran. In the midst of war, 1981 was riddled with interclerical rivalry and terrorist attacks which killed several prominent revolutionary leaders. In October 1981 Khamenei became president and held the position until 1989 when he assumed the position held by Ayatollah Khomeini. What followed was a dual leadership on top with Rafsanjani's presidency and Khamenei's dubious role as the supreme religious leader.

During the 1980s the bureaucracy was streamlined, the educational system went through a major overhaul, and middle-level clerics were placed in various ministries including the Ministry of Education and Training. The end of the Iran–Iraq War (1988) and Khomeini's death (1989) not only intensified clerical rivalries, but also emboldened those who wished for more reforms, better relations with the world, and the relaxing of moral restrictions. Throughout the 1990s Iran flirted with reform and experienced factional struggles, assassinations and murders, and oppression. The regime resembled a clerical feudalism with a complex set of patronage–client relations colored by personalistic politics. From the standpoint of one scholar, the Islamic Republic today is "an authoritarian regime that permits limited pluralism, in which the government is responsive but not accountable to the people"; yet, the system operates through "personalistic patronage networks" outside the state apparatus.[55]

State–minority relations evolved in a revolutionary environment. Some scholars argue that the phases of Iranian Revolution fit Crane Brinton's model: specifically (1) the rule of the moderates, (2) the accession of the extremists and the "reign of terror and virtue," and (3) Thermidor and the return to normalcy. Brinton himself had reservations about the neat division amongst these three.[56] While events in this study indicate stages in state–minority relations, it cannot identify clearcut phases. The worst years for religious minorities were from 1981 to 1984–85; this intensification of state intrusion into their lives coincided with widespread cultural cleansing and the "reign of terror and virtue." By the mid- to late 1980s the approach to religious minorities was already routinized. Although some policy shifts were apparent, the reasons for change differed. A host of mitigating factors was important, including the impact of the personalistic approach, center–provincial differences, the Iran–Iraq War, and the reaction of recognized religious minorities.

Two more details must be covered before turning to unique features in the investigation of religious minorities: the general view of non-Muslim minorities in Islamic interpretation and the expressed views held by the ideologues of the regime. The following section sets the stage for the ideological state of the revolutionary republic.

Islam and Ahl al-Ketab

The presence of diverse religious and linguistic minorities in the geographical area known as the Middle East has been traced to its geopolitical setting which served as a roadway to religious conceptions including ancient Persian and Indian religions, and a variety of cultures from Central Asia and the Mediterranean region. Communal identities have been marked by localism and acquired "religious coloring."[57] Early empires did not make political demands on their subjects and remained relatively aloof from communal issues. Loyalty to the top ruler, payment of taxes, and occasional service in the army were the main demands made by the supranational state. The rise of Islam in the seventh century did not destroy this system but further nurtured it.[58] John Esposito described the early years as such:

> Muhammad was not the founder of Islam; he did not start a new religion. Like his prophetic predecessors, he came as a religious reformer. Muhammad maintained that he did not bring a new message from a new God but called people back to the one, true God and to a way of life that most of his contemporaries had forgotten or deviated from. Worship of Allah was not the evolutionary emergence of monotheism from polytheism but a return to a forgotten past, to the faith of the first monotheist, Abraham.[59]

Scholars have argued that, on a wide range of issues, early Islam differed significantly from what followed.[60]

In practice, most interpreters and rulers believed that Islam recognized no nation but the nation of Islam, thereby creating the cultural underpinning of state and religion. In literal interpretation, Islam recognized only one other group of "legitimate" peoples, the Ahl al-Ketab (the People of the Book) and they were often granted the status of Ahl al-Dhimma (the Protected People). These in practice have been Christians, Jews, Sabeans, and Zoroastrians (particularly in Iran); in some cases adherents to other religions (e.g., Hindus) were granted protected status.

Ahl al-Ketab were initially Jews and Christians based on the possession of divine books of revelation. Their privileged position was conditional based on the submission to Muslims and payment of jazieh (a special tax paid by the non-Muslims to the Muslim rulers). In return they were guaranteed freedom of worship, humane treatment, and protection. The Prophet Mohammad is believed to have said: "He who wrongs a Jew or a Christian will have myself (the Prophet) as his accuser on the day of judgment."[61]

The problems faced by Jews and Christians have their nexus in the Muslim theologians' belief that the Ahl al-Ketab have falsified the true contents of their own holy scriptures which prophesied the coming of the

Prophet Mohammad and the rise of Islam. Quranic verses and actions of the Prophet, his companions, and followers are used as evidence.[62] Both Sunni and Shii Islam recognize Noah, Abraham, Moses, and Jesus, "until in the succession of the prophets, Muhammad is reached."[63] Islam is seen as the last major religion revealed through the last prophet necessitating the final conversion by People of the Book and others. In line with this core belief, widespread among Muslims, those Muslims who turned away from Islam were apostates and their penalty for refusing to recant their false ways was death.

In time, as intolerance increased, restrictions against the Ahl al-Ketab became more rigid. Dhimma status was granted by the rulers of a Muslim state to the non-Muslim subjects; some saw it as a superior's granting of rights to an inferior based on the former's recognition and possession of the truth:

At the same time, the individual had to be subject to the general rules of the state, pay a special tax, not show "insolence" towards the dominant confession, bear the external marks of recognition of his status as a "protected person" . . . and non-member of the dominant community, and not proselytize among members of the dominant group.[64]

Some contend that this historical issue should not be taken lightly and "glossed over." The dominant was "being defined as tolerant, and therefore worthy of gratitude, only because the dominated" were despised.[65]

Others have argued that dhimma status was directly connected to the overall Islamic worldview and analysts should not confuse practice with theory. In practice, the treatment of non-Muslims differed from one locality and historical period to the next based on the individual ruler's preferences. In theory, texts of Islamic law reflect varied views among the jurists on the treatment of People of the Book and Protected People with differences emerging in four main Sunni schools of law: Maliki, Hanafi, Shafii, and Hanbali. According to this view, non-Muslims' submission to Muslims is in legal and political terms and not in terms of beliefs and metaphysics. The existence of stages of tolerance of non-Muslims demonstrates that they were not regarded as second-class citizens.[66]

In practice, however, the overall treatment of the People of the Book in the history of the Islamic rulers fell short of the ideal. At the mercy of unjust rulers, they were more "helpless" than their Muslim counterparts and lacked the protection of Islamic law and the "feudal customs,"[67] a general "political incapacity" that could have been overcome by converting to Islam.[68]

Discussion of the complexity and variance in old texts of Islamic law are outside the scope of this work. A few points, however, are relevant and more directly related to the subject of this book. The first issue is the position of Zoroastrians in Islam. In the Quran they are referred to by the original Greek name, Madjus, but are not directly named along with the Christians and Jews as Ahl al-Ketab. However, in practice the Zoroastrians paid special taxes and were treated on a par with the People of the Book. Several explanations are offered in Muslim texts: (1) early on, for practical reasons, in order to rule over a religiously diverse population, Islam extended the status of Ahl al-Ketab to non-Muslims other than the Christians and Jews (including the Hindus and the Zoroastrians), (2) the founder of Zoroastrianism, Zoroaster, was viewed by some Arab Muslims as neither a prophet nor a polytheist but an intermediate figure not to be dismissed, (3) Arabs could not conquer and maintain control of Zoroastrian Persia by treating them as polytheists; even when the Muslims conquered Bahrain, Oman, and Yemen, the Madjus paid jazieh and were treated like Christians and Jews.[69] The Shafii legal school endorsed the payment of jazieh by Zoroastrians because it considered them to be one of the People of the Book. The Hanafi legal school of thought endorsed the payment of jazieh for a different reason; it viewed Zoroastrians as ajam – non-Arab people.[70] For practical reasons even the title Madjus with the connotation of the Protected People was extended to non-Zoroastrians such as the Scandinavians and the Berbers.[71] Despite these explanations, in historical Arab texts, the Zoroastrian Persians are regularly referred to as "heathens."[72]

The second issue relevant to this study is the worldview of Islam in relation to non-Muslims. This view is shaped by the concepts of Dar al-Islam (the territory of Islam where Muslim authorities are in charge and enforce Islamic laws) and Dar al-Harb (the territory controlled by non-Muslims where non-Islamic laws are applied and which is identified as the enemy). Since religion is not separated from politics, Dar al-Islam and Dar al-Harb become two opposing abodes in a constant state of conflict and war. Regardless of any theological justification, this dichotomy creates a clear concept of "the other," which can easily trigger hostility and turn into an actual state of war. Constant tension (and its consequent contradictions) in Muslim political thought has the potential of turning into an unending source of anti-other verbal diatribes. Within this paradigm, some scholars believe that Shii political thought has distinguishing features separate from the Sunni mainstream. Hamid Enayat refers to Sunni optimism and Shii pessimism about the nature of man, the Shii preoccupation with righteousness and justice, emotionalism manifested in rituals, and ultimately Shii idealism.[73] Moojan Momen sees Islam for the Shiis, even more so than the Sunnis, to be "a religion of rituals, obligations, and prohibitions,"[74] and points to the presence of "the Shii worldview" in popular manifestations of the religion. This view emphasizes themes such as "martyrdom and patient suffering" and "the need for a scapegoat": "This worldview is as much present among the ulama as among the ordinary people and usually it has been the ulama who as the natural leaders of the community, have directed the people as to the identity of the scapegoat."[75] Both Enayat and Momen trace the presence of such intense peculiarities to Shiism's minority status in Islam and their perpetual persecution. In other words, historical persecution can instill a persecution complex leading to a pessimistic outlook and rejection of an objective condition: "the most outstanding feature of Shiism is an attitude of mind which refuses to admit that majority opinion is necessarily true or right, and – which is its converse – a rationalized defense of the moral excellence of an embattled minority."[76]

The third issue relevant to this study concerns the legal rights of Muslims versus non-Muslims, particularly Christian and Jewish subjects in Dar al-Islam. Several prominent contemporary Sunni Islamic thinkers have argued for a broader and more rational interpretation of Islamic laws dealing with non-Muslims and other issues. One of the principal founders of Islamic reformism, Mohammad Abduh of Egypt (1849–1905), emphasized the primacy of public interest, and recommended comparison and synthesis of the four Sunni legal schools (including opinions of independent jurists) in order to derive legal rulings from the Quran and the Hadith. Inherent in Abduh's approach was the urgently felt necessity to adjust Islamic laws to the changing contemporary world.[77]

However, legal rights pertaining to Muslims have never been the same as those for non-Muslims; differentiation and discrimination have been deemed natural and necessary. One scholar sees culture and tradition behind the contradictory claims of contemporaries who, on the one hand, argue that Islam recognizes "the principle of equality" and, on the other, insist on preserving "premodern Islamic rules" on the separate, different, or inferior status of non-Muslims in the Islamic polity.[78] Many religious laws remain unchanged (though they are not always applied), such as prohibiting non-Muslims from serving as judges or forbidding a Muslim woman from marrying a non-Muslim man.

The modern state, however, by necessity shapes the meaning of certain legal interpretations. One case in point historically is the payment of jazieh by non-Muslims. Jazieh is generally translated as a poll tax, but since poll taxes were unilaterally based on the will of the ruler, a more accurate translation may be "a protection and security tax."[79] Despite differences among jurists, conditional exemptions exist in Islam. The most relevant is the argument that, in the modern state, if a non-Muslim joins the Muslim army, he and his family are exempt from the payment of jazieh.[80] In other words, the institutions of the modern state and the obligations placed on its citizens make the principle of jazieh unnecessary. Yet, the modern state still remains within the domain of Dar al-Islam and some issues cannot be changed. Regardless of the degree of freedom of expression, a non-Muslim's criticism of the Prophet Mohammad or Islam is seen as an action against the state.[81] Uniformity in the educational system is essential, and, unless the "spirit" of the curriculum conforms to the Islamic public school, there can be no separate school for non-Muslims. While teaching of language, customs, and religion of non-Muslims is allowed, a non-Muslim cannot object to his children receiving Islamic education.[82]

The fourth issue, the scholarship of which is still in its infancy, is differences of interpretation between the Sunni schools of thought and the Shii on the relations between Muslims and non-Muslims. Historical works describing these relationships will be discussed later. During the late Safavid period (1501–1722), when the ulama were becoming more assertive, the Shii theologian Mohammad Baqer Majlesi (d. 1699) is credited for producing several important writings in Persian, and for popularizing the Shii ethos among ordinary people. A major religious figure in Isfahan, he condemned Sufi influence on Shii clergy and set out to eradicate it. His style is described as "dry, formal, dogmatic, legalistic,"[83] an embodiment of his version of Shiism. Among Majlesi's many works is *Hilliyat al-Mottaqin*, in which he sets out strict rules of behavior for a Muslim, basing it on the Hadith about the Prophet and the Shii Imams. Some of the rules involve non-Muslims; for instance, commenting on the vital importance of greeting (salam) in Islamic conduct, he explains that certain types of people should not be greeted by a Muslim including Zoroastrians, Jews, Christians, pagans, chess players or other gamblers, musicians, and homosexuals.[84]

The most dramatic difference with the Sunnis is over the sources of pollution (nejasat). The Shii theological writings advocate avoiding contact with non-Muslims (including physical contact with a non-Muslim or a non-Muslim corpse, consuming food and drink prepared by non-Muslims, and using utensils used by non-Muslims) and offer detailed guidelines on cleansing in cases where such contact has taken place. The consumption, for example, of meat of those animals ritually slaughtered by the Jews was not prohibited by Sunnis. In contrast, the Shii authorities declared the preparation or physical contact of a Jew (or any non-Muslim) with the meat as najess (impure) prohibiting its consumption by Muslims.[85] In extreme cases the Shii codes of pollution are extended to the Sunnis as well.[86] Some suggest that the major source for the concept of impurity lies in the pre-Islamic religion of Persia,

Zoroastrianism.[87] "Like Hinduism, Zoroastrian doctrine holds that all non-Zoroastrians are ritually unclean . . . As a result, there were numerous religious stipulations that regulated and limited contact between Zoroastrians and non-Zoroastrians."[88] The practice of purity also included marriage to non-Zoroastrians, and Zoroastrians who had to come into contact with others would undergo purification rituals. Converts to the religion in the fourteenth to early nineteenth centuries had to go through purification practices but this ceased afterwards and only Zoroastrian priests were required to observe purification rituals.[89]

The adoption of the codes of pollution and a "segregative tendency" by the Shii Iranians may have been caused by the prolonged period of Islamization under direct Arab rule (more than 200 years), the question of whether or not the Zoroastrians could be considered as People of the Book, and the status of the Shii as a persecuted minority.[90] For centuries, especially since the Safavid era, Shii religious leaders, local governors, and kings added their own regulations to the codes of pollution; the end result was an ambiguous cultural practice with local and personal variations throughout Iran.[91] Most religious leaders wrote and preached approvingly of the codes of pollution on non-Muslims, ideological baggage which was carried into the Islamic theocratic regime with the 1979 Revolution. This subject will be covered in more detail later in the discussion of the policy sphere regarding non-Muslim religious minorities.

Regime ideologues: the core mentalité

Through direct clerical rule beliefs which were once in the domain of religious schools and households spilled into the political realm, molding the foundation of state ideology on non-Muslim citizens of Iran. Laws governing religious minorities were based on the belief of Islam's (particularly Shii Islam's) superiority to other religions. The founding of a theocracy meant putting specifics into practice. Direct legalized application of the mainstream view became ideological orthodoxy. Details of discriminatory laws will be discussed later; suffice it to say here that not since the inception of the Pahlavi dynasty in 1925 (and on some details, the Qajar dynasty, 1795–1925) at least had the country experienced such a wide and systematic scale of legally institutionalized discrimination and segmentation.

A work first published in Persian in 1966 became the benchmark for the treatment of People of the Book, Iranian Christian converts, and the Bahais in post-revolutionary Iran. The author, Sultanhussein Tabandeh, was the leader of the Nematollahi Soltanalishahi Sufi Order centered at Gonabad in Khorasan. The Nematollahi order was founded in early 1400

AD by Seyyed Nur al-Din Shah Nematollahi; his shrine is near Mahun in Kerman. Tabandeh's group was a special section of the original Sufi order. The foreword to the book, written by Abulfazl Hazeghi (a four-time Parliament deputy from Jahrom, Fars, and three-time leader of Iranian pilgrims to Mecca), claims that the work presents an Islamic perspective on the Universal Declaration of Human Rights and that a copy was given to every representative of the Islamic countries attending the 1968 Tehran International Conference on Human Rights.[92] Tabandeh maintained that he had never been in politics and his motive was purely religious: the purpose was to show that what men were attempting to establish in modern times had already been set out in Islam in the seventh century AD. Yet he lamented that political leaders of Islamic countries rarely followed the commandments of Islam.[93]

The work has the appearance of an objective account, and provides references to Plato, al-Farabi, and Western thinkers. Nevertheless, the Shii perspective is obvious from the start as Shah Ismail (the founder of the Safavid dynasty) is called a champion of "the oppressed."[94] It reviews every article of the Universal Declaration of Human Rights and outlines each article's possible application (if any) to a Muslim country. The following is a brief summary of Tabandeh's views on the non-Muslims, later to be put into practice, almost verbatim, in the Islamic Republic of Iran:

(1) He endorses the law of retaliation or retribution (later adopted in Iran as qesas) which in criminal law sets out different and more severe punishments for non-Muslims. Two instances stand out:

   (a) if a Muslim murders another, he should be killed by the next of kin of the murdered Muslim; if the murdered person is a non-Muslim, then the Muslim cannot be put to death by his kin – punishment through payment of a fine and lashing should suffice; and

   (b) the punishment for a Muslim male who commits adultery is shaving of his head, 100 lashes, and one year in prison, but if a non-Muslim man commits adultery with a Muslim woman his penalty is execution.

The reason is that Islam is considered the superior religion and those who have not accepted this are "reckoned as outside the pale of humanity; and their existence is considered injurious to the generality of mankind." They resemble a political party that is against general welfare and must be banned and, if necessary, treated with violence in order to stop their carnage. People of the Book "have not reached the highest level of spirituality" and continue to obey commands which have been replaced by Islam. They are "on a lower level of belief and conviction."[95]

(2) Islam is strict with "polytheists and idolaters" and association with them is forbidden. They are "lower than wild beasts."[96]

(3) While there are diverse views on the issue of marriage of a Muslim male to a woman from the People of the Book, all agree that a Muslim female cannot marry a "polytheist idolatrous" or a member of a "People of the Book." A woman who knowingly enters such a union "must be punished" and children born of such a union are "illegitimate." The reason: since men are considered guardians of women, and women are required to obey their husbands, marriage to a non-Muslim man means that a Muslim has placed herself in a subordinate position coming "under the authority" of a non-Muslim. "Islam and its peoples must be above infidels, and never permit non-Muslims to acquire lordship over them."[97]

(4) On freedom of thought and religion, Tabandeh makes these exceptions:

(a) While People of the Book can pursue their religion and communal life, following of religions "contrary to Islam, like those who demand Islam's extirpation," are prohibited. This includes "a community which under the name of religion is organized to be against Islam."[98] (This is a clear reference to Bahaism.)

(b) No non-Muslim should hold government posts; members of the judiciary, legislative body, and cabinet must be Muslims.[99]

(c) There is no freedom of choice to change one's religion from Islam. Anyone who strays away from Islam is motivated by lust, bribery, or is converting out of spite. The act is apostasy and a Fetri apostate, one whose parents were Muslim but who has deserted his faith, is "a diseased member of the body politic, gangrenous, incurable, fit only for amputation, and must be executed."[100] If one is born into another religion, converts to Islam, and then recants Islam, he is called a national apostate. He "must be reasoned with for three days to win him back," but when all hope is lost for repentance he too should be executed. If, having reconverted, he repeats this pattern again, the third time he will be identified as a Fetri apostate and no repentance will be accepted:[101]

No man of sense, from the mere fact that he possesses intelligence, will ever turn down the better in favour of the inferior. Anyone who penetrates beneath the surface to the inner essence of Islam is bound to recognise its superiority over the other religions.[102]

Tabendeh also has an extensive discussion on women in Islam riddled with fundamental mistakes; however, every point he makes became the law of the land immediately after the Revolution and before the activation of reformism from pro-regime women. Placing Tabandeh's views in the context of modern human rights, Ann Elizabeth Mayer reflects:

Instead of the concern that one finds in international human rights law for the freedom of the individuals involved, the concern is for the prestige of the Muslim community, the honor of which is sullied if one of their number is subordinated to a member of the inferior group, the non-Muslims.[103]

Overall policy, decrees, and authorized and unauthorized actions were shaped by written and expressed views of regime ideologues. Many provincial lower-ranking mullahs achieved upward mobility through and because of the Revolution rather than their own religious learning and merit. The process of building a theocracy attracted many ambitious characters and plenty of opportunists (who are never in short supply in such situations). Lacking in-depth religious learning, they were anxious imitators of the most negative views on non-Muslims. A few had a very large impact in proportion to their numbers.

The superiority of Muslims to the adherents of other religions was frequently addressed by the clerical ideologues. It was a state of mind, a source of self-legitimation with constant repetition. "There is only one true religion in every epoch and it is essential for all to follow it," wrote Morteza Motahhari, a professor of theology and a member of the Revolutionary Council. He called the idea that all "heavenly religions" are equal "a false thought." Belief in God and one of the "heavenly religions" was not sufficient. Even positive comments and acknowledgment of the holiness of the Prophet Mohammad and Imam Ali were not acceptable. And the existence of several religions did not mean that people could choose one over another. Submitting to God meant the acceptance of His "last command," which was revealed to the Prophet Mohammad.[104]

To Motahhari, the Muslim believer was like a patient under the care and supervision of a physician, but the non-Muslim believer was a patient under no supervision acting recklessly by taking any medicine and food in sight. The latter was taking a chance and he would eventually hurt himself. A non-Muslim's belief in God was not sufficient since he lacked a correct blueprint, but the Muslim was being guided by a comprehensive correct program. However, Motahhari made a distinction between People of the Book and the heathens: under "some conditions" the former may end up in heaven but the latter were lost forever. (The specific conditions for ascending to heaven were left out.)[105] To Motahhari, Jews and Christians who insisted on maintaining their religions were suffering from the condition of kafir-e majerai. Kafir means infidel; the religious meaning of kafir-e majerai is one who is quarrelsome and denies facts.[106] Therefore, they became a special type of infidel, inferior child-like entities whom Muslims tolerated. Compared to Judaism and Christianity, Islam was a more perfect religion necessitating a final conversion.

The belief that Islam was superior to all other religions was so deeply ingrained in the psyche of the revolutionaries that even the so-called moderate elements believed in its truth. Mehdi Bazargan, an engineer by training and religiously devout by family line and personal practice, became the prime minister of the Provisional Government in 1979. He believed that man must have one of the monotheistic religions in order to battle selfishness, materialism, and communism. Yet, the choice was not a difficult one. "Among the monotheist religions, Zoroastrianism is obsolete, Judaism has bred materialism, and Christianity is dictated by its church. Islam is the only way out."[107] In this line of thinking there is no recognition of Hinduism, Buddhism, Bahaism, or other religions.

The views on the Jews were particularly negative. The highly respected Ayatollah Mahmud Taleqani, who was revered for his humanity and modesty and who often preached about cessation of discord, was puzzled by the support Christians were giving to the Jews. Weren't these the same Jews responsible for the killing of Christ? Why weren't Christians cooperating with Muslims whose religious book, Quran, had praised Christ? Yet, Taleqani's language was softer compared to other clergy; he believed that both Jews and Christians had used the teachings of their prophets for political and economic gains.[108]

As the leader of the Islamic forces who seized power in 1979, Ayatollah Khomeini, more so than any other visible high-ranking clergy, held views that directly influenced and shaped state ideology. His written work and lectures were widely used to reenforce attitudes and to make policy. Remaining generally aloof from the details of policymaking made his comments even more poignant. In his pre-revolutionary work addressing Islamic justice, Ayatollah Ruhollah Khomeini argued that, despite the Prophet Mohammad's benevolence and kindness toward thieves and non-Muslims, he was compelled to destroy the Jewish tribe of Bani Quraizeh because they were promoting corruption in Islamic society and were harmful to Islam.[109] In anticipation of a possible departure to Lebanon from Iraq in 1971, he lamented that even the Iraqi Jews were treated better by Iraqi authorities than the Shiis and Iranians. The Jews were given six months to prepare for exodus and their possessions were sold at a fair price, he claimed.[110]

In his attack on the institution of monarchy, Khomeini rarely left out the non-Muslim minorities or Israel. The television stations in Iran and throughout the Islamic world were in the hands of Israelis to broadcast whatever they wanted.[111] "Jewish thieves" were responsible for cursing Muslims while declaring they were "the chosen people."[112] Criticizing monarchical Iran and the Turkish Republic for their pro-Israel stand, he declared: "Sunni brothers will think that the Shiis are Jew-worshippers [Yahudi parast]."[113] The Jews and Israelis were interchangeable entities who had penetrated all facets of life. Iran was being "trampled upon under Jewish boots."[114] The Jews had conspired to kill the Qajar king Naser al-Din Shah and had a historically grand design to rule through a new monarchy and a new government (the Pahlavi dynasty): "Gentlemen, be frightened. They are such monsters."[115] In a vitriolic attack on Mohammad Reza Shah's celebration of 2,500 years of Persian monarchy in 1971, Khomeini declared that Israeli technicians had planned the celebrations and they were behind the exuberant expenses and overspending.[116] Objecting to the sale of oil to Israel, he said: "We should not ignore that the Jews want to take over Islamic countries."[117] Then, condemning the concerns and fears of the ulama and their quietism, Khomeini reflected on his own life. His murder was not expedient but he wished the royalists had killed him: "What do I want this life for? Death to this life that I have. Do they threaten me because they think I like this life? . . . the sooner I get killed the better."[118]

Ayatollah Khomeini was asked a series of questions on business matters involving the relationship between Jews and Muslims. Could Muslims work in Jewish-owned businesses if these businesses were helping Israel even if the Muslims were not aware of such transactions? He responded that in either case this was unlawful and religiously prohibited (haram). On a related question, he saw no problem if an institution was owned by a Muslim but Jews worked there and had a few Muslims working for them as long as the Muslims did not serve Israel. However, it was "a shameful act" for a Muslim to work for "this sect [ferqeh]." He was asked if believing Muslims could have business transactions with Jews in order to eventually take over their businesses. Khomeini responded that, if the Muslims were certain that they could eliminate Jewish domination from the Muslim bazaars, then their business dealings with the Jews were acceptable.[119]

In an address to the Syrian foreign minister after the Revolution Khomeini lamented: "If Muslims got together and each poured one bucket of water on Israel, a flood would wash away Israel."[120] In other words, Muslim unity would destroy Israel. To Khomeini the world was a hostile place with enemies lurking in every corner; these enemies were all in collusion against him and the Muslim brethren. Metaphorically, the United States was "Israel's mother and Saddam [Hossein of Iraq] [was] Begin's [of Israel] younger brother" as they all engaged in propaganda against Muslims.[121]

Bahais for Khomeini were a mere political party materializing in Iran to guarantee Zionist domination of the Iranian economy. Bahais were a simple extension of a foreign plot, and both Jews and Bahais were the oppressors of the Muslim people.[122] He flatly prohibited trade with the Bahais.[123]

Khomeini's attitude toward Zoroastrianism was one of disdain. He called the religion "an old and inveterate sect," the Zoroastrians "fire-worshippers," and their intentions "reactionary."[124] Mohammad Reza Shah's orders in the early 1970s to change the Iranian calendar from Islamic to the monarchical history outraged the clerical establishment. For Khomeini this was an act of "treason" and a direct insult to the Prophet Mohammad, Islam, and all Muslims; it was an attempt to restore Zoroastrianism, set up "fire-temples," and destroy Islam. He regularly referred to Zoroastrians with the derogatory term "gabr."[125]

Khomeini saw pre-revolutionary Iran as an environment where all "stray sects" were busy plotting against Islam. Christians with the support of foreign governments were sent to Iran to evangelize through their schools and institutions. Printing non-Islamic religious texts (implying the Bible) was allowed, and the only prohibition was directed at "the Muslim ulama and Islam."[126]

Before the takeover of the revolutionaries, many religious figures, in interviews with the European press, said that the rights of the People of the Book would be protected. In a typical commentary, Ayatollah Allameh Yahya Nuri blamed concerns over the status of religious minorities on "colonial and despotic forces." In his position as an "Islamic authority" he issued a declaration to the Christians, Jews, and Zoroastrians that their rights would be more assured under an Islamic system than any other political system.[127] Ayatollah Nuri later wrote about equality and justice in an Islamic state arguing that "an individual's geographical, national, ethnic, or linguistic background" was not important; as long as "they share[d] the beliefs of Islam," there would be no discrimination.[128] Therefore, not being a Muslim was grounds for discrimination in an Islamic state.

Research on non-Muslim religious minorities

In 1991 the report of the special representative of the Commission on Human Rights, Reynaldo Galindo Pohl, referred to the investigation of Iran as "particularly complex and complicated." Politicization of every issue inside and outside Iran by opponents and proponents of the regime had created enormous difficulties. He saw this as the result of "the radical polarization of political forces, the conflict between opinions that have turned into preestablished, inflexible, intransigent credos and the struggle between national and international political interests." The human rights situation in Iran was said to have "gone on in prejudiced and speculative terms, which have been accompanied by reactions of hypersensitivity."[129]

One of the most striking features of research on non-Muslim minorities has been the abundance of rumors and misinformation against the Islamic Republic: for instance, the allegations of kidnapping of Zoroastrian girls from Yazd by Revolutionary Guards, or reports that Christian Iraqi prisoners of war were being forcefully converted to Islam.[130] Christian fundamentalists also propagated outrageous lies in the West, claiming that mass executions (hangings) and imprisonments were taking place in Iran. Ironically, their publications often gave the impression that the Muslim world was a killing field for all Christians, and Islam was portrayed as an aggressive, bloodthirsty religion.[131]

Policy motives are not always easy to discern. Numerous detailed discussions as well as confrontations in the Majlis (parliament) have occurred in committees and behind closed doors. Sometimes the nature of the controversy has been brought to the floor of the Majlis during open sessions; many times these issues have not been discussed publicly. The complex web of the state bureaucracy encourages secretiveness, which is common to bureaucratic administrations. As Max Weber explains:

Bureaucratic administration always tends to be an administration of "secret sessions": in so far as it can, it hides its knowledge and action from criticism . . . everywhere that the power interests of the domination structure toward the outside are at stake . . . we find secrecy.[132]

In the Iranian case, the personal element plays a crucial role in maintaining secrecy. Muslim or non-Muslim, both resort to concealment; this conduct is prevalent and accepted as routine. A scholar is always aware that facts may be missing due to the secretiveness of the polity. As James Bill eloquently states:

The processes of power and decisionmaking are usually hidden within the deepest recesses of society, where they exist in a state of constant flux . . . Many of the shrewdest and most influential political figures in Iran have intentionally avoided the blinding sunlight of publicity and have sought to exert power in the more shadowy corridors of the political system.[133]

With intense clerical rivalries in the midst of an ideological state, it is impossible to distinguish personalism from political views. The exact nature of factionalism has always been a difficult and complex issue. Ambiguity extends to stands taken by individual clergy vis-à-vis non-Muslims as well. This author was unable to find any written works by clergy that presented a message radically different from what has already been discussed. However, the evidence presented in this book shows an inherent dualism. For instance, recognized non-Muslim minorities were unanimous (evidence supports their sentiments) that Ayatollah Mohammad Beheshti was protective of their rights. It is also correct that institutionalization of restrictions began in 1981, the year of his assassination. Yet, it was Ayatollah Beheshti who initiated the criminal laws of qesas (retribution) before his death. He also reassured the minorities that he would personally protect their rights, and they need not worry about discriminatory clauses in the law. Or, take the case of Ayatollah Hossein-Ali Montazeri whose written work shows adherence to the idea of najess (impurity), discussed later, but who in practice advocated a liberal treatment for the Armenians; or, Bazargan, a noncleric, who believed and wrote about the inferiority of all religions other than Islam, but opposed the criminal laws of qesas. Some were not high-ranking clergy (such as Rafsanjani with personal ties to some non-Muslims), but were astute politicians who were focused on existing opportunities rather than on an ideal status for non-Muslims. However, the evidence presented in this book points not only to an inherent dualism but also to a change of what is stated over time. Yet, these changes in position have been a tradition among the Shii ulama. Historically, they have altered their views "at different periods in their lives according to circumstances."[134] In the policy sphere, increasingly, the gap between expressed ideas and actual practice widened with the passage of time. The why and the how of the change (or pretended change) cannot be reliably assessed for research purposes. A host of internal and external circumstances or personal alienation from those presently in power may be responsible for the change of tune of individual clergy and their cronies. In a secretive and conniving world of Iranian politics, when radicals of yesterday become today's moderates, regardless of the niceties with which they sugarcoat their words, their sincerity remains in doubt.

One additional point requires further explanation. Due to the condition of marginality, minorities in the Arab world, Iran, and Turkey have been attracted to secular ideologies and political parties. The Baath, the Syrian Social Nationalist, and the Communist Parties are some examples. In the Iranian case, there is evidence that non-Muslim citizens have been active in various leftist parties.[135] While there is truth to this, the majority of adherents to various left-wing organizations, including the Tudeh (Communist) Party, have been of Shii background. The left and the Communists have not always been dogmatically anti-clerical. The Tudeh Party, for instance, nominated Ayatollah Taleqani as its candidate for parliament in the 1940s. After the 1979 Revolution, the same party backed Ayatollah Khomeini and undermined other leftist groups. Even after the Tudeh Party was systematically persecuted by Islamic authorities, there was evidence that ex-Tudeh members continued to function in the government bureaucracy under the banner of Islam.[136] Non-Muslim communities had a similar experience with their own far leftist factions.

Iranian intellectuals, acting individually, have initiated shifts in their allegiance from liberal/socialist secularism to Islamism. For instance, Homa Nategh, a university professor in Tehran during the Revolution, shifted from her leftist view to Islamism, and then renounced both. While a professor, she had written so harshly against the clergy that the religious elements had asked for her dismissal from the university. But, during the first few months of the Revolution, Nategh wrote in their defense, purposefully leaving out negative information. She condemned women's objections to veiling and urged them to vote for Ayatollah Taleqani for president and Masud Rajavi, the head of the Mojahedin Organization, for the Majlis. She is, however, one of the few who, with astonishment, admitted to her sudden ideological shift. "It was as though logic was taken away from me, as though I wasn't thinking."[137] This is not an isolated case. Earlier, Jalal Al-e Ahmad, a well-known writer and intellectual, also exhibited the same tendency. The son of a cleric, he was first attracted to communism, then liberal secularism, and eventually to Islam.

Shifting political allegiances may demonstrate an inherent disdain and distrust for the state. Individuals may be truthful each time they change political allegiances; they may also be motivated by fear, opportunism, or political expediency. Or they may simply transform a search for personal identity to the political arena, seeking in the outer world an answer to the contradictions they feel within. What concerns us here is the acknowledgment that the phenomenon exists and may have a bearing upon speeches, statements, and the behavior of authorities and religious minorities. Therefore, the parameters of determining true loyalty and allegiance to one's own community alone becomes uncertain. There can very well be a multitude of crosscutting allegiances manifesting themselves at different points in time. This pertains as much to minorities as to the majority.

The non-Muslim minority issue was not created by the Islamic Republic. Their history is intertwined with the history of the Iranian state. The state's nationalist agenda, local clergy's manipulation of events, anti-Western sentiments, and the tension between the secular rulers and the ulama made the non-Muslims easy prey. The next chapter identifies the religious minorities and explores their history.

1 Ethnic anatomy and politics of non-Muslim minorities

The scholarly literature on non-Muslim minorities is highly uneven, complex, and thinly researched. This chapter is not meant to be an exhaustive historical analysis; rather the main purpose is to introduce each community and examine its overall relations with Iranian society and the state. Several patterns in state–minority relations are identified at the conclusion of the chapter.

The sources for this chapter are secondary and include publications in Armenian, Persian, and English; there are noticeable differences in the quality of the sources. Every attempt has been made to deal constructively with contradictory cases, and the strengths and weaknesses of writings about each group have been carefully assessed. New historical works on religious minorities may clarify certain events and situations. For the purpose of this study, enough information is available to shed some light on the sociopolitical condition of Armenians, Assyrians and Chaldeans, Jews, Zoroastrians, and Bahais during the twentieth century.

The Armenians

The background of the Armenians has been traced to prehistoric times, to communities living in eastern Anatolia and the outskirts of Mount Ararat. From about 500 BC, Greek and Persian sources refer to the land of "Armenia" and its people as the "Armenians." By 70 BC, the Armenian Empire stretched from the Caspian Sea to the Mediterranean. The territory was frequently a focus of power struggle between the Roman and Parthian Empires. The Armenian Apostolic Church, an ancient and autocephalous branch of Eastern Christianity, became the church of the Armenian state circa AD 314. It, along with the Armenian alphabet (created in AD 404), enhanced the distinctive identity of the Armenians.

During the sixteenth century the Persian and Ottoman Empires competed over Armenia along with other territories in the region located between the two empires. In a settlement in 1639, the Ottomans took over

most of the Armenian enclave. During the first three decades of the nineteenth century, Russia annexed nearly all of Persian territory north of the
Arax (Aras) River, including its Armenian enclave. Through bilateral
treaties between Persia, Ottoman Turkey, and Russia, Armenian lands
were reshuffled and Armenians residing in some areas were forced to
migrate. Until the first two decades of the twentieth century, the fate of
the Armenian population was closely intertwined with one or more of
these three dominant powers.[1]

Between 1894 and 1920, the Armenians living under the Ottoman
Empire experienced the destruction of more than two-thirds of their population in a series of massacres, culminating in the genocide of 1915. On
28 May 1918 for the first time in centuries, an independent state was
established. The Armenian Republic lasted only two years; its collapse
was due to several factors, including: catastrophic economic conditions,
starving refugees from Turkish Armenia, reliance on unfulfilled promises
of the Allied powers, Kemal Ataturk's successful military ventures against
the Allied powers, ideological and personal friction combined with political immaturity within the Armenian leadership; and the advance of
Bolsheviks into the Caucasus. While the Turkish army took a large
portion of western Armenia, the Bolshevik Red Army occupied the
eastern section and established the Armenian Soviet Socialist Republic at
the end of 1920.[2]

The cultural links between the Armenians and the Persians can be
traced back to Zoroastrian times. For twelve centuries, Armenia was
under the direct or indirect rule of the Persians. While much influenced
by Persian culture and religion, Armenia also retained its unique characteristics as a nation. Later, Armenian Christianity retained some
Zoroastrian vocabulary and ritual.[3] Both peoples claim to be of Indo-
European origin. Although the presence of Armenians in Persia predates
the Safavid era (1501–1722),[4] the bulk of the Armenian population was
transported from their ancestral lands during the early seventeenth
century by Shah Abbas. This forced relocation of the population (within
the same empire) was preceded by the destruction of the famous town of
Julfa and nearly everything between Erzerum and Tabriz.[5]

Two reasons are often cited for the deportation: it was (1) a protective
military measure against the incursions of the Ottoman Empire, and (2)
part of a grand plan to modernize the capital city of Isfahan by advancing
international trade. The processes leading to the population relocation
have been reported differently by European and Armenian historians.
The fact remains that these people were captives whose lands and livelihood were destroyed intentionally.[6] While there is general agreement that
the treatment of Armenians was fair under Shah Abbas, this was not the

Table 2. *Ethnic anatomy of non-Muslim minorities*

Ethno-religious group	Estimated size	Religion	Location	Extension across Iranian borders	Recorded uprisings in the twentieth century	Degree of assimilation before 1979
Armenians	250,000 (mid-1970s); between 150,000 and 200,000 (1990s)	Apostolic (some Catholics and Protestants)	Major cities, especially Isfahan, Tehran, Tabriz	Armenia, throughout the Middle East and Turkey, Europe, the USA, India and southeast Asia, Ethiopia, South Africa, Australia, Uruguay, Venezuela, Brazil, Argentina	No recorded uprising against the state	Avoid intermarriages with non-Armenians; some intermarriages with Assyrians, very few with Muslims
Assyrians and Chaldeans	30,000 (mid-1970s); 16,000–18,000 (1992)	Mostly Nestorian, some Chaldeans (Roman Catholic)	Major cities especially Tehran and Urmieh (Rezaiyeh); for Chaldeans, the Khuzestan region, especially Ahvaz	Iraq (tribal Nestorians, Chaldeans), Syria (Jacobites), Lebanon (Jacobites), Turkey (Nestorians, Jacobites), Russia (Nestorians). There are smaller offshoots inspired by the missionaries in these countries. There are signicant Assyrian communities in the United States, Canada, Britain, Australia, Greece, Germany	No recorded uprising against the state	Avoid intermarriages outside their denomination; some intermarriages with Armenians. Compared to the Armenians, however, many more have married and mixed with different Christian groups and Muslims

Group	Population estimate	Religion	Location in Iran	Diaspora	Uprising	Intermarriage
Bahais	Estimates vary and are unreliable 150,000–300,000	Bahai	Major cities and smaller towns. More spread throughout the country than any other non-Muslim religious minority	United States, Europe, India, Canada, Australia, New Zealand, Uganda, Panama, Western Samoa, China, Japan, South Africa, Brazil (plans for and attempts at expansion in Africa and Latin America). The Bahais enjoy a consultative status among the non-governmental organizations of the United Nations Economic and Social Council.	No recorded uprising against the state	Intermarriages are strongly resisted but occur more frequently than among other non-Muslims. Bahais are highly assimilated into Persian society
Jews	Around 80,000 (1970s); between 20,000 and 30,000 (1990s)	Judaism	Major cities, especially Shiraz and Hamadan; no village population. Mainly concentrated in Tehran	Israel, very few in Syria and Turkey, Persian Gulf, some in Egypt and north Africa, Europe, the USA, the former Soviet Union, Latin America, Canada	No recorded uprising against the state	Mostly marry other Jews; some marriages with Bahais and Muslims. Highly integrated into Persian society by the 1970s
Zoroastrians	30,000–35,000 (1970s); 50,000 (1990s)	Zoroastrian	Major cities but particularly in Tehran, Yazd, Kerman. Some village population around Yazd	India, Pakistan, very few in the United States. Their estimated world population is around 125,000	No recorded uprising against the state	The most assimilated among the recognized non-Muslim minorities. Intermarriages with Muslims are more common than among other minority groups

case with his successors. Forced conversions to Islam, discriminatory measures, high taxation, and instances of clerical agitation against the Christian population abound in eyewitness accounts.[7]

The relationship between the Armenian community and the Safavid state was shaped by a millet-type administration. The New Julfa Armenians had internal autonomy; their relationship to the state was mediated through the patriarchs of the church and individuals appointed as the shah's representatives in the administration of the community's affairs. Armenians in Isfahan have been given credit for a number of industrial inventions such as the Safavid artillery; they also were successful merchants of different commodities, especially silk.

By the twentieth century, there were significant Armenian communities in northwestern Iran and the capital, Tehran. Although Armenians in Persia excelled as small artisans, were involved in international trade, and were basically integrated into the modern Iranian economy, they never dominated the economic sphere of the country. Similarly, their political role remained limited. During Qajar rule, however, Armenian ambassadors were dispatched to Europe[8] and Armenians played an active role in the liberal, left, and constitutional movements in Iran in the early twentieth century.[9]

The Reza Shah era was a much more difficult time for the community than the Mohammad Reza Shah reign. Although the Armenians were given cultural and religious autonomy in communal affairs and were allowed one additional deputy to the Majlis, Reza Shah closed down their schools in the years 1938–39 and threatened their internal autonomy. The Armenians were denied government jobs and employment.[10] During this time, accusations and criticism in the government-controlled media against the Christian community was mainly directed at the Armenians and the Assyrians. While the British saw this as part of a pro-Nazi tendency designed to arouse the fanatical religious segments of the population,[11] most Armenians attributed it to Reza Shah's connection to and personal admiration for Kemal Ataturk of Turkey. Others have seen it as part of the grand plan of pan-Iranist activities in the country.[12] Many villages in Iranian Azerbaijan had ancient Armenian names until the 1930s when Reza Shah Persianized their names.[13] Both closure of minority schools and the changes in the names of villages, cities, streets, etc. were part of Reza Shah's general policy framework designed to strengthen the state and diminish foreign dependence.

Mohammad Faghfoory's research on ulama–state relations between 1921 and 1941 shows that as early as 1921 Reza Khan had used ethnic/religious identity to achieve his political goals. He set out to eliminate his rival and partner, Seyyed Ziya al-Din Tabatabai, by exploiting his relationship with non-Muslim groups, especially the Armenians. Ziya al-Din's arrest of a well-known cleric and deputy from Isfahan was blamed on the Armenians. By manufacturing an Armenian, British, and Ziya al-Din front, Reza Khan won the support of the ulama to oust his rival.[14]

During the rule of Mohammad Reza Shah, Armenian internal autonomy was fully restored.[15] The power of the state apparatus provided security for minority communities. As in his father's reign, a strong state under Mohammed Reza Shah prevented the arbitrary exercise of power by local clergy. The general policy of economic development, modernization, and Westernization furthered the communal life and the socioeconomic condition of religious minorities. In the shah's authoritarian system, minority deputies to the Majlis (similar to Muslim deputies) were mere figureheads, some with close business ties to the royal family and their friends.

Various publications with themes such as the Armenian Republic of 1918, the Armenian grievances against the Turkish government, and details pertaining to the genocide of 1915 were published in both Persian and Armenian. Armenians were active in most sectors except politics and the military. While the former was viewed by the Armenians as a troublesome area to be shunned at all costs, the avoidance of the latter was prompted by government suspicion that the deeply felt affinity with the Armenian Soviet Socialist Republic might result in the disclosure of military and intelligence secrets to the Soviets. Armenians, however, served in the lower echelons of the military. They could serve as assistant ministers, but no ministerial or visible high political office was open to non-Muslims.

Despite relative freedom and even expressed admiration and trust by the Persians, Armenians have been acutely aware of their marginal status in Iran. They have preserved themselves by paying homage to the top leadership in the hope of receiving in exchange a safe livelihood and protection from Muslim religious extremists. For much of the twentieth century, as indigenous Christians more at ease with Western ways, they satisfied the Iranian thirst for Western economic connections, lifestyle, and ethos. With no territorial claim on Persian sovereignty, the Armenians were safe subordinates who could not and would not rebel. They really had no basis for a rebellion; they had cultural autonomy and relative respect.

The Armenians are the largest Christian minority and probably the largest non-Muslim community in Iran.[16] During the 1980s and 1990s, their numbers were estimated to be around 200,000.[17] The bulk of the population belongs to the Apostolic Church, which has archdioceses in the cities of Tehran, Tabriz, and Isfahan. However, a small number of

Armenians are Catholics and Protestants. The population is urban, with some in villages around the cities of Isfahan and Tabriz, and between Arak and Hamadan. Since the Pahlavi era, the Armenians have been politically represented in the parliament by two deputies, one each from the north and the south. They are the only non-Muslim minority to be represented by two members.

The Assyrians and Chaldeans

It is impossible to provide a simple explanation for the evolution of the Assyrians and Chaldeans in the modern Middle East. Because of religious schisms and the active involvement of Western powers with various segments of the Christian population, the Assyrians and the Chaldeans are the most complex non-Muslim religious minority to study historically.

The majority of Christians in Mesopotamia and Persia belonged to the East Syrian Church (known as the Nestorian Church), which later evolved into two dominant groups: the Assyrians and the Chaldeans (Catholics). Those who belonged to the West Syrian Church were known as the Jacobites, who flourished in Syria. The Catholic–Protestant schism was one of many sectarian conflicts among Christian Middle Easterners. From the end of the nineteenth century those Nestorians who refused to be identified with Catholics called themselves Assyrians. Anglican missionaries were responsible for spreading the idea that the Nestorians were descendants of ancient Assyria (Ashurestan). Commonalities and similarities in languages, physiognomies, and customs of the two reenforced the theory of sameness.[18]

Another theory is associated with the names "Syria" and "Assyria" and states that both have the same root, and notes that those who call themselves Syrians are ethnically Assyrians.[19] There is a tendency, however, to refer to most Christian denominations as Assyrians. For example, members of the Jacobite community in Turkey are referred to as Assyrian Jacobites;[20] Chaldeans are referred to as Assyrian Roman Catholics;[21] Assyrians are also referred to as Nestorians as opposed to Chaldeans. One writer asserts that the Assyrians are followers of Nestorianism, who include Catholics and Protestants.[22]

These different references are extremely confusing and stem from a very simple premise of whether the Assyrians are an ethnonational group or a religious community. Arian Ishaya sees them as a distinct ethnic group which has resided in the lands around the present Irano-Turkish borders. She believes that their presence in Iran dates back to at least the first century AD and maybe even to a much earlier time. Within this ethnic point of view, Assyrians are divided along various denominations including the Nestorian Church, its Chaldean offshoot, the Russian Orthodox Church, Protestant churches, and the Jacobite Church.[23] From this perspective, the Chaldeans are ethnically Assyrians who refuse to give up their traditional name. These are merely confessional divisions and do not impact on the social and cultural unity of the ethnic identity. The Catholic Church, however, is larger than the Nestorian Church, which has only one diocese in Tehran. The Catholics have three dioceses, in Tehran, Urmieh, and Ahvaz.[24]

There is no problem in identifying any group members along ethnic lines. The problem arises when either their numbers or political clout overshadow a smaller group and define their identity regardless of their wishes. There are many more who identify themselves as Assyrians in Iran than who refer to themselves as Chaldeans. If, for example, the Chaldeans see themselves as an ethnic group separate from Assyrians, then they might ask for separate representation. It was no coincidence that the Assyrian/Chaldean deputy in the Assembly of Experts, during the discussions on the constitution of the revolutionary regime in 1979 on the specific question of the number of deputies for religious minorities, protested having only one representative for Assyrians and Chaldeans combined. He asked for one deputy for each group.[25] The request was rejected. As in the earlier 1906/07 constitution, the Assyrians and Chaldeans together were given one deputy.

The problem of defining the ethnic identities of either Chaldeans or Assyrians is related to the convoluted and complex history of their social and political evolution. During the pre-World War I era, there were many Christian groups in the Ottoman Empire, Persia, and Russia. Many of these communities resided in the Azerbaijan area, mainly in villages and in the town of Urmieh (Rezaiyeh).[26] According to John Joseph, the Nestorians of Urmieh were under the jurisdiction of Mar Shimun in Hakkari (Iraq); they had accepted his authority in the seventeenth century when the patriarch resided in the Azerbaijan region.[27] In 1897, the Iranian Nestorians headed by the Azerbaijan Assyrians asked to join the Russian Orthodox Church. The Russian influence in the area increased and the number of other Western missionaries was reduced. The Russian influence in the area was a mixed blessing. On the one hand, it increased Christian–Muslim antagonism and "encouraged" inter-Christian rivalry. On the other hand, the presence of Russian cavalry gave Christians a sense of security and protection from attacks, especially by the Kurds.[28]

The quarrels among the Assyrians, some Armenians, Kurds, and Azeris had deep roots, in the 1800s. The worst event for the Urmieh

Christians was the Kurdish attack in autumn 1880. It is said, however, that Shii villagers suffered more destruction than the Christians.[29] Urmieh remained under Russian influence until the beginning of World War I. The British continued to compete with Russian influence in the area. Meanwhile, the Constitutional Revolution of 1906, through its supplement of 1907, gave Assyrians one delegate to the Majlis. Due to the concentration of Assyrians in Azerbaijan at the time, the delegate had to come from Urmieh. Yet, the infighting among various Christian denominations in Urmieh undermined the selection of one deputy. Decisions reached by the Nestorians, Roman Catholics, and the Presbyterians were vetoed by the Russian Orthodox. The latter argued that their denomination was the main representative of the Christian (non-Armenian) community. Until late spring 1911, no final decision was reached.[30] There were no representatives between World Wars I and II, and the first Assyrian deputy was elected for four years in 1959.[31]

Most scholars are in agreement that foreign missionaries with semi-political goals were responsible for the disintegration of the Christian community in the area, hostility between Christians and Muslims, and mistrust between Persian authorities and the Assyrians.[32] The story of the events in Iranian Azerbaijan during the war years, especially those between 1917 and 1918, is often recounted with different emphases.[33] These were the years of anarchy and weak central government in Iran. Social problems and conflicts among the Christian population were aggravated by large numbers of Armenian and Assyrian refugees flooding into the region from the north and the northwest (then part of the Ottoman Empire). The Russian departure prompted the local Christians to arm themselves in self-defense. Between January and July 1918, many Christians and Muslims perished in local conflicts.[34]

At the end of World War I, a mixed group of self-appointed officials claiming to represent the Assyrians attended the Paris Peace Conference. Of seven claims submitted by this group, three concerned the Persian Assyrians.[35] Although Britain planned to settle the Assyrian problem somehow, lack of leadership due to the disunity among various denominations prevented any positive development. Joseph describes their problems thus: "the mountaineers of Hakkari were against the plainsmen of Urmiyah, the Protestants against the 'Nestorians', and the pro-patriarch faction against its rival party."[36] By this time tens of thousands of Assyrians had already emigrated to the West, especially to Europe, Canada, and the United States.[37]

In Iran, during the post-war era, Reza Khan defeated the Kurdish Simko forces, resulting in the return of large numbers of Nestorians from other Persian cities back to Urmieh. The activities of missionaries flourished again, and a period of relative calm and protection by the Reza Shah regime prevailed in the area. Because of their past quasi-political role, the foreign missions were considered a destabilizing force. In the late 1920s, the regime began imposing general restrictions on mission schools. In 1934, the government asked all foreigners to evacuate the Azerbaijan region. Some believe that this decree resulted from the 1933 uprising and subsequent massacre of the Hakkari Assyrians in Iraq. Reza Shah was concerned that missionaries' work might indirectly give rise to separatist tendencies among the Assyrians of Azerbaijan, similar to those of Iraq.[38]

Mohammad Reza Shah's regime was a peaceful one for the Assyrians and Chaldeans, whose numbers had already dwindled considerably compared to the early 1900s.[39] The official Iranian press referred to them as Assyrian Church of the East and the Chaldean Catholic Church. By the mid-1970s at least half of the 30,000 Assyrian population lived in Tehran, and some 40 percent still resided in Urmieh and its surroundings.[40] During the 1990s, the number of Assyrians and Chaldeans together had shrunk to an all-time low of between 16,000 to 18,000 in Iran, the majority being Assyrian.[41] The bulk of the Chaldean population of Iran adhere to Catholicism and traditionally reside in the Khuzestan province with concentration in Ahvaz. Their patriarchal seat is in Baghdad (Iraq) and their liturgical and vernacular languages are Syriac and Arabic.[42]

Missionary activities

Christianity in Persia dates back to the pre-Islamic era beginning with the Parthians (171 BC–AD 224), when several bishoprics were founded and the Persian church was involved in proselytizing outside Persia including in China and India. During Islamic rule, various Christian groups (mostly Nestorians) were residents of Persia. Groups from several religious orders from the Roman Catholic Church were sent to Persia during the reign of Shah Abbas I (1588–1629), among them the Carmelites, who settled in Isfahan. It was only in the nineteenth century that the French Roman Catholics and Protestants went to Iran as missionaries.[43]

It is also clear that, regardless of denomination, Assyrians were at times resentful of the missions, while Armenians were almost continuously so. At one point the Anglican Church had to give assurances that it would not accept Armenians.[44] The bickering between Iranian Armenians and the Roman Catholic Church dated back to as early as 1700.[45] This does not indicate some type of unique religiosity on the part of the Armenians. It is simply a sign of an earlier and a more solidified ethnonational identity meshed with Christian Apostolic Church traditions. Anything that posed a threat to it was viewed with suspicion, be it Christian or Muslim.

Much of the attraction of the missionaries was their schools and hospitals. Among the Muslims, it was mainly the children of the elite who attended these schools.[46] Reza Shah's regime began to limit missionary activity in Iran. In 1931, village evangelism was prohibited and in 1932 Persians of any religion were prohibited from attending missionary schools.[47] In addition to prohibition, the rise in the number of schools for girls and boys under Reza Shah in the 1930s reduced interest in missionary educational activities.

The basic point remains that missionary work and foreign penetration went hand in hand and were deeply resented. This was evident in the order to close the Christian hospital in Isfahan in 1951; the hospital was run by the local Anglican Church Missionary Society. The order was reversed when the Mossadeq government fell. However, reflecting on the event decades later Bishop Dehqani Tafti, the head Anglican priest, wondered whether his church would have been better off if it had nationalized its hospital, thus reducing a heavy managerial burden. He felt that the closing of seven hospitals in northern Iran by the American Presbyterian missionaries was a wise move.[48] He also attested that, in the post-1952 era, his church was closely watched by the shah's secret police (the SAVAK) as well as the Islamic groups. He elaborates on acts of vigilantism against the church which had no protection from the Iranian authorities. To him and his church members the shah's regime was tantamount to a police state.[49]

It is difficult to obtain accurate figures for Protestants (all denominations) and Catholics in Iran. Complicating the matter is the mixture of ethnic identity with religious affiliation, and the number of Muslim conversions to Christianity. Most informants often referred to "only a few thousand" in estimating the overall numbers of nonethnic Christians in Iran. One source states that by 1994 all Protestant churches in Iran claimed an ethnic and Iranian membership of some 15,000.[50] This author has also been given the figures 5,000, 8,000, and 10,000. It is important to note that the inclusion of ethnics, on the one hand, serves the purpose of hiding the number of Iranian Muslim converts to Christianity and, on the other hand, of inflating the number of adherents. The fact is that ethnic Protestants retained their ethnic identity, while intermingling with their own group (e.g., Armenian Protestants with Apostolics), while Muslim converts referred to themselves as Christians.

The Jews

The Iranian Jews are the most researched non-Muslim religious minority in Iran. There is a gradual mushrooming of anthropological and historical works, beginning especially in the 1960s. Editors of a well-known volume on Jewish ethnology in the Middle East see this as part of a general trend encompassing all Middle Eastern Jewry. They attribute it to the emigration of most Middle Eastern Jews to Israel, their curiosity about their past, and the rising social problems in the Israeli state and polity.[51]

Any study of the Jews always faces the issue of religious versus ethnic identity. As one scholar of ethnic politics put it: "Judaism, although a religion of revelation and universal principle, is not a proselytizing faith. Over the years, it has often become difficult to distinguish between religious community and ethnic identity as the essential bond linking Jews."[52]

The presence of Jews in Persia predates the Christians. At least since the conquest of the Babylonian Empire by Cyrus the Great in 539 BC, Jews with a distinctive identity lived within Persian borders.[53] Jews wrote in Judeo-Persian (classical Persian in Hebrew letters) and their prose and poetry reflected a synthesis between the Persian and Jewish cultures.[54] Jewish sectarian movements have also existed in Iran, and one scholar suggests a "Jewish development parallel to the appearance of numerous proto-Shi'ite sects with messianic overtones during the final years of the Omayyad caliphate."[55]

Although there is evidence of Jewish persecution in pre-Islamic Iran, most scholars point to the official adoption of Shiism as state religion and the Safavid Dynasty (1501–1722) as the beginning of the worst era in Persian–Jewish relations. The mistreatment was so intense and extensive compared to the past that some even concluded that Shiism may have been solely responsible for anti-Jewish sentiments.

The fact remains that in a number of discriminatory spheres the Jews shared their persecution with Christian minorities. For example, during most of the Safavid era the Jews, Christians, and Zoroastrians paid special taxes through appointees to the local authorities. The law of apostasy rewarded those non-Muslims who converted to Islam by making them the sole inheritors of the property and possessions of all relatives, even distant ones. Since non-Muslim religious minorities were dependent on the clerical leaders of the dominant Muslim community, the type of treatment they received, as well as the severity of persecution, varied locally. Many scholars also believe that the persecution of Jews was more severe, and one of its consequences was Jewish conversion to Islam in significant numbers.[56] Another important historical point is that Jewish persecution was not limited to parts of Persia. From the late eighteenth through the nineteenth century, expulsion or violence against the Jews increased throughout the Ottoman Empire and Morocco.[57]

Why were the Jews a special target? While this question cannot be answered with certainty, some scholars have offered explanations of their own. Their answers can be classified as: (1) compared to the Christian population, they did not have the same strong backing and overall protection or intervention from the Western powers (and some missionary groups), and this turned them into an easy target; or (2) the local Christians shared the Muslims' bias against the Jews for one (or a combination) of these reasons: (a) their strong religious views, (b) anti-Jewish European ideologies, and (c) as non-Muslims were forced into vocational specializations due to their status, fierce economic competition resulted, and there was an incentive to eliminate Jewish competition from the local scene. This last reason, however, cut both ways, since the Jews were also competing with other non-Muslim minorities (for example, with the Zoroastrians in Yazd) for an economic share of the limited local markets.[58]

On the issue of the intervention of Western powers on behalf of the Jews, it is known that as early as the 1870s European Jewry had tried to help improve the condition of the Jews in Iran. The British government also made attempts, and the United States government intervened as early as 1894. These diplomatic initiatives continued in the period after World War I. In fact, beginning in 1898, the Alliance Israelite Universelle (an educational organization founded by Jewish intellectuals in Paris in 1860) opened its first school in Tehran, followed by schools in the cities of Isfahan, Hamadan, Kermanshah, Shiraz, and Seneh in subsequent years. The teachers in these schools, who were foreign nationals, intervened on behalf of the Jews quite regularly.[59]

The Constitutional Revolution of 1906 was viewed by many Jews as a positive development. The new constitution granted one representative to the Jews. As with the Armenians, the Jews at first were not allowed to send a deputy from their own community to the Majlis and were represented by a Muslim clergyman.[60] The ascent of Reza Shah brought temporary relief to the Jews and other non-Muslims. However, during the late 1920s, Jewish schools were closed. In the 1930s Reza Shah's pro-Nazi sympathies seriously threatened Iranian Jewry. There were no persecutions of the Jews, but, as with other minorities, anti-Jewish articles were published in the Persian media.[61] Unlike the religiously motivated prejudice, anti-Jewish sentiments acquired an ethnonational character, a direct import from Germany. This time well-educated and "progressive" individuals were in a leading position, seeing themselves as the "superior Aryans" and "genuine Iranians." One rumor exemplified the easy marriage between the Shii religious and ultranationalist secular prejudice. It was rumored that Hitler had been secretly converted to Islam and his Muslim name was Heydar (one of the titles of Imam Ali – meaning the lion); around his neck hung a silver necklace with a picture of Ali. Hitler was going to reveal his religion to the world after defeating the deceitful British and the anti-God Russians, and finishing off the Jews. A popular poem of the time went: "Imam yavar-e ma, Hossein sarvar-e ma. Agar alman naresad, khak bar sar-e ma [Imam is our supporter, Hossein is our master. If Germany doesn't arrive, dirt on our heads]."[62]

The founding of the state of Israel in 1948 prompted the mass emigration of Jews from Iran. Not all were Iranian Jews; many Iraqi Jews were part of this exodus via Iran as well. In two major waves between 1947 and 1951, most Iraqi Jews came to Iran on their way to Israel. The first wave of Iraqi Jews was wealthy, well educated, and spoke English well; many of them made Iran their permanent home. In addition to business opportunities available in Iran, the state of war with its Arab neighbors and the socialist lifestyle of citizens made Israel an unappealing place to live.[63] Between 1948 and 1953, more than one-third of the Jewish population of Iran emigrated to Israel.[64] Most of the emigrants from this wave were from the provinces and belonged to the lower classes; the wealthy Jews, particularly from Tehran, preferred to remain in Iran. As the state of Israel was declared, however, posters in the Tehran bazaar asked Iranians to boycott merchandise sold by Jewish merchants and to join Arab armies in their fight against Israel.[65] The Mossadeq era in the early 1950s saw another rise in politically motivated public anti-Jewish sentiments. Both cases were correlated with a substantial weakening of the central government and increasing strength of the religious forces.

Mohammad Reza Shah's reign was the most prosperous era for Iranian Jewry. Jewish organizations, synagogues, and other associations operated freely at both the provincial and national levels. Intermarriages with Muslims, especially among the college-educated, increased in the 1970s but the numbers still remained negligible. However, one scholar suggests that the Iranianization of the Jews, particularly during Mohammad Reza Shah's reign, weakened their "Zionist and Jewish values."[66] In 1979, 2 of the 18 members of the Royal Academy of Sciences, 80 of the 4,000 university lecturers, and 600 of the 10,000 physicians in Iran were Jews. For the first time ever, about 50 percent of Jewish children of elementary school age attended Hebrew schools and received lessons in Hebrew.[67] The economic status of the Jews in Iran improved dramatically compared to the past. Estimates seem to vary; however, by 1968 Iran already had the wealthiest Jewish community in all of Asia and Africa (with the exception of Israel and South Africa).[68] According to one source, by 1979, the overwhelming majority of Jews were middle class, 10 percent were wealthy, and another 10 percent were impoverished.[69]

A crucial factor in the dramatic improvement of the lot of Iranian Jews was the close connection between the shah's regime and the state of Israel. Details of the relationship between the two state actors and the exact role of Iranian Jewry still await rigorous exploration.[70] However, this relationship had a dramatic impact on the situation of the Jews during and immediately after the 1979 Revolution.

In the 1970s, the number of Jews in Iran was estimated to be around 80,000; within one year of the Revolution their numbers declined dramatically to about 50,000–60,000.[71] By the mid- to late 1980s, the number of Iranian Jews was estimated to be between 20,000 and 30,000. For the mid-1990s the number of Jews was reported to be unusually high, around 35,000.[72]

The Zoroastrians

Zoroastrianism arose out of complex religious conditions in ancient Persia. It is known by the name of its Prophet Zarathushtra (Zoroaster) who most probably lived in what is today eastern–northeastern Iran between 1700 and 1500 BC.[73] In the tradition of Indo-European religions, Zoroastrianism was dualistic in ethics and monotheistic in belief. There is little doubt that it influenced Buddhism, Judaism, Christianity, and Islam throughout the centuries. Three pre-Islamic Persian empires adopted Zoroastrianism as the state religion, the last being the Sassanian Empire in AD 226; this version, by most expert accounts, was far removed from its original.[74] The Muslim Arab conquest of Persia (in the middle of the seventh century) gradually led to the reduction of the Zoroastrian population. At first the Zoroastrians, through their community regulations, maintained exclusivity; but eventually, through conversions to Islam and intermarriages with Muslims, the community lost its economic and social domination.[75]

Most research has focused on the Zoroastrian religion rather than the actual treatment of its adherents by local or state authorities, the ulama, and their cronies. There is, therefore, little information about their perils. It is known, for example, that during the ninth and tenth centuries, the Zoroastrians were oppressed so severely that a large group emigrated from Khorasan area to the state of Gujarat in Western India and later became known as the Parsis.[76] Throughout centuries, their priests and representatives made regular visits to Iran whenever they were allowed to do so, and the practice has continued during the Islamic Republic.[77]

Some have argued that the Parsis were responsible for reinvigorating the Persian Zoroastrian communities, especially in Kerman, during the end of the nineteenth century. Reinvigoration was vital, due to restrictions placed on these communities (including on their movement and dress codes) in the early nineteenth century. Some of these restrictions continued into the twentieth century.[78] The Zoroastrians of Kerman and Yazd paid jazieh to the local authorities until the abrogation of this tax in 1882; the new governor of Kerman reinstituted it thirty-seven years later. At the urging of the Tehran Zoroastrian community, the central government intervened, reversing the Kerman governor's decision.[79] The treatment of Zoroastrians differed from one locality to another and maltreatment by the local population and the Muslim clergy was harsher in Yazd than Kerman.[80]

Zoroastrian intellectuals, like other non-Muslim minorities, took an active role in the pro-constitution movement in Iran. Wealthy Zoroastrian families helped the movement financially and lobbied the Muslim merchants, ulama, preachers, and the press for the passage of provisions on equal rights of all citizens.[81] However, unlike the Jews and the Armenians, the Zoroastrians did not relinquish their representation to Muslim clergymen, and were represented by one deputy in the first Majlis.[82]

The Reza Shah era had a peculiar relevance to the Zoroastrian community. On the one hand, their schools and worship centers were subjected to restrictions similar to those on other non-Muslim minorities. On the other hand, they became a unique instrument for the nationalist ideology of the new monarch. Ancient Persian symbols (closely associated with Zoroastrians) became the cornerstone of modern Iranian nation building. The most obvious was the 1934 declaration by Reza Shah that foreigners call the country "Iran" rather than "Persia." "Iran" derived from an expression in the Zoroastrian holy book, Avesta, and in the new ideology it was closely associated with the glorious past of Persian kingdoms in the period before the Arab invasion.[83] Naturally, many Zoroastrians welcomed the new system and some were ardent supporters of Reza Shah. Among them was Arbab Keikhosrow Shahrokh, the Zoroastrian deputy in the Majlis, who worked tirelessly to improve the condition of the Zoroastrian communities throughout the country and who was a strong advocate of development programs for Iran. Yet even he could not outlast Reza Shah, who many believe ordered his assassination.[84] This incident is more of a reflection on Reza Shah's ruling style than on his policy toward the Zoroastrians.

Mohammad Reza Shah's government was certainly better than any previous regime in its relations with the Zoroastrians. The first Zoroastrian World Congress met in Tehran in 1960 and one member of the community was placed in high position in the government. Similar to other non-Muslim minorities, some of its members joined left-wing groups and particularly the Tudeh Party of Iran.[85] Although official state–minority relations were good, prejudice and discrimination at the provincial level lingered on.

The concentration of Zoroastrians in Tehran during the last few decades has been a trend similar to that of other non-Muslim minorities. Most migrants have come from Yazd and Kerman. One source states that the number of Zoroastrian residents in Tehran increased from only 300 in the first decade of the twentieth century to around 15,000 in the 1980s.[86]

Worldwide their numbers are about 125,000,[87] concentrated mainly in India, Pakistan, and Iran. Before 1979 their numbers in Iran were 30,000.[88] By the mid-1990s, the Zoroastrian population numbered 50,000.[89] Today, in addition to the above-mentioned cities, Zoroastrian worship centers can be found in Shiraz, Isfahan, and Ahvaz. There are still Zoroastrians residing in villages, especially around Yazd.

The Bahais

Two movements in the nineteenth century led to the inception of Bahaism. Shaikhism was a movement among the Shiis whose proponents expected the return of the hidden Twelfth Imam in 1844. Babism, first developed as a faction of Shaikhism, departed from it when its youthful leader, Seyyed Ali Mohammad Shirazi (1819–50) declared himself to be the gate to the Hidden Imam and later the Hidden Imam himself. Known as the Bab, he denied being a new prophet, and his early teachings were within the bounds of Shiism, often interpreted as a more progressive and reformist form of Islam.[90] In a pioneering study of Babism, Abbas Amanat highlights the unconventional and revolutionary nature of the movement:

At the heart of the Babi ethos was a spirit of rebellion against social injustice and moral mischief, for which the Babis held both the ruler and the 'ulama responsible. The Babis were unanimous in their condemnation. The methods they prescribed, however, differed widely.[91]

Amanat also identifies tension within the movement between the moderates and the militants, the latter intensifying the clash with government authorities. Babism did not last long; its proponents were exterminated by the government. Bab was executed in 1850 and the rest of the leadership perished within the next two years.

Bahaism emerged from Babism. One of Bab's followers, Mirza Hossein Ali Nuri (1817–92), known as Bahaullah, declared in 1860 that he was the divine manifestation of God, the messianic figure predicted by Bab. Despite the ensuing disbelief and sectarian splits, from the late 1860s to the 1890s Bahaism as a distinct religion spread rapidly outside Iran, mainly in Third World countries and from the 1890s to the 1920s in Europe and North America.[92] Bahaullah was besieged by Persian and

Ottoman officials, Islamic clergy, militant Babis, and his own brother, Mirza Yahya, known as Sobh-e Azal, and his adherents (known as Azalis). Despite overwhelming odds he maintained a pacifist stand advocating world peace, universal education, an end to racial and religious prejudice, and several fundamental social reform issues. His religious views embraced and recognized other major religions such as Christianity, Judaism, Zoroastrianism, and Islam. He was exiled, ending up eventually in Acre in Palestine where he died in 1892. Today, in addition to Acre, Haifa is also significant for Bahaism, as the remains of Bab and his devotees were taken there and buried.[93]

Following Bahaullah, the religious leadership of the Bahai community became an arena of controversy and conflict. Bahaullah appointed his eldest son, Abd-al-Baha, as the successor in 1892; Abd-al-Baha appointed his grandson, Shoghi Effendi Rabbani, to be the leader after his death. Both were challenged by family members and their Bahai supporters. Shoghi Effendi died in London in 1957; as he was childless and had excommunicated eligible relatives, there was no one to succeed him. A global congress in London elected members to the Universal House of Justice, its seat in Haifa, Israel, to take over the role of religious authority. Even at this juncture of history, another leader declared himself the successor to Shoghi Effendi and with a small number of adherents formed what is known as the Remey movement.[94]

A great deal has been written about Babi and Bahai religious beliefs.[95] Some Zoroastrians but many more Jews converted to Bahaism, particularly in the nineteenth century.[96] Bahais see themselves as the advocates of universalism and peace on earth; their main book of laws is originally in Arabic, *al-Ketab al-Aqdas*, and they adhere to certain rituals, observances, and pilgrimage which have gone through changes over time. Bahais emphasize that Bahaism, as it stands today, is a distinct religion for the modern world. They emphatically deny being either a sect or a reform movement within Islam. The Bahai concept of progressive revelation has set them on a direct collision course with the Muslims. Progressive revelation is the belief that "God has been sending manifestations of God, whether prophets or messengers, since the inception of the human race, and will continue to do so in the future." These successive manifestations bring in "increasingly sophisticated religious teachings over time."[97] Bahaullah, their spiritual leader, recognized Moses, Christ, Mohammad, and other prophets to be, like himself, the historical manifestations of God. The idea of progressive revelation clashes with the Islamic worldview which sees Mohammad as the last prophet and Islam as the last major religion.

Bahai history in Iran is marred by perpetual persecutions since the faith's inception. During the Constitutional Revolution, the Bahais took an ambivalent position, which was caused by a combination of factors. Bahaullah's writings had endorsed a constitutional form of government, yet the Bahai community did not openly take a position for fear of reprisal from either side. Bahaullah's successor, Abd-al-Baha, urged involvement in the constitutional process in 1906 but became "disillusioned" after the Revolution had succeeded and declared that Bahais should "dissociate themselves from politics . . . a policy which gradually became frozen into a Bahai principle."[98] This is a common argument made by Bahais even today, but others have disputed this assertion.[99]

Direct, violent, and public persecution of Bahais ceased during Reza Shah's rule, as part of attempts to avoid an impression of anarchy and chaos. His grand plan for modernization and Westernization of Iran resulted in giving important positions to Bahais in the civil administration, especially in finance. In the 1930s the Bahais became subject to the same restrictions that had been imposed upon legal non-Muslim minorities. Despite the tendency in pro-Bahai popular sources to present the events of the 1930s as purely Bahai persecution, many reported acts such as attacks in the Iranian press, closing down of some centers, closing of Bahai schools, demotion or denying access to government jobs for Bahais, and a ban on the publication of Bahai literature were similar to measures directed at Armenians, Jews, and Zoroastrians. Only one of the reported measures, namely nonrecognition of Bahai marriages, was specifically targeted at the community.[100]

The popular notion among Iranian Muslims and other non-Muslims is that the Bahais enjoyed a privileged status during the reign of Mohammad Reza Shah. There is also a public perception by all groups that, since the Bahais were evangelizing their faith, intermarriage with Muslim and non-Muslim citizens was a tactical device for their missionary work. This perception misses the point that, since Bahaullah recognized all major religions, it was only logical to permit intermarriages.[101]

Most Bahai sources emphatically deny having had a privileged status by emphasizing the persecution of Bahais during the month of Ramadan in 1955. These purges had the strong backing of the Marja-e Taqlid (Source of Emulation) of the time, Ayatollah Mohammad Hossein Borujerdi (d. 1962). The vehemence of the ulama in pushing the shah's government to engage in an anti-Bahai campaign resulted in the direct participation of officials in the physical destruction of the dome of the Bahai center in Tehran.[102] The shah's government grew cautious following international protests launched by the Bahai lobbies in Western countries.[103] There is evidence that throughout the 1960s and 1970s Islamic groups continued their harassment, and even collaborated with the government's secret service agency, the SAVAK, against the Bahais.[104]

Overall, Bahais argue that, since the Iranian civil code required applicants to identify their religion, Bahais were not employed in government services. Consequently, employment in private industry became the only option. This, combined with the fact that education was highly valued in the socialization of Bahai children, turned many into a qualified pool of professionals in the modernizing/Westernizing Iran of the shah.[105] The relative betterment of the condition of the Bahais was not without its price. The attained wealth of some Bahai families "rekindled dormant prejudices and provoked anger and resentment"[106] toward the community. While the expanded land ownership of the Bahais is acknowledged, the Bahai sources cite high taxes especially targeted at their community and their land holdings, as well as the 1975 formation of a single-party state, with the only party, Rastakhiz (Resurgence), being one which the Bahais declined to join on religious grounds, as additional measures of subtle oppression by the regime.[107]

Iran is not the only Islamic country that has undertaken the direct (or indirect) persecution of the Bahais. In 1962 Bahais were persecuted in Morocco; in 1960 Bahai activities were banned in Egypt, and from 1970 in Iraq.[108] Though the understandably one-sided publications from the Bahai quarters as well as the persistent bias of secular or religious, educated, or noneducated Iranians against them must be taken into account, one simple fact remains unchanged. Of all non-Muslim religious minorities the persecution of the Bahais has been the most widespread, systematic, and uninterrupted. Persecution does not lie only in the action of a state or a community but in the mind of every individual. The Bahais represented everything that it was sanctioned (by the state, the ulama, the Shii Muslim community, and the secular, even Western-educated) to hate – namely, apostasy, association with the West and Israel, pro-monarchism, and an elite club bent on self-promotion and propaganda.

Estimating the number of Bahais in Iran has always been difficult due to their persecution and strict adherence to secrecy.[109] The reported number of Bahais in Iran has ranged anywhere from the outrageously high figure of 500,000 to the low number of 150,000. The number 300,000 has been mentioned more frequently, especially for the mid- to late 1970s, but it is not reliable. Roger Cooper gives an estimate of between 150,000 and 300,000.[110] In contrast to other non-Muslim minorities, the Bahais have been spread throughout the country in villages, small towns, and various cities, fueling the paranoia of the prejudiced.

Comparative dynamics

In pre-revolutionary Iran several patterns may be identified.

Differential legitimacy zones

Non-Muslim minorities have had differential relations with the Shii authorities. Assyrians and Chaldeans, whose history has been more intensely intermingled with the missionaries, have played a less dynamic role in the shaping of the modern Iranian (nation-)state. The Jews for most of the twentieth century were impoverished, by necessity bent on survival, and lacked a strong religious leadership. Vilified by the Shii Muslim ulama and living under the perpetual threat of assault, the Jews were unable to participate visibly and actively in national events. Bahais, never recognized, relied on their own internal solidarity (with latent international networks) to live in their homeland. Both Jewish and Bahai communities prospered under the reign of the second Pahlavi king.

The Armenians and Zoroastrians stand out as the most dramatic actors in the Iranian political scene. With strong communal organizations and better leadership, they related to the local ulama and ultimately to the Qajar kings directly. Both groups were active during the Constitutional Revolution and, even with the advent of Reza Shah, they were directly involved in the passage of legislation favoring all non-Muslim minorities. Their legitimacy zone has always been more solid and stable compared to other non-Muslim minorities.

Perpetual clerical bigotry

During the pre-Reza Shah era, the clergy exercised excessive power at local levels, and the non-Muslim communities were at the mercy of their whims; in addition, the clergy played an active role in politics, cooperating with political groups and government officials. The religious leaders and government authorities had a long history of cooperation and coexistence. The high-ranking clergy were prominent in rival political groups, and "more often than not supported, or were compelled to support, government policies."[111] And, despite the constitution and later the end of legal discrimination under Reza Shah, the clerical anti-non-Muslim tendencies did not cease. Although at first Reza Shah manipulated their bigotry to facilitate his move into power, and then suppressed their voice, religiously motivated attacks against non-Muslims were reported in provinces and towns throughout the country following his exile.[112] Yet, the disturbing tendency, more obvious to non-Muslims than Muslim secularists, to blame non-Muslims or to associate them unfairly with political rivals in order to fulfill political and personal ambitions (and to know that this policy will work with the clergy and their adherents) remains a sour point in modern Iranian history. The repetition of these patterns under Mohammad Reza Shah was blatantly demonstrated in the 1955 incident against the Bahais. The state knew how to pay lip service to the religious elements even in the most "secular" era of Iran.

Nationalist xenophobia

Most might not realize how easily nationalist tendencies can move toward fanaticism and become, similar to religious bigotry, a force wrapped in intense ethnocentrism and chauvinism. Reza Shah's rule brought relief and provided a security blanket for the non-Muslims; centralized uniformity protected them from the tyranny of the local religious zealots. Yet, the sharp ideological shift to strict Persianization deprived them of their small gains. All ethnic and religious minorities suffered the harsh consequences of the new nationalist ardor. The irony is that ultranationalist fervor does not stop with one or two acts but spills over into bigotry similar to religious zealotry. For example, Abrahamian reports that the Armenian schools lost their license to operate in 1938; this was bad enough, but even worse and more troublesome were a series of articles in the newspaper, *Ettela'at*, attacking Iran's Christians, referring to them as "dangerous criminals."[113]

Here the religious bigots were replaced by secular educated nationalists who defined everyone's identity based not on adherence to Islam but on an obscure identity envisioned through state ideology. In many ways, perhaps, this was worse than religious bigotry; here there were no alternative textual interpretations or religious men with spiritual insight to interfere and redirect the currents of prejudice. The vibrations of the nationalist xenophobia of the 1930s continued in the sleek era of the 1960s and 1970s, where messages of integration were mainly a window dressing, symbolic gestures took precedence over reality, and shallow sloganeering replaced the substance of the complexity of nation building.

Two faces of the era of the shahs

During the Reza Shah era, and particularly during the reign of his son, the pull to the capital was strong for both Muslim and non-Muslim citizens. The economic prosperity of the country was good for both groups. Development of a middle-class sector, education, and increases in the professional and technical citizenry were impressive. The power of the modern state with a centralized authoritarian apparatus defined national identity for all of its citizens. The use of brute force by Reza Shah was replaced by more subtle coercion and "positive incentives" – rewarding those who acculturated – under Mohammad Reza Shah. The Pahlavi rule promoted homogenization; religious minorities were to join "the national mainstream."[114] Differences were theoretically nonexistent or of minimum importance; everyone was equal before the law; everyone was welcome into any profession. The sameness of all citizens was reiterated, and every ethnic and religious minority was referred to as *Irani* first and foremost.

There was another Iran as well. Provincial life, more so than Tehran, exemplified this difference; discrimination and prejudice were daily experiences for many non-Muslims. Granted, they were often subtle, more individualized, and rarely involved killing, and the intensity varied by the event and the community in question. Yet the idea circulating among the "modernized" Iranians was that non-Muslim minorities had attained positions of authority and responsibility. The Bahai physician of the shah, for example, has often been mentioned, along with a handful of non-Muslim wealthy industrialists, as being among those who had co-partnerships in business ventures with the court. Three crucial questions are never raised or addressed: (1) the simple issue of the qualifications of non-Muslim individuals for attainment of their positions; (2) the nature of the relationship of these persons to their own communities: for instance, how involved were they? Did their connection in any way cause the prosperity of their own community or (as with the Muslims) were their own families the main benefactors?[115] And, (3) the motivation behind having a non-Muslim in a certain position: for example, was a Bahai physician more trustworthy because he was less likely to poison or misdiagnose the shah? Or, why would Reza Shah appoint Bahais mainly in finance or entrust the Zoroastrian deputy in the Majlis, Keikhosrow Shahrokh, with several burdensome tasks, all of which involved financial responsibilities? Was a Zoroastrian perceived as less likely to steal from the national treasury? Studies of ethnic groups have shown the purposeful use of ethnic identity in government and state appointments in authoritarian systems; what would prevent similar peculiar considerations in the selection of non-Muslims to sensitive posts? Would there have been a close relationship between the Jewish diaspora and Israel if these connections were not endorsed and encouraged by the shah's government?

The non-Muslims had a different story to tell: they were often placed in positions of secondary importance; lacking visibility, they would help an important minister or head of a section (who did not do the work) look good. A prevalent mindset, especially among ethnic non-Muslims, namely Jews, Armenians, Assyrians, and Chaldeans, was that Muslim Iranians should be viewed with care because of the presence of a constant duality in their words and actions. They could be supportive one minute but turn against a person or an issue the next minute. Ironically, this view was also expressed by Shii Muslim Iranians about themselves, demonstrating a profound cynical sense of self and the other in a whole (nation-) state.[116]

Several facts have accompanied the reality of life for religious minorities: (1) they have been a minute group; (2) unlike some Muslim ethnic groups, they have had no claim to any discrete part of Iran's territory – in fact, geographically they have not been outsiders; (3) having experienced local tyranny, they have been obedient subjects of the modern state system, always aware of the menacing alternative; and (4) affected by the reverberations of national ideology and identity, education, and economic well-being, many minorities have achieved upward social mobility and have come to see themselves as Iranians.

Yet, none of the above situations prevented a direct assault on the identity, loyalty, and integrity of the non-Muslim community in 1979 and after. Their legal, social, economic, and religious lives were to go through a major overhaul with the Bahais bearing the largest brunt of the change. Debates over the constitution of the revolutionary regime were the first public forum in which patterns of conflict and accommodation emerge.

2   The Assembly of Experts: debut in the year of destiny

The constitution of the Islamic Republic of Iran was the first significant document marking the ideological direction of the new state and the status of its religious minorities. The open proceedings put on display a multitude of issues including differing views on the legal status of religious minorities, the powerful role of Ayatollah Beheshti, and the critical impact of the non-Muslim deputies on the final draft of the constitution.

The constitution was written in the summer and autumn of 1979 during an extremely tumultuous revolutionary atmosphere. The year was marked by the executions of former military and civilian officials, clashes between various leftist forces, fighting between the leftist and pro-Khomeini supporters, battles between government troops and various Muslim ethnonational groups in provinces (including fighting between the Kurds and the Azeris), a series of assassinations including the killing of Ayatollah Morteza Motahhari (one of the main ideologues and a member of the Revolutionary Council) and the wounding of Ali-Akbar Hashemi Rafsanjani in Tehran (in May), the closing of some two dozen opposition newspapers (in mid-August), and the takeover of the American Embassy (in November).

The exact details of what transpired before or during the publication of the first draft constitution endorsed by Ayatollah Khomeini and the draft which was adopted and developed by the Assembly of Experts (Majlis-e Khebregan) is unclear. What is clear is that religious and ethnic minorities were deeply concerned about their rights within the new system, and the prime minister of the Provisional Government, Mehdi Bazargan, was cognizant of these concerns.[1]

The first draft constitution had been written before Khomeini's return to Iran. After his return, the draft was again worked on and its final version was published in June 1979. This document had several features: (1) it made no special provisions for the clerical domination of the state, (2) it did not mention the vice-regency of the faqih (the supreme jurist), (3) it was approved by the Revolutionary Council and Ayatollah Khomeini without objection, (4) Ayatollah Khomeini had proposed a referendum to finalize the draft and did not particularly favor a constituent assembly, and (5) the Islamic Republican Party (IRP) did not condemn the document. Rather, the opposition parties were the ones who objected to anything short of a constituent assembly to discuss the draft.[2]

The small number of members for the Assembly of Experts was a compromise, but when the elections were called, several important secular parties and parties representing ethnic groups boycotted the elections. The political parties that participated in the elections comprised a complex set of coalitions, the largest falling under the IRP.[3] Of seventy-three deputies elected, fifty-five were clerics and over fifty were on the IRP coalition slate, thereby giving them a clear majority.[4] The Assembly was in session for a little over three months from August through November 1979 for the sole purpose of devising a constitution. The end result was a major departure from the early draft. The concept of the supreme jurist was incorporated into the document, though it did allow for presidential and parliamentary elections.

The open proceedings were affected by the political climate outside the Assembly. Most groups, including non-Muslim minorities, were attentive to how developments might affect their interests. Formal and informal meetings were arranged with the authorities to ask questions and convey community concerns. At one point, for instance, Sadeq Tabatabai, deputy prime minister and the spokesman for the Provisional Government, attended a meeting in the Tehran Diocese Councils to reassure everyone that the elected deputies to the Assembly of Experts would be free to voice their opinions on any issue of concern. Along with this reassurance, Tabatabai refuted the restrictions against Christians reported in Italian, German, and American press reports calling them "thoroughly unfounded" and part of Western "propaganda."[5]

During the convening of the Assembly of Experts, two individuals led the Tehran Friday Prayer congregations consecutively, Ayatollah Mahmud Taleqani and Ayatollah Hossein-Ali Montazeri. Neither expressed or encouraged negative feelings toward non-Muslims. Ayatollah Taleqani, whose illness and subsequent death were a major blow to the more progressive Islamic forces, made only one reference to non-Muslim minorities. Most of his sermons were addressed to the Muslim population urging them to cease discord, cooperate, and respect one another. The Assembly of Experts was not devoid of shortcomings, he admitted, but he dismissed complaints about lack of freedom.[6] He addressed the non-Muslims in only one sermon. Referring to the Iranian Jews as "brothers," Taleqani warned: "This Zionist danger is not directed only at the world of Islam and Christianity, but it is also directed at you."[7] He continued, saying that Jerusalem belonged to all religions and not to a select group; that the "pretense" of being oppressed by the Nazis no longer existed; and that the truly devout and progressive Jews should dissociate themselves from "the bloodthirsty" Zionists and their agents.[8] Once, at Ayatollah Khomeini's house, he encountered the Armenian representatives; reassuring them of their rights, he called Islam "the creed of freedom."[9]

Ayatollah Montazeri took over the Friday Prayer sermons after Taleqani's death while continuing to chair the Assembly of Experts. Occasionally he raised controversial issues discussed in the Assembly, such as whether the rule of the supreme jurist (Velayat-e Faqih) was Islamic. He was more concerned with the overall relationship of religion and politics and the ethnic uprisings than the religious minorities.[10] Jews were the only non-Muslim minority to appear several times in his speeches and always in the context of Zionism, Israel, and American domination. While Israel was the "the illegitimate child of imperialism,"[11] he was careful not to disparage Iranian Jews. When saying "Yahud" he explained he did not mean the Jewish minority whose religious and communal rights along with the Zoroastrians and Christians were protected in Islam: "Do not be mistaken if I said Jew, we do not oppose all Jews." Then, directing his comments to the army and the Revolutionary Guards in particular, he reiterated: "Do not assume the Jewish problem" was being raised; the problem was "Zionism."[12] In his sermons and throughout the duration of the Assembly of Experts, Montazeri maintained a careful and sensitive tone.

While minority representatives in the Assembly of Experts lacked direct political authority, they enjoyed relative freedom to voice their opposition to the work being done in the Assembly. It is clear that the deputies, the chair (Ayatollah Montazeri), and the vice-chair (Ayatollah Beheshti) were responding, often defensively, to allegations made against them. The political climate forced these deputies to address issues that otherwise would have never been raised. The environment lent to the Assembly of Experts a fluidity and openness which was a novel experience in Iran. Despite the clerical and IRP domination of the Assembly, the debates were lively and rigorous. Every article was discussed in detail and although much rewriting took place in closed committees, the open sessions still exposed some problematic areas and forced further rewriting of the articles. Quite often issues discussed in committees, especially strong disagreements, resurfaced during the open public forum, which became rancorous at times.

Much time was allocated to debating procedural matters. The dialectic style of argument and counterargument (characteristic of Shii religious education) was often a source of conflict. At the third meeting Ayatollah

Beheshti tried to discourage spontaneous interruptions, instructing the deputies that debates in the parliamentary medium differed from general discussions where one directly and immediately responded to another person's comments; here the deputies must take notes and then respond when it was their turn to speak up.[13] At one point, Ayatollah Montazeri gave a lengthy explanation of the peculiar nature and format of clerical debates, as learned in religious schools, in which argument was made by contradictions. He asked the print media to reflect all facets of the debates and not to leave out counterarguments which were designed to answer questions.[14]

Interruptions and out-of-order expressions of opinion prevailed throughout the meetings. When Ayatollah Montazeri spoke out of order to rebuke a deputy at one point, Beheshti reminded him: "The chair must await his turn; he should not speak whenever he wants." Montazeri thanked him and obliged.[15] In another case, one deputy used strong words to criticize the chair for reading the recommendations of the deputies and then ignoring them; "they disappear into thin air," he said.[16] These problems seemed to continue throughout the Assembly of Experts; during the thirty-second session, the frustrated Zoroastrian deputy, Priest Rostam Shahzadi, commented: "Either do not bother to write your names down, or if you do, you gentlemen must speak in turn!"[17]

Constant tension between the religious right and the nonclerical deputies resonated throughout the proceedings. For instance, at one point when the only nonclerical representative from Azerbaijan complained that they were moving too fast in reviewing the draft of the constitution, he was placed on the defensive for the use of the word "progressive" in describing himself. "What do you mean?," he was asked. "Aren't they [the clerics] progressive?"[18]

Many exchanges reflected a conscious awareness of parliamentary procedures involving time limits for speakers, arguments for and against various articles, and unresolved conflicts within the committees, which often spilled over into the floor debates. Several times committees were urged to rework the draft and resubmit it for public debate. Some deputies protested the hasty and unorganized manner in which laws were written in the committees then rushed to the floor for debate, while others defended the process.[19] Personalities did stand out in opposition to one another or as they responded to the media or their own constituency. At one point even the chair, Ayatollah Montazeri, and the vice-chair, Ayatollah Beheshti, who was in charge of the Assembly at the time, clashed over the language of the description of the Islamic Republic. Montazeri voiced his opposition to the statement ironed out in one of the committees, "Jomhuri-ye Islami nezami ast tohidi [the Islamic Republic is a monotheistic system]" and went on to explain his position. Beheshti clearly did not want Montazeri to continue the discussion and would not allow him to speak. An angry Montazeri accused Beheshti of being an opportunist. Other deputies intervened and the debate continued, eventually the word "tohidi" was replaced by "iman be khodaye yekta [belief in a single God]"; yet Montazeri was not allowed to explain his position even once.[20] This forceful, skilled, and shrewd handling of proceedings, skewing situations to adhere to his preferences, was typical of Ayatollah Beheshti. Despite officially being vice-chair, he was clearly in command both privately and publicly.[21]

Overall, the debates were strikingly candid and personalized; yet the sweeping clerical domination impacted voting results. The bulk of the discussion remained within the boundaries of Islamic ethos and on a number of issues the results were a foregone conclusion.[22] The cornerstones of the debates were the structure and the extent of Islamism.

While many important discussions ensued in the Assembly of Experts, the focus here is on the cases involving religious minorities. Among the deputies in the Assembly, four represented religious minorities, one from each group; these were the Armenians (Hrair Khalatian), Assyrians (Sergen Bait Ushana), Jews (Aziz Daneshrad), and Zoroastrians (Rostam Shahzadi).[23] The swearing-in ceremony was conducted uniformly for all deputies of the Majlis-e Khebregan; all members swore to God, the Quran, and other divine books to observe the continuity and solidarity of the Islamic Republic, its territorial integrity, and union of all Iranian ethnic groups.[24] Compared to the restrictive text of the oath of office for the Majlis, which was adopted later, the language of the text of the oath for the Assembly of Experts was more universal and liberal.

Ethnoreligious sensibilities were apparent among the deputies. The Muslim ethnic minorities (mainly representatives from provinces with large non-Persian populations) were cognizant of the special consideration given to the non-Muslim religious minorities by the leadership of the Assembly of Experts. They showed discontent with the center's (Tehran's) institutional domination of policy and polity. This sentiment was shared by both the Shii and Sunni ethnic groups. The underlying premise of this belief was that the center defined every aspect of life for minorities, thereby eliminating local initiatives. More importantly, they alleged, Tehran did not trust non-Persian ethnonationals.[25] Tensions between center and periphery resurfaced over and over again in debates on various articles of the constitution. One draft article mentioned that the center of the Islamic Republic of Iran was Tehran; opposition was widespread and provincial deputies, including ethnic ones, voted against it. As a consequence it was dropped from consideration altogether.[26]

Halfway through the proceedings, ethnonational desires were still voiced forcefully. One representative blatantly asked for the right of self-determination of ethnonational Azeris, Baluch, and Arabs. Separating the concept of self-determination from secession, he argued that none of the movements led by ethnics had ever been separatist in nature. The cultural, national, and religious desires of all ethnic groups, including the Kurds and the Turkmans, must not be ignored. One said, "I don't believe that your intention is to turn millions of people, constituting two-thirds of this country's population, into Persian-speaking Shiis."[27]

Reflecting concerns voiced to the Provisional Government before the activation of the Majlis-e Khebregan, throughout the proceedings the Sunni deputies remained uneasy about proclaiming Iran a Twelver Shii state. They protested vociferously, asking either for a neutral reference to religion, or that Sunnism, as with Christianity, Judaism, and Zoroastrianism, be mentioned as a recognized state religion. This prompted long analytical debates on the floor.[28] In one of the earlier sessions, a deputy from Baluchestan, Molavi Abdol-Aziz, argued that, similar to Arab countries, Iran must be declared an Islamic state and make no references to Shii or Sunni. He added: "Article 14 states that Zoroastrians, Jews, and Christians are recognized religious minorities in Iran. How is it that we officially recognize the religions of Israel and the United States who are our formal enemies and their religions are obsolete, . . . but we do not accept Sunnism?"[29]

At the end of his speech, Ayatollah Beheshti (chairing that session) politely reminded the deputy that declaring Iran Shii did not mean that Sunnis were not recognized. Also, he hoped Abdol-Aziz's comments were not misinterpreted; Christians, Jews, and Zoroastrians had always been welcomed in Islam. He allowed comments in response from the Jewish deputy, Daneshrad, who began his speech by citing his past anti-Zionist publications. After making it clear that he was anti-Israel, the deputy asserted that he respected Islam as much as "his father's religion," emphasized the common belief in One God, and pointed to the rarity of practice of true religion by attributing several quotes to Imam Ali. Neither was the religion in Israel Judaism, nor the religion of the United States Christianity: "The Israeli government is a government of no religion and its foundation is not based on religion but on the politics of usurpation which is hated by all believing Jews." In conclusion, he added that, since Imam Khomeini had given his approval to respecting the rights of religious minorities, it was best not to make comments which violated the principles of brotherhood and cordiality.[30] The Baluch deputy responded that his comments had been interpreted negatively; of course, he believed that everyone had rights.[31]

The move to make the constitution all-inclusive persisted. Midway through the proceedings even the Armenian deputy, who often limited his comments to the Armenian concerns, appealed in a long speech for "the recognition of the rights of all ethnic and religious communities" naming the Fars, Baluch, Kurd, Turk, Arab, Lur, Turkman, Armenian, Assyrian, Chaldean, Jewish, Zoroastrian, Shii, and Sunni communities, and "other religions, denominations, and ethnics."[32] The push for general references to "other religions" was repeated by other religious minority deputies and could signify their indirect reference to the rights of the Bahais who came under attack in the following years.

Anti-Bahaism was obvious throughout the proceedings. This was most apparent in haggling over every word and expression of certain articles to assure the exclusion of the Bahais. For instance, Article 26 of the constitution addresses the right to form political parties, societies, and professional associations whether they be Islamic or belong to one of the recognized religious minorities. In the ensuing debates the original version referred to "official religious minorities." The speaker of the committee that had worked on the wording of the article explained that the expression was selected on purpose in order to insure that the Bahais would not be included.[33] In another discussion over the issue of freedom of the press, a deputy commented that, if the press was allowed to operate freely, "the stray Bahai sect" through their publications would "seduce" the people.[34]

Interactions between the non-Muslim and Muslim deputies

There is little doubt that many deputies, but particularly Ayatollah Beheshti, were respectfully attentive to the four deputies representing recognized religious minorities (RRMs). He frequently intervened to clarify, to cut off, or to urge deputies to refrain from direct comments against the religious minorities (except the Bahais). Beheshti remained a strong link between these four and the rest, providing a protective buffer against any possible verbal attacks. No matter how harsh and critical the comments of any of the four deputies were, he reiterated that they had an obligation to reflect the discontent of their constituency. During the longest debate on the issue of the governance of the supreme jurist, for example, one of the deputies referred to "the minorities and the dissatisfied." At the end of the session, Beheshti immediately interjected that the deputy was not referring to religious minorities but to the "minority thinkers in society (those who go against the majority favoring the rule of the supreme jurist)."[35]

The subject of religious minorities, in fact, was raised on the first day of the meetings. In his opening speech Ayatollah Montazeri said that he had hoped for a constitution that was 100 percent Islamic and progressive, and that protected "all segments, even the non-Muslims, in Iran."[36] During the third session, Deputy Mohammad Karami, leaving out any reference to the word "progressive," reassured religious minorities of their indisputable rights to life and liberty in the Islamic constitution.[37]

Rumor, innuendo, and speculation circulated outside the Assembly, and the RRM deputies were certainly a target and were cognizant of the fact. At one point the Armenian representative, in private, conveyed to Ayatollah Montazeri the adamant position held by some that religious minorities must not be allowed to express themselves on any issues other than those directly concerning them. The chair disagreed and pointed out that as deputies to the Assembly of Experts all four could comment on any aspect of the constitution. "There are no differences; because this [the right to speak up] is a public right and their election to the Majlis-e Khebregan was for this reason."[38] Later in the proceedings the opposite sentiments were raised. Ayatollah Montazeri referred to a letter addressed to him where he was accused of not allowing the RRM deputies to voice their views. He denied the allegation and each RRM deputy took turns to deny the content of the letter and to state that whenever requested they were given ample time to speak.[39] Even in his concluding remarks, Ayatollah Beheshti referred to the RRM deputies as "four friends" and the recognized religious minorities as "the non-Muslim countrymen [ham mihanan]," thanking them and asking for their active participation in the new system.[40]

Although all four deputies were viewed by the Muslims as collectively representing religious minorities, the reality was somewhat different. Each deputy's first priority was his own constituency. The representatives, each with a unique personality and a different political persuasion, dealt with the Assembly differently. Each possessed a unique worldview. They acted independently and at times appeared in opposition to one another. Sometimes they met as a group in closed sessions discussing articles concerning religious minorities; at other times they met in general committees with other deputies to discuss various articles of the constitution. While the majority of the Muslim deputies perceived the RRM deputies as a unitary whole, the RRM deputies reflected clearly distinct positions. Developments regarding two articles of the constitution concerning religious minorities provide evidence of this.

Article 13 of the constitution of the Islamic Republic of Iran reads: "Zoroastrian, Jewish, and Christian Iranians are the *only* recognized religious *minorities* who are *legally* free in the practice of their religious ceremonies, on matters of personal status and religious education [emphasis added]." This article was debated at length during the eighteenth session of the Assembly of Experts. All four deputies presented their own version of this article to the vice chair, Ayatollah Beheshti. Their version departed from the final text (above) in three important ways: they neither wanted to be referred to as a "minority [aqaliat]," nor did they want the insertion of the word "only [tanha]" in the statement. They also opposed the term "legally [dar hodud-e qanun]"; in its place they recommended the word "officially [rasmi]." The term "minorities [aqaliatha]" in their version was replaced by "communities [javame]."[41]

The version submitted by the four deputies gave the Zoroastrians, Jews, and Christians much more latitude and it also left room for inclusion of other religious groups. This is clear from an interesting exchange between the Armenian and Assyrian representatives. The latter delivered a lecture during heated debates in which he argued for the inclusion of the Sabeans as a religious minority; this was a departure from the original draft submitted by the four deputies. The Armenian representative immediately voiced his objection, reminding his Assyrian colleague, Bait Ushana, that he had moved away from their joint version in closed session where they had agreed to replace "aqaliat [minority]" with "jameeh [community]" and not to mention the Sabeans.[42]

There was clearly a spontaneous, free-ranging exchange between all the deputies. Interestingly, at another point, the Armenian deputy demanded that Armenians and Assyrians (as national groups) be mentioned after "Christians." It was important, he said, "to clarify who is meant here; many in this Assembly still think that we and the Western Christians are the same." Khalatian went on at some length to point out the historical relationship between Iranians and Armenians. He reiterated that clashes between Maronites and Armenians in Lebanon were a clear case in point that the word "Christian" alone would not be enough. The word "jameeh" exemplified "a unique social, national, religious, denominational, cultural, and historical system" and therefore was a more accurate representation.[43]

While the Armenian deputy's request was consistent with the request to be referred to as a "community" rather than a "minority," one point of contention remained: this change would have created a serious problem for other nonethnic Christians. However, there was a possibility that the forum was being used to convey a message to those who had equated Western imperialism with Christian minorities in Iran. The deputy might have already known that there was no chance for the inclusion of his version, but the point had to be made to affirm the nativeness of Iranian Christian communities. Conveying certain – often very obvious and even elementary – points was a common feature of the discussions in the

Assembly of Experts; it was meant for educating the ignorant inside the Assembly as well as for public consumption.[44]

Repeated self-identification and self-legitimization in a revolutionary environment dominated by the ignorant and the extremists was a necessity. Some deputies were in the habit of taking cheap shots at the recognized religious minorities. A case in point was Deputy Rabani Shirazi who regularly either objected to whatever the RRM deputies said or made sarcastic remarks. At one point, for example, misparaphrasing the Armenian deputy, Shirazi claimed that Khalatian "threateningly" had said that, if the Islamic government did not officially recognize the religion of the Armenians, the Christian governments of the world would be upset. Khalatian immediately responded: "no, they will be happy because they will take advantage of it!"[45]

Discussions over Article 13 provided ample opportunity for each deputy to put his own group in a favorable light by emphasizing the historical connection between it and the Muslims. For instance, the Jewish deputy portrayed the identity of the Jews in the context of other RRMs. He pointed out that: (1) Jews and Christians had lived in Iran for over two thousand years; (2) historically thousands of Jews either left the country or converted to Islam (implying that some Muslims might have had Jewish ancestors); (3) the positive and the negative aspects of Iranian Jewry were the same as those of other Iranians – in social and economic life Muslims and Jews were intermixed; (4) wealthy industrialists were not all Jews, but included Muslims and other minority religions; (5) there were many impoverished Jews in Iran, especially in the slums of Gorgan and Nezam Abad; and (6), personalizing the identity issue, Daneshrad reflected on his background and emphasized how he insisted that his son should study the Quran and remain in religion classes on Islam.[46]

Priest Shahzadi, in his first speech to the Assembly of Experts, explained that many Zoroastrians did not wish to be considered a religious minority because they had a unique connection with the land and its people. When Iranians converted to Islam they only changed the name of their God and God's prophet, but they preserved many of their Persian traditions like the New Year; "an Iranian Muslim cannot be considered equal to an Arab Muslim."[47] He brought home the nativeness of the Zoroastrian community several times by emphasizing that Muslims and Zoroastrians were the same people. Reminding deputies of mixed schools and clinics in Yazd and Kerman, he urged unity and coexistence.[48]

Several Muslim deputies spoke in favor of or against various recommendations made by religious minorities on Article 13 and engaged in a spirited discussion over every word. Those who objected to the minorities' version and voted in the majority for the version of Article 13 that was adopted had specific concerns including: (1) political groups could claim to be communities and therefore win or demand recognition (Bahais were definitely in everyone's mind); (2) "legal" must be used instead of "official" since the base reference was Islam and groups were either legal or not (official and nonofficial did not project as big a gap: nonofficial groups could become official one day) but the Islamic edicts were unchangeable; (3) the focus was on recognized religious minorities, therefore, there was no need to mention national groups; and (4) since Ismailis and Sabeans were already recognized in Islam, there was no need to be repetitive. There were obvious attempts to specify the exact wording in order to achieve controlled legalization. The final voting with fifty-nine deputies present was: fifty-one for, six against, and two abstentions.[49] The version passed by the Assembly, instead of the terms "legally" or "within the bounds of the law" used today, contained the expression "within the bounds of Islamic regulations [dar hodud-e moqararat-e Islami]." It is unclear when the change came about, but the RRMs' discontent over the ambiguity of the expression was voiced throughout the proceedings.[50]

Another article directly related to religious minorities dealt with the election of representatives. Article 64 (originally Article 50) stated that the Islamic Assembly would have 270 members. "After every ten years, if the population of the country has increased, representatives will be added to each electoral district at the rate of one per every 150,000 additional people. The Zoroastrians and Jews will each elect one representative; Assyrian and Chaldean Christians will jointly elect one deputy; and Armenian Christians in the south and north each will elect one representative." For every decennial increase of 150,000 in the population of each minority community, an additional deputy would be allocated to it in parliament.

Three arguments dominated the discussion of Article 64. First, significant disagreement occurred over having one deputy for every 150,000 people. This prompted a representative from Baluchestan to suggest a change in numbers so that more cities could have deputies. He complained that the three cities of Zahedan, Khash, and Sarvan together had only one representative.[51] Beheshti assured him that in the future this issue would be considered. Although the exchange did not cause a major controversy, it was an additional indication of the intent of ethnonationals not to be left out. Issues of appropriate representation for them were raised several times in discussions on other articles of the constitution.

The second area of concern was how an increase of 150,000 in the population of religious minorities would affect their representation. Some of the comments made on the floor of the Assembly of Experts were: "What if in one year, they go up 150,000? Do they get one deputy by the end of the year?" "Even if one hundred years go by the number of Zoroastrians will never increase by 150,000!" "Even in ten years the total number of religious minorities will not increase by 150,000, so there is nothing to worry about."[52] The debate, however, forced the inclusion of every ten years in the second part of Article 64.

The third disagreement over Article 64 centered around a protest made by one of the RRM deputies. Bait Ushana, the Assyrian deputy, protested electing one deputy jointly for the Assyrians and Chaldeans. He claimed that the version presented to the open session of the Assembly of Experts differed from what was previously agreed upon. He claimed that the number of Assyrians and Chaldeans was 200,000, but that most of them resided outside Iran. Ayatollah Montazeri asked how many resided in Iran, and Bait Ushana responded that their numbers were around 70,000–80,000, similar to the size of the Armenian population. "Why should the Armenians have two deputies and we have one?" He maintained that the number of Armenians was 300,000, and that most of them resided outside the country. Although his numbers were incorrect (Armenians numbered around 250,000 in 1979 and most did not reside outside the country), the Armenian deputy did not protest. One deputy responded that, since the main basis was religious creed, Chaldeans and Assyrians were the same and their numbers were less important.[53] The issue was brushed aside by others. It was clear that the subject had received much discussion in closed meetings and it was a fait accompli. The debate, however, prompted a Baluch deputy to stand up and ask for more deputies for his region, to no avail.[54]

The four RRM deputies seized the opportunity to voice discontent with discriminatory practices against their constituency. The Zoroastrian deputy cited several cases, such as an edict issued by the head of the Ministry of Education and Training in the city of Shiraz forbidding all RRMs to teach in schools, attacks by religious extremists upon the holy places of religious minorities,[55] and the case of a teacher in a secondary school and of Ayatollah Sadeq Khalkhali who had labeled Zoroastrians fire-worshippers. When a cleric and a teacher insulted a religious minority in this way, Priest Shahzadi said, what were we to expect of ordinary citizens:

Does freedom within the legal boundaries of Islam mean that because some Muslims are in a majority and uninformed about the teachings of the prophets of other religions, they have the right to accuse and insult religious minorities? And, if religious minorities direct similar accusations at the Muslim populace what will their reaction be? Isn't it better if those who consider themselves learned and informed clerics spend a little time in getting to know other religions and familiarize themselves with their teachings . . . in order not to make religion an instrument of conflict?[56]

The Armenian deputy, in less direct and more cautious language, also pointed to similar difficulties, such as imposing job restrictions on Christians. Clearly, he was reluctant to go into details but was concerned that outmigration from Iran was being encouraged by discriminatory practices in the job market. Less condemnatory than Priest Shahzadi, Khalatian expressed his confidence that government officials would block "the opportunist elements."[57]

In terms of frequency of participation on the floor, Bait Ushana, the Assyrian deputy, far exceeded anyone else; he commented on many issues and articles not involving the RRMs.[58] The least vocal deputy was Khalatian, the Armenian. Each deputy had his own style reflecting his own group's psychological mode and historical relationship to the majority of Muslims. The Armenian deputy was cautious. Although he commented and asked questions about a variety of issues, he was mainly concerned about the realm of minority and particularly Armenian rights. The Jewish deputy, Daneshrad, was in the most precarious position. A climate of fear and insecurity prevailed in the Jewish community and many were leaving the country. Meanwhile, in Israel there was public talk of probable military action against Iran if the Jews came to harm.[59] While commenting on a wide range of issues, Daneshrad directed all of his energy in proving to everyone that he and his people were loyal citizens of Iran and were avid anti-Israelis. Being aware that he was often treated with prejudice, suspicion, and accused of opportunism, Daneshrad reiterated his oneness with Islamic elements and the government,[60] and even, in a lecture at the last session of the Assembly of Experts, called the constitution "the most progressive constitution" in Muslim and Christian countries of the world.[61] These were not the expressed views of other RRM deputies.

The Zoroastrian deputy, Priest Shahzadi, boldly and frequently pointed to the shortcomings in the constitution. The religious minorities, he said, were treated as though they were fighting Islam until yesterday and just today had put down their arms and taken refuge under the protection of Islam. What was meant by the term "moqararat-e Islami [Islamic regulations]" in Article 13, he asked. No one could provide him with a clear meaning, and the inherent ambiguity could unleash serious problems. Article 13 exemplified the "governing prejudice" in the Assembly of Experts. Minorities were denied the presidency, the prime ministership, the ambassadorship, ministerial posts, and top-level military positions. "How far down is this retrogressive prohibition going to descend?" Referring to India, Priest Shahzadi attempted to show how a constitution could be worded so as not to foment discrimination.[62] In another lecture he said that the Provisional Government and the

Assembly of Experts had disappointed the Zoroastrians; as natives of Iran with no alternative home country, they were treated as second-class citizens without equal rights in political, military, and legal arenas and, ironically, they enjoyed these rights in both Pakistan and India.[63]

What distinguished the Zoroastrian deputy from other RRM deputies was his all-inclusive language and style. Frank, feisty, extremely well-versed in Persian and in Islam, and very wise, Shahzadi, a Zoroastrian priest, acted as the conscience of the nation and was hard to be reckoned with. Fearless and righteous about his view of the land of Persia, his comments on RRMs encompassed all, and on matters of the state, Priest Shahzadi always redirected discussions by asking if something was good and beneficial for the country.[64] He was the first RRM deputy to speak in the Assembly of Experts and, being acutely aware of the prejudicial sentiment shared among some deputies, he placed special emphasis on the teaching of the Persian language in the new regime.[65] Later, in debates over Article 16 on the instruction of Arabic in schools, Deputy Eshraqi took a shot at the Zoroastrians with his snide remark that during the previous years the attempt to expand the Persian language in Iran was due to a plan to expand a certain religion (meaning Zoroastrianism).[66] This was an ironic statement, considering that not only was he conversing in Persian but the whole proceedings were in Persian.

It is impossible to delve into the proceedings and not sympathize with the burdensome task of the RRM deputies. They played a crucial role in securing some rights for their constituencies under the most strenuous circumstances. The proceedings show that with the shrewdness of Beheshti and Montazeri's sympathy, the RRM deputies, by insisting on their own inclusion, reduced the repetitive references to Islam in the language of the constitution. They were instrumental in softening the language of several (non-RRM related) articles as well and replacing constant references to Islam with universal vocabulary. No opportunity was missed to expand and stretch the concept of "rights" and by asking "How about us?" their impact in proportion to their numbers was remarkable.[67]

Conclusion

Overall, the proceedings of the Assembly of Experts showed two contradictory tendencies existing side by side. There were accommodative tendencies on the part of religious minorities as a result of thousands of years of existence in Iran. Their numbers altogether did not even reach 1 million; this compared to some (at that time) 35 million Muslims. The environmental milieu was not lost on any of the four deputies. While some were more cautious and restrained than others, they all knew their limitations. They expressed loyalty to the Revolution, to the person of Ayatollah Khomeini, and Islamic doctrine.

While the four deputies were accommodative, they also forcefully represented their own constituency and voiced the fears, needs, and demands of their own people. While they were often treated by other deputies as one collectivity, they did not always speak in one voice. They were extremely attentive to what was said about them by other deputies; they corrected inaccuracies and protested against certain remarks. They condemned biased characterizations of their peoples and asked the vice-chair and the chair of the Assembly to back them publicly. Their strongest protests were aimed at being called "a minority," having to adhere to an abstraction called "Islamic regulations," and not being allowed to serve as president, prime minister, ambassador, or chief of the armed forces. They reported and protested the job dismissals, beatings, and looting experienced by their constituencies and were encouraged to do so by Ayatollah Beheshti.

This was not a democracy but it definitely signaled a major departure from the past. Not every move was or could be orchestrated to convey a unified front. Political views simply could not always be subject to control. While those preferring a direct clerical rule of the state dominated the proceedings, the debates reflected the dynamic revolutionary temper outside the Assembly of Experts.

3 Policy sphere of recognized religious minorities

On the surface, the theocratic state granted the recognized religious minorities (RRMs) the same rights they had held before. Each enjoyed political representation, and their communities were guaranteed freedom of religion, language, and culture. The new regime, solely based on its constitution, could rightly claim a policy of continuity vis-à-vis the Armenians, the Assyrians and Chaldeans, the Zoroastrians, and the Jews. The exclusion of the Bahais was also consonant with past practice.

In reality life became more taxing and complex for the minorities. Readers should keep in mind the impact of the Revolution and the subsequent eight-year Iran–Iraq War as intervening variables in the analysis presented in this and the next two chapters. Just as important is the use of religion as a political ideology, which led to contradictions, fusion of myth with reality, a struggle between religious principles and the quest for power, a breakdown of hierarchical order, and eventually unprecedented confusion on human rights. The end result was development of a sharp "us"–"them" distinction involving the Muslim citizens of Iran and the non-Muslims. In contrast to the previous regime which stressed homogenization, the Islamic Republic accepted pluralism but pursued either exclusion or subordination, with coercion or the threat of coercion, based on ideology. The theocratic character (fused with a strange version of leftist ideology) of the state had created a new set of relationships between the state and the religious minorities, constituting compartmentalization and segmentation. Yet the noncentralized character of the political system had allowed for variations, flexibility, and changes over time.

George Eaton Simpson and J. Milton Yinger, in a classic text on racial and cultural minorities, identify six major types of policies often utilized by a dominant group (in this case the Shii theocracy): assimilation, pluralism, legal protection of minorities, population transfer, continued subjugation, and extermination.[1] These six general policy domains are not mutually exclusive; many may be practiced simultaneously. Some are conscious long-run plans; some are ad hoc adjustments to specific situations; some are the byproducts (perhaps unintended) of other policies. In some instances they are the official actions of majority-group leaders; in others they are the day-by-day responses of individual members of the dominant group.[2]

During the 1980s in Iran, two general policies involving recognized minorities can be identified: legal protection of minorities and continued subjugation. Legal protection of minorities, while noble and surely guaranteed in the Islamic constitution of Iran, implies that a special group of people neither "accept the pattern"[3] nor fit the dominant mode, and require special treatment. Continued subjugation basically means keeping the minority "in their place";[4] this often involves a secondary or subservient position. It can be subtle or undisguised depending on the nature of minority–majority relations.

Important details leading to legal protection in the constitution have been discussed above (chapter 2). This chapter analyzes the practical domain of legal protection and its ramifications for the recognized religious minorities.

Religion

Religious practice has been the most tolerated of all legal rights of the RRMs. They are allowed to observe their religious services, ceremonies, and holidays. The government, however, must be notified beforehand about the religious significance and exact dates of these observances. The text of any talk delivered to public gatherings must be submitted to the Vezarat-e Farhang va Ershad-e Islami (the Ministry of Culture and Islamic Guidance)[5] for approval. The non-Persian texts were to be submitted in the original along with a copy translated into Persian to the Department of Religious Minorities within the ministry.

One of the main message-transmitters on religious duties and obligations is the publication of yearly calendars by religious minorities. Every year, before final printing, these calendars are subjected to review (or censorship) by the ministry's Department of Publications. The main target of restrictions is religious books, particularly the Bible, which can neither be imported to nor printed in Iran. The ramifications of this are serious for future generations of religious minorities.

From the beginning all RRMs were warned to refrain from any type of proselytizing. Most took strict measures not to allow anyone outside their own group to attend religious ceremonies. Religious leaders were asked to sign a form confirming that Muslims would not be allowed into their religious centers. Bishop Haik Hovsepian-Mehr, president of the Council of Protestant Churches in Iran, was the only Christian church leader who refused to sign the form.[6]

At the outset of the Revolution, however, there was no significant destruction or confiscation of churches, temples, or synagogues. Most problems were sporadic and localized rather than a matter of state policy. It is common knowledge, for example, that in 1979, two holy Zoroastrian temples were desecrated and that in the early 1980s Armenian graveyards and religious centers were vandalized in the northern cities of Rasht, Anzali, Gorgan, and Sari.[7] In one incident, the Revolutionary Guards burst into the main Armenian church in Tehran; inspecting religious paintings inside the church, they protested the semi-nude portrayal of Christ, and ordered the covering of the pictures. The painter, who resided outside the country, had to fly to Tehran to put clothes on Christ's body. Also, Revolutionary Guards would climb up the walls surrounding the courtyard (from outside) where the church and its administrative offices were located and keep vigil night and day.[8]

Community and religious centers in the south and southwest lost population because of the Iran–Iraq War, with a particularly sharp decline among Armenians, Assyrians, and Chaldeans. The ramifications of the war and the population exodus were the loss or abandonment of buildings. For example, the Armenian church and school in Abadan were taken over by the local government with a promise of restitution after the war. The church building was used as a center for the local revolutionary committee as well as the headquarters of the Pasdaran (the Revolutionary Guards).[9]

The issues involving ahval-e shakhsieh (personal status) such as marriage, divorce, custody, and inheritance were handled through committees under the supervision of the religious leadership for each community. Final decisions, however, were made by the state agency in charge of the particular case. Although the agencies often adhered to the minority committee and religious rulings, problems were caused by bureaucratic incompetence or disagreeable personalities. In one case involving inheritance, for example, an elderly woman was denied inheritance despite having all the right paperwork and religious endorsements. This was due to a bad-tempered bureaucrat who believed that women should not inherit. Although she took legal action and a Muslim judge ruled in her favor, the individual refused to carry out the court's orders. Eventually, his superiors intervened and the case was resolved.[10] These types of problems were faced daily by all Iranians regardless of their religious affiliation.

Family matters including requests for divorce or custody of children are also handled in the same manner. The ruling of the committee along with the paperwork was sent for final appeal to the dadgah-e madani-ye khass (Special Civil Court).[11] The Special Civil Court can accept or reject the committee ruling; yet, in most cases, it affirms the decision. Even if a minority appeals directly to the court with the intent of circumventing the mandate of its own group, the court often asks for the opinion of the committee on the matter. Despite having control, the court does not usually evade or violate the committee's authority. In this area, even though the state is the final arbiter, the relationship with the RRMs has been harmonious and the abuse of state authority minimal.

Education

Education became the most difficult issue for the recognized religious minorities, despite clear guarantees in the constitution. In fact, one finds policy shifts over time. At this point it is unclear what specific factors or personalities pushed for these changes. As with many other public policies of the Islamic Republic, the exact policy factors may never be known. Factionalism, power struggles, and the presence of ideological extremists or those eager to please superiors with some vague notion of religiosity combined to contribute to policy changes. In terms of timing, there appears to be a strong correlation between attempts to centralize state power and tightening the controls on recognized religious minorities.

From 1979 to 1981, a period characterized by political participation of a diverse group of revolutionaries, minority schools operated as they always had. Three individuals were credited for the smooth operation of schools: Mehdi Bazargan, Mohammad Beheshti, and Mohammad-Javad Bahonar.[12] The removal of Bazargan, the outbreak of the Iran–Iraq War, the bomb blasts in June and August 1981 that killed Beheshti and Bahonar, and the power struggle over political dominance all led to a different approach to the education of religious minorities. The new government policy of pressure began in late 1981 and intensified in 1983. Many in the minority communities concede that, after the death of Bahonar, religio-educational issues became highly politicized.

The conflict revolved around several specific issues. Some schools were ordered to change their names. The Assyrian girls' school Sussan, for example, changed its name to Mariam. The Zoroastrian schools, however, bore the main brunt of the name change policy and tried to resist. Some succeeded, such as the famous Anushiravan boys school in Tehran. Most of the pressure was directed at schools bearing the names of kings and queens.[13] This was part of an overall pattern of name alteration which swept the country for a decade involving towns, cities, streets, and so forth.

The government ordered the separation of schools by sex; it was left up to the minority to decide which schools were for which sex. Another decree prohibited having a school on church, synagogue, or temple grounds. The purpose was to prevent exposing Muslims who attended the minority school to a different religion. In Jewish schools (e.g., Abrishami and Rah-e Danesh in Tehran), where the synagogue was located on the top floor, this was not an issue. But the order was carried out in the Armenian Kooshesh boys' school in Tehran where a wall was built to separate the church from the school building. In the case of an Assyrian school, separation was impossible because of the school's small size. The result was the state's takeover of the school and its subsequent closure. The Assyrian community continued to protest this action long into the 1990s;[14] the protests have not (as of yet) come to fruition. Even as late as 1997, the Jewish community was still asking for the return of a confiscated boys' school in Tehran.[15] What is significant, however, is that such protests could take place at all without repercussions. This open exchange between the RRMs and state authorities remained the least noticed and most impressive character of the theocratic state.

Due to lower student enrollment in many Zoroastrian, Jewish, and Assyrian and Chaldean schools, these institutions were forced to take in Muslim students. (These students attended different classes on religion.) The severe shortage of schools for Muslims also contributed to their placement in minority schools. Minority students did enroll in Muslim-dominated schools, but at much lower rates than in pre-revolutionary times. Partly due to the large numbers of students and the unceasing persistence of the Armenian Apostolic Church leadership, most Armenian schools were populated solely by Armenians (and in some cases by Assyrians and Chaldeans).[16]

Three other changes made it clear by early 1983 that the educational autonomy the RRMs had enjoyed for decades was being seriously threatened by the new regime. The three interrelated issues were: the appointment of Muslim principals, teachers, clerics, and radical elements to minority schools; teaching time reduction or outright elimination of teaching of languages other than Persian; and direct interference in the teaching of minority religion. While the language issue had no impact on Zoroastrians and only a minor effect on the Jews, it represented a dramatic departure from the past for the Armenian and the Assyrian and Chaldean communities. For the last three groups, the issues of language and religion were closely intertwined.

The practice of appointing Muslim principals and teachers was prevalent in pre-revolutionary times as well, but the distinguishing features this time were the widespread scale of such appointments and the arbitrary practice of power by these individuals.[17] Depending on the character of the teacher or the principal, curriculum and classes were dramatically impacted, touching off protests from parents and religious leaders. For instance, the state-appointed principal of the Tehran Anushiravan school regularly made fun of Zoroastrian beliefs and prevented the meeting of Zoroastrian religious classes on Fridays, the official day of rest for all agencies. On her own initiative, she convened a class on the study of religions, where her comments caused an uproar among the Zoroastrian students.[18] In the Armenian Alishan school, a Muslim clergyman taught religion to Christian children for one year and in Gohar boys' school the principal made students chant the Islamic phrase "allah-o akbar [God is great]" before going to class. When they refused to repeat the phrase, he prevented students from attending classes and closed down the school for several days. After protests, Ershad intervened and classes resumed.[19] These issues were raised repeatedly in speeches delivered by representatives of religious minorities in the Majlis.[20]

Being the largest recognized religious minority in Iran, the Armenians shouldered the brunt of the combined effect of restrictions on language and religion. Zoroastrians and Jews taught in Persian, and the Assyrian and Chaldeans were so few in number (especially the children and the youth) that their protests were either merged with the Armenians' or they conceded to the new system by agreeing not to pursue Aramaic. Therefore, the conflict became primarily an Armenian issue.

The first confrontation erupted in November 1981 when government authorities prohibited the teaching of the Armenian language in Armenian schools. In protest, Armenian schools stopped operating for one week all over the country. Then students returned to school but refused to study and participate in classroom activities. No directives formalizing the language ban were ever issued by the Ministry of Education and Training (MET). Meanwhile, pressure on the Armenian community increased as some in government expressed a desire to take over the famous Ararat sports stadium in Tehran, which belonged to the Armenians.[21] This move may have originated autonomously or may have been part of an organized attempt to increase pressure in general in order to obtain consent. This was followed by a circular issued by the supreme council of the MET stating that religious teachings had to be in Persian.[22]

The conflict continued throughout 1982, marked by an exchange of letters, negotiations, and continued discussions between community leaders and government authorities. During this period, some Muslim principals and teachers who taught in Armenian schools vehemently opposed instruction of the Bible altogether, while the MET attempted several times to reinstate the study of religion in Persian. Armenian schools refused, and language and religious instruction in Armenian continued.

By early 1983 it had become clear to the Armenian community that the educational and linguistic autonomy its members had enjoyed for centuries was seriously threatened by the new regime. In a formal letter to the MET, the prelate, Archbishop Artak Manukian, outlined the desires and expectations of the community. In concrete and clear terms, the letter asked that: (1) only Armenians register in Armenian schools, (2) the Armenian Apostolic religion be freely taught, (3) the Armenian language remain part of the regular curriculum, (4) the school environment be in compliance with the Armenian church, religion, and culture, (5) schools affirm the religious customs of the Armenian church, and (6) principals and teachers of these schools remain, as much as possible, Armenians. Should this prove impossible, they should then be individuals who, in addition to respecting the religion, had the necessary qualifications for the job.[23]

Throughout this ordeal, the Armenian Majlis deputies continued to stress the interconnectedness between the Armenian language, culture, and religion. In the past, the teaching of Christianity took place in Armenian; therefore, they raised a point to which Muslim clergy were sensitive, namely that teaching Christianity in Persian might be interpreted as proselytizing.[24] This appears to have been a political move on their part with no positive outcome.

In responding to the demands and protests of the Armenian community, the minister of the MET made the following announcement: (1) religious teaching in minority schools must be in Persian, and (2) the time allocated to the teaching of the Armenian language must be reduced and possibly eliminated from the curriculum in order not to cause hardship to the students.[25]

The next major confrontation occurred at the end of the 1983 academic year. The supreme council of the MET sent instructions to the prelacy asking it to develop questions for the final examination in religion. Questions were presented in Armenian. Next, the ministry asked for a translation of these questions; a Persian translation was sent. The ministry then demanded that these translations be used as formal final examination questions. In response, the prelacy reiterated that, as in the past years, the examination must be administered in Armenian. There was no response from the ministry, but on the day of the examination, the Persian translation was distributed among the fifth-graders (ten- to eleven-year-olds) for their final test in religion. In some places, the students were told that the prelacy had agreed that the test be administered in Persian. This caused confusion, and most refused to take the test. Despite immediate protests by community leaders, the same was done for third-graders (eight- to nine-year-olds), who in response handed in white sheets and walked out of the examination session. The education authorities retaliated by failing all of the students.[26]

Subsequently, a formal directive was issued from the MET in November 1983 to the principals of schools belonging to all religious minorities. It reiterated in clear terms points that had been raised since 1981: religious education must be in Persian; a single religious text written by the authorities for all recognized religious minorities must be taught in all their schools; schools must seek special permission for conducting any ceremonies, including religious ones; female teachers and students must observe the Islamic dress codes; and the teaching of the Armenian language must be reduced to only two hours per week.[27]

Despite this clear directive, diversity persisted in the educational sphere. Some schools continued as before, some removed Armenian from their curriculum, some had two hours of language instruction, some continued to teach religion, and others did not teach it at all. During 1984, pressure increased as the Interior Ministry canceled scheduled elections for the Diocesan Council.[28] By spring 1984, the conflict over the teaching of religion in Armenian climaxed in the abrupt closing of more than a dozen Armenian schools in Tehran.[29] The government orders for closure seem to have come the same day that Archbishop Manukian was meeting in Qom with Ayatollah Hossein-Ali Montazeri, then the named successor to Ayatollah Khomeini and a reputed sympathizer with minorities.

This action increased tensions between the authorities and the Armenian community, but this time the government did not back down. In the Friday prayer sermon, the Majlis speaker at the time, Hashemi Rafsanjani, pointed to the conflict: "Armenian students want their religious books to be taught in the Armenian language, not in Persian, but this is against the constitution of the Islamic Republic . . . The Armenians can read their religious books in Armenian outside the state schools."[30] The statement misrepresented both the wording and the intent of Articles 13 and 15 of the Islamic constitution, which were unambiguous on the linguistic and religious freedom of recognized religious minorities.

Later, in a letter to Ayatollah Montazeri, Archbishop Manukian wrote with uncharacteristic bluntness:

Despite your comforting words, not only did the problems raised in connection with the schools remain unresolved, but recent orders have actually exacerbated the situation: the unwarranted replacement of school principals, the dismissal of several teachers of the Armenian language and religion, and the closure of a number of schools.[31]

By the summer of 1984, the international media had picked up on the conflict, and it was being reported all over the world. In response, a cautious statement from the Armenian Archdiocese of Tehran criticized and condemned outside interference and called the conflict an internal matter to be resolved quickly. The statement stressed the Armenian people's solidarity with the Muslims in the Revolution and the war with Iraq.[32] The community was uneasy and suspicious about any international voice raised in defense of Armenian rights and against the Iranian state, viewing it as potentially part of a larger conspiracy designed to either capitalize on Armenian problems in order to undermine the Islamic Republic, or simply as a plot to worsen Armenian relations with the state. Armenians believed that they could solve their problems amicably through direct talks with government authorities. In other words, their negative reaction to the international community was not coerced by the government. Iran was engaged in a war with Iraq, which had the help and support of the West and particularly the United States. Judgments as to a community's concerns should be placed in their proper political context. It was in fact reasonable to be suspicious of a world community that suddenly became so interested in the linguistic and religious rights of Iran's Armenians.

The resistance of the community was nurtured by the post-revolutionary political environment of divided authority and a decentralized system of governance. Ayatollah Ruhollah Khomeini, in his typical style, remained aloof; he never made a public statement on this issue. Ayatollah Montazeri (whose eventual public opposition to the blatant violations of human rights resulted in his resignation from the position of successorship) was sympathetic to the plight of the Armenians. Despite being involved, he could not or did not play a decisive role in the final result. Characters in a secondary position of leadership were the most active players reimposing their own views. The views of the extremist faction, therefore, were brought to bear on this issue.

Yet, an additional element, independent of religious ideology, may have prompted the regime's uncompromising stand on this issue. In some meetings between the authorities and community representatives the comment was made that, if Armenians were granted linguistic freedom, other ethnic groups, particularly Arabic- and Turkish-speaking citizens of Iran, would demand the same.[33] If this was indeed a concern, it signifies a meeting of two ideological interests: the religious extremists' program of Islamization or "Shiization" and the remnants of ardent Persianization, the views of which, at least on linguistic policy, echoed the ultranationalist ideology of Reza Shah Pahlavi.

Ultimately, the government directives prevailed, but instead of eliminating the Armenian language classes, they reduced them to only two hours per week, too little time for instruction in any language. Often, by the time the academic calendar drew to an end, the students had covered barely half of the text.

Much diversity existed not only among the schools, but also across cities. In Isfahan, for example, the hours spent in Armenian language class were much longer, ranging from six to eight hours a week. Similarly in other cities, such as Rasht and Tabriz, the local authorities were more flexible. Tehran stood out as the harshest and the strictest enforcer of government decrees. An active observer of these events attributed the variation to the type of government organ dealing with such issues. In Tehran, applications and requests had to be made to the MET, while in the provinces requests were submitted to the local city's Education Department; in the first case the community was dealing with politicians, in the latter with technocrats.[34] Others have attributed it to the close relationship between the Armenian religious leadership in Isfahan (and other cities) and the local Islamic clerics.[35] In 1995, the times allocated to the Armenian language classes increased from two to five hours per week in Tehran, as in other areas.

These conflicts over education demonstrate several factors about the theocratic regime vis-à-vis its RRMs: (1) inconsistencies are part of the Iranian scene, reflected in matters involving Muslims as well; (2) the theocratic state never acquired the structural and institutional rigidity of the shah's regime, and the clerics' diverse views on issues, as well as the local "coloring," were not suppressed; (3) state–minority relations have been localized, perhaps out of necessity, so that variations can occur where local permission is required on an ad hoc basis or at the level of policy implementation. These are, in turn, affected by the history of the Muslim community's contact with the minorities, the nature of the personal relationship between the high-ranking clerics and the religious leadership of the community, and the local authorities' overall attitude and willingness to adhere to the center (Tehran). Tehran, however, represented the national center of the theocratic state and required a show of rigidity and closer supervision.

Direct interference in the religious teaching of RRMs was the third major change in the RRMs' education, with likely profound future impact on the next generation. Numerous exchanges and meetings between the religious and political leadership of the RRMs and the authorities were unsuccessful. The MET wrote and printed a textbook on religion for minority students. The book, *Talimat-e Mazhabi Vizheh-ye Aqaliathaye Mazhabi (Kalimi, Zarthoshti, Masihi)* (Religious Studies Specifically for Religious Minorities: Jews, Zoroastrians, Christians), written anonymously, is used in the only course of religion allowed in RRM schools. The course is taught by Muslim teachers for at least three hours a week.

The contents are partly Islam and partly some form of New Age spirituality. Chapter titles include: "Life is not pointless," "Human evolution," "Apple tree," "Green leaves of plants," and "The beautiful books of knowledge of God."[36]

The religious leadership of all recognized minority groups sent letters of protest to the MET on several occasions but to no avail. Their objections were: (1) that the textbook was a violation of Article 13 of the Islamic constitution guaranteeing freedom in religious teaching; (2) that there were overt and covert passages from the Quran, which had the effect of evangelizing Islam to minority students; and (3) the issue of who wrote the book and what their qualifications were. It was stressed that only Jews, Zoroastrians, and Christians could write religious texts for their own communities. These letters were sent individually as well as collectively (one letter was written and signed by all Christian denominations in the country). The height of the letter-writing period on this issue was 1982. All letters and requests by the RRM religious leadership were completely ignored; they never received a response.[37]

In addition to the special religious studies text, as in the pre-revolutionary era, non-Muslim students read the same texts used by Muslim students throughout the nation. A major overhaul of school textbooks, which began only nine days after Ayatollah Khomeini stepped on Iranian soil, was completed by 1981. Textbooks were agents of socialization for the new generation, with the goal of forming a "new Islamic person" in Iran. Western nationalism, Eastern socialism, Zionism, and secularism were attacked, and role models were not scientists or writers but "Islamic scholars and religious leaders."[38] Consequently, the RRM children ended up with a double dose of the Islamic version of Iranian theocracy. They were targets of socialization and indirectly, it was hoped, of Islamic proselytizing. The religious text, about the contents of which no RRM religious figure was ever consulted, was written to fulfill what many Shii Muslim clergy believed to be the ultimate faith of all People of the Book, namely their acceptance of the last Prophet of God. The RRMs were viewed as evolutionary transients on their way to becoming Muslims and the role of a theocracy was to facilitate this change, gradually, while maintaining their rights as the respected and protected People of the Book.

The university curriculum was identical for all students. For the RRMs in the early years the main problems began in high school. Two important factors for the RRM students were passing the examination on religion basically requiring knowledge of Islam, and obtaining approval from the ministry on their moral conduct or qualifications. The examination was extremely difficult to succeed in, especially in competition with Muslim students. The second was affected by malicious Muslim principals who purposefully graded down students on their enzebat (basically a reference to appropriate conduct) in school. According to a MET directive, students who received below a minimum score could not take the entrance examination to the university.[39] Therefore, on the one hand, the RRM students were at the mercy of their Muslim government-appointed teachers and principals, and, on the other hand, they had to pass a test on Islamic theology. While minority students continued to attend universities and major in various fields, their numbers compared to the pre-revolutionary era went down considerably. As in other areas, regulations pertaining to religious exams for RRMs have evolved into a new form. Application forms that the individual student who wishes to take the university entrance examination must submit ask for their religious affiliation. If the student identifies herself/himself as an RRM, s/he will be exempt from the exam on Islamic religion. In exceptional cases, minority students do not identify themselves as an RRM for fear of discrimination, preferring to take the exam on Islam.

It is important to add that character investigation was part and parcel of the new regime, and involved Muslim Shii students as well. From 1981 to 1984 the investigation of the moral character of those intending to enter university became more systematic and organized. It involved not only the principals and teachers but also "neighbors, members of the Islamic Association of Students, and representatives of local mosques." Intense public criticism and increased need for better-educated citizens lessened the practice considerably in the following years.[40]

On a related educational matter, the number of Muslim Iranians taking Armenian language courses at university level increased significantly. Ershad and other government agencies, including the intelligence units, provide a unique employment opportunity for such graduates.[41]

Communal life

All aspects of the RRMs' communal lives were affected by theocratic rule. Some of the changes were due to long-range official policy; others were short-range policies or actions which were revised due to impracticality or protests from the minority groups. In addition, day-to-day operations of an overzealous security force, combined with revolutionary paranoia and, as usual, unauthorized individual initiatives, caused a multitude of actions against the RRMs, especially during the first half of the 1980s.

At the beginning of the Islamic regime, sweeping changes were directed at big industrialists (including Muslims) and those sectors of the economy involved in food consumption. In the case of the Coca-Cola plant, for example, the owner (an Armenian) fled the country, the factory was confiscated, and Armenian workers were fired. Several years later, the family members were allowed to oversee the daily operations of the plant, and Armenians were allowed to work at the clerical level; however, the production workers remained Muslim. Armenian workers were never rehired on the grounds that non-Muslims should not touch the bottles or their contents, which may be consumed by Muslims.[42]

For other minority-owned and -operated factories a combination of Muslim workers and mechanization was used in order not to expose Muslims to the najess (impure) non-Muslims. Concerns with purity were reflected in trade as well, especially on food items such as meat, which was imported from Muslim countries, including significant amounts from Indonesia.

The infiltration of nejasat-consciousness into the policy sphere was a natural byproduct of the theological discussions by religious leaders. Ayatollah Hossein-Ali Montazeri saw nejasat in twelve items including blood, dogs, pigs, wine, and kafirs.[43] A kafir is defined as a person who denies God or does not accept the prophethood of Mohammad. Montazeri's definition of kafir was broad enough to include those Muslims who doubted and did not pray or fast.[44] A kafir's body, including hair, nails, and body fluids, was to be avoided.[45] The purchase, sale, or receiving of meat and fat from either non-Muslim countries or a kafir were forbidden.[46]

To Montazeri the philosophy behind a kafir's nejasat was different from the other eleven items. A kafir's impurity was "a political order from Islam and must be adhered to by the followers of Islam, and the goal [was] to promote general hatred toward those who are outside Muslim circles" in order to prevent Muslims from succumbing to corrupt thoughts. Of course, if a Muslim had hostility toward or cursed one of the twelve Shii Imams, he, too, became polluted. Yet, Montazeri also included an unusual clause: if People of the Book avoided impurities such as pigs and wine, their purity was not impossible.[47] Only a small minority of ulama have made any exceptions for Ahl al-Ketab; one scholar attributes Montazeri's flexibility to early differences between Shii and Sunni and amongst the Shii ulama.[48]

Ayatollah Khomeini addressed the nejasat issue in some detail. When asked what the status of Ahl al-Ketab was in relation to purity, he responded: "Non-Muslims of any religion or creed are najess."[49] Khomeini was asked a multitude of questions about contact with non-Muslims. In his view, a handshake with a non-Muslim was not najess unless there was contact with the body fluids of the non-Muslim (e.g., the hand of the non-Muslim was sweaty). Dry cleaning of Muslim and non-Muslim clothes together was also not a problem as long as the clothes were clean (though why already clean clothes would be dry cleaned was not mentioned); but if there was exposure to fluids or humidity, then the clothes were najess.[50] Khomeini was asked whether eating in a restaurant frequented by non-Muslims but owned and operated by Muslims was a problem. He responded that, if the food and the utensils were not najess, there was no problem.[51] He was asked about a Christian supervisor of a cooking oil factory. The Christian had to touch the oil occasionally to measure the flow. What was the religious implication? This was najess, in Khomeini's view, but if there was doubt as to whether or not the Christian had touched the oil, then it was pure.[52] If a dress washed by a non-Muslim had dried in the sun, was it pure? If the dress had come into contact with the sweat of the non-Muslim without the purification ritual being performed, then it was najess.[53]

The questions asked were reflective of the state of mind of Khomeini's followers. Their inquiries were specific: non-Muslims such as Christians and Zoroastrians took telephones and similar items to repair shops; were these objects pure? Should these shops accept or reject repairs?[54] A flower pot made of clean clay was sold by a Hindu. It was not known whether the maker was a Muslim or not; was the pot pure? Would leaving it in water for a few days purify the pot? According to Khomeini, having knowledge of the nejasat of these items made the items impure.[55]

Many of Khomeini's fervent religious supporters, including the Hezbollah (Party of God – an amalgamation of the most radical elements) and the Pasdaran (Revolutionary Guards), believed in ritual purity and impurity, and the nejasat issue continued to be addressed by many lower-rank clerics.

While the nejasat issue directly and dramatically singled out the non-Muslims in the policy arena, codes of purity and impurity were numerous, covering various aspects of a Muslim's daily life in contact with impure items. Many practicing Muslims remained uninterested in nejasat, and strict adherence by some members caused discord within the same family.[56]

Shops that sold foodstuffs associated with minorities (such as sandwiches or bakery goods) had to display signs which read "makhsus-e aqaliat" or "vizheh-ye aqaliat" (especially for minorities). If the food was baked by Muslims and those who served the customers were Muslims, then no signs were necessary even though the owners were from the RRMs.[57]

In practice, a policy sphere based on segmentation between the impure non-Muslims and the pure Muslims did not mean that all clerics believed in it or adhered to it, including those at the top official levels of leadership and high-ranking clerics.[58] Noncompliance was evident in practice. In one case, a clergyman would regularly frequent a food store owned and operated by non-Muslims. In order to evade recognition, he would visit through the back door dressed in civilian clothes.

As with most policies in Iran, considerable variations were visible at the implementation level. Many Shii Muslims remained uninterested in such distinctions in their daily contacts with minorities. Stores owned and operated by minorities were still frequented by Muslims who cared more about the product than obeying a state decree. Cities and towns throughout the country varied as well, depending upon the local authorities' will to implement the rules, and the general public's desire to adhere to them. And, as usual, laws, public policies, and government directives could go only so far. By 1997 government officials, concerned with the country's international image, ordered signs removed from the windows of minority-owned and -operated stores. Nevertheless, the law remained unchanged.

Putting into practice the nejasat regulations from the early months of the Revolution had an ideological basis but had pragmatic results in the policy sphere. Economically, the Islamic regime used every avenue to provide more employment for the Muslim loyalists during the 1980s.

Job discrimination became rampant throughout the 1980s. During the early years discrimination was blatant. For example, an advertisement for training in the academy and subsequent hiring in the police department listed several conditions, one of which was being Muslim. Zoroastrians protested by asserting that, if dying for Iran in the war with Iraq was acceptable, then so should the employment of minorities in the police force be acceptable. They obtained a letter from Ayatollah Kashani which stated that Zoroastrians were not foreigners, that they were authentic Iranians and loyal subjects and therefore should face no barriers. Shortly afterwards, the advertisement changed, replacing the reference to the Muslim religion with the language of being a follower of "one of the recognized religions of the country: Islam, Christianity, Zoroastrianism, Judaism."[59]

Not all problems were resolved by a letter from a high-ranking ayatollah or a change in job description. RRM representatives in the Majlis complained often, and letters to the editorial sections of minority publications indicated discrimination in government agencies, particularly the MET. Some of the employment advertisements blatantly stated that they were not hiring religious minorities and that they need not bother to apply.[60]

One of the most conspicuous policy spheres of discrimination was the military. The Iran–Iraq War prompted a situation in which RRMs served as soldiers and support personnel at the front, and significant numbers of Armenians, Assyrians and Chaldeans, and Zoroastrians were killed in proportion to their population. Yet in ensuing discussions in the Majlis on the laws and regulations of the Islamic Republic's military in 1987, one of the conditions of employment was adherence to Islam. The religious minority representatives objected to the article and suggested its replacement with "adherence to one of the recognized religions of the country." The Zoroastrian representative, Malekpoor, served as the group representative. He told other deputies that the Majlis Defense Committee (working on the draft) had expressed concern that inclusion of non-Muslims would raise objections of the Shoraye Negahban (the Council of Guardians) which oversaw legislation passed by the Majlis. As far as Malekpoor was concerned, the council was working in accordance with the constitution and Islam; neither was being violated with the inclusion of the RRMs. If they could serve as soldiers, they could also be hired in the professional military. Not hiring any RRMs meant that they would be denied employment in all those industries connected to the Ministry of Defense. A Muslim delegate objecting to the hiring of minorities argued that the problem was one of Islam and the constitution. If an RRM reached a high rank in the military, he would be in a position of command. This meant a non-Muslim would be issuing orders to a believing Muslim of lower rank, and this was against the Quran. The inclusion of minorities would also violate the constitution, which stated in clear terms that the army had to be Islamic. Discussions in support of Malekpoor's proposal by another Muslim deputy raised the point that the whole country operated under Islamic rule and the Quran, including minorities. If they had served in other capacities, if they had already been martyred for Iran, and if the religion issue was not raised then, why should it be raised at all? The secretary of the Majlis Defense Committee praised the minorities and explained that the only reason the committee placed a religious requirement on employment was out of concern for nonapproval of the Council. Undersecretary of Defense Malekzadeh stressed the contribution of minorities and announced that the government had no opinion one way or the other. (The tone of the discussion leaves a different impression.) When the votes were cast, the RRMs' proposal was defeated.[61]

Two main employers – namely, the nationalized oil industry and the government – continued discriminatory practices against minorities. The oil industry in particular had significant number of RRMs; they were either demoted or persuaded to resign or retire, and their hiring came to a halt. Religious minorities were often replaced by incompetent religious ideologues. From the early to mid-1980s, RRMs raised objections to every discrimination case, but by the end of the decade the practice was so firmly institutionalized that no one bothered to raise the issue again. As a result, an overwhelming majority of the RRMs sought employment in the private sector.

The social life of the RRMs as a group came under scrutiny in the early 1980s. After a series of ad hoc actions, RRM representatives were summoned to a meeting with Morteza Hosseini, the prosecutor of courts in charge of combating vice (dadsetan-e dadgahaye mobarezeh ba monkerat) in 1982. They were told to observe Islamic laws in all walks of public life. Special emphasis was placed on the women's hejab (Islamic headcover). Hosseini singled out the Armenian Ararat club and sports stadium in Tehran, indicating that women and men frequent the place together. The Islamic regime had left minorities alone in their households but Ararat was a public arena and as such was subjected to Islamic rules. "On the other hand, some refer to us and ask that we pursue a harsher line in such cases," Hosseini emphasized.[62]

In this meeting, each RRM representative responded differently. The Jewish representative affirmed that his community had no problem with restricting the use of alcohol and requiring the hejab; he only asked for more cooperation from the authorities. The Zoroastrian representative asserted that hejab was part of an ancient Zoroastrian gown and was being observed. He asked the authorities not to view them as Protected People but as fellow countrymen. The Armenian representative, whose community was singled out in the meeting, was more candid. On the issue of mixed company (men and women attending places together), he said it was a common cultural practice. The Ararat stadium, schools, and places where weddings were held were like homes to the Armenians. An attempt would be made not to allow the presence of Muslims in such places. He went on to state that those in charge of implementing Islamic rules were imposing their personal preferences and making "unnecessary problems" for the Armenians. "We hope that, just as we respect all Islamic laws, brothers would have mutual respect for ours." The representative of the Presbyterian Church stated that general guidelines on Islamic rules were necessary and these guidelines should be mindful of Christian faith. "If we are a minority in Iran, it is because we love Iran and respect Islamic laws. Otherwise, we could have left Iran but we did not and are not going to. We are trying to live side by side with our Muslim brothers in harmony."[63]

The first official announcement on a possible policy directive on recognized religious minorities surfaced later in the same year. Musavi Tabrizi, the prosecutor general of the Islamic Republic, published an article in which he outlined the conditions that must be observed in order for minorities to live safely in Iran. They had to refrain from fighting the Islamic government, harming Muslims, drinking alcoholic beverages or eating pork in public, building new religious centers, adultery with or marriage to Muslim women, and diverting Muslims from Islam with fraud, deceit, and propaganda. Non-Muslims had to pay jazieh and accept the social, legal, penal, and economic rules of Islam.[64] The payment of a religious tax, however, never materialized. The religious justification may have been that, since the state was already Islamic and the RRMs were serving in the Iran–Iraq War, jazieh was unnecessary.[65]

The forced Islamic headcover imposed on religious minorities faced objections from Christian and Zoroastrian women. In meetings with their own community leaders, these women were adamant that the government's order requiring non-Muslim RRMs to wear Islamic dress went against the constitution, which permitted every community to adhere to its own traditions. A small group of Armenian women in defiance wore the traditional Armenian head band and lace in public but were ordered by Islamic authorities to stop. The women's objection was also directed at the children's and young schoolgirls' Islamic dress codes. In 1985–86 all Christian school girls, who were already wearing headscarves, were ordered to wear the Islamic headcover. Muslim teachers instructed mothers to cover the head of the female children while testing them on spelling and dictation at home. In this way, children would become accustomed to hearing muffled words through the headcover. The Armenian women's objections continued for several years.[66]

It was not by accident that Rafsanjani, then head of the Majlis, while providing detailed instructions on women's dress codes, behavior, and even manner of speech and voice, mentioned the RRM women: "You are not obligated by God [to cover yourselves] but you live in a society which has laws and rules. We have laws for our streets, offices, and environment, and you must obey these laws. To observe the laws of a society where a person lives is everyone's responsibility."[67]

Harassment of minority gatherings continued intermittently. At some times in the Ararat Club and sports stadium males and females were separated. At one point, the Pasdaran broke into an Armenian social and cultural organizational meeting and arrested the president of the group. They declared that women should not be present in such meetings without the hejab; if they must attend, then their seating should be segregated and the women's section should be separated from the men's by a curtain. The organization was closed down for three days and then was left alone. The obsession with headcovers and mixed-sex gatherings continued. In April 1990, guards entered an Armenian community center unannounced. They closed it and detained the office clerk and three members of the board. The charge was allowing girls to be present without wearing headcovers. The detainees were sentenced to seventy-four lashes; they were then allowed to "purchase" the lashes.[68]

Various RRM social gatherings, especially weddings, were interrupted by the Revolutionary Guards. Although an official permit was required for weddings, it rarely made any difference to the security personnel, who would break into the gathering unannounced.[69] In 1987, it was reported that the Pasdaran broke into a Jewish wedding celebration; finding alcoholic beverages, they arrested some 120 guests and gave each 75 lashes as punishment.[70]

Similar random actions continued well into the 1990s and, although some Muslim weddings were also broken into, the non-Muslim minorities were a particular target. Non-Muslim gatherings provided opportunities for finding women without the hejab, and alcohol (which non-Muslims were permitted to consume). Muslim victims of such actions believe that the main motive by the late 1980s was bribery rather than the safeguarding of public morale.

It is a mistake to assume that the RRMs passively accepted the restrictions. In 1985, in an eloquent letter to the head of Publications and Advertisement of the Ministry of Islamic Guidance (Ershad), Priest Rostam Shahzadi responded to each restrictive inquiry on the Zoroastrian minority. In Zoroastrianism, he wrote, there were no restrictions on the use of alcohol and music. The doors and windows of the community centers were of double thickness so that sound could not be heard outside. Dancing and chanting were joyful expressions and were not prohibited, and socializing with followers of every religion and denomination was an essential part of peaceful coexistence in the Zoroastrian religion.[71] Yet, on some points the Zoroastrians were made to adhere to the new rules. For example, an invitation from the Zoroastrian Assembly of Tehran to a Zoroastrian celebration in the mid-1980s requested Zoroastrian guests to observe the following rules: they could neither consume alcoholic drinks nor have them in their possession, women must observe the proper attire inside and Islamic attire outside, Muslims would not be allowed to attend (as required by government orders), and Zoroastrians were warned not to gather outside the Zoroastrian center after the celebrations were over, and not to honk automobile horns.[72]

Armenians, Assyrians, Chaldeans, and Jews followed similar restrictions. Each socialized within its own clubs and community centers; some prohibited only Muslims, others went further and forbade the entrance of anyone other than members of their own community. If an Iranian Muslim was caught in a minority setting, the place would be closed down for good. No one wanted to take the risk. This insulation of RRMs from the rest of the population, and partially from each other, was a policy with serious repercussions for cross-socialization of the next generation. The

practice led to the compartmentalization of people into religious groupings. As government restrictions were relaxed, the RRMs were allowed to
play music, but the records and tapes had to be reviewed and approved by
Ershad in advance.

The RRMs were allowed to hold their religious/cultural feasts and holidays with prior permission of the government. Although a list of set occasions was provided, RRMs had to ask and receive formal approval every
year. In addition, religious minority members were allowed to form societies, groups, and organizations, such as their own women's organizations, student groups, professional and benevolent associations, and
cultural groups with branches in different cities, with the permission of
local and national government officials. Also, in contrast to some of the
rigid decrees and announcements, some schools and community buildings were renovated or built anew on an ad hoc basis.[73] Colored by localism and personalism, "policy" meant one thing in one period and a
different thing in another, and exceptions were made so frequently that
flexibility became the norm in state–minority relations on communal
affairs.

Throughout the 1980s, the Iranian state exhibited varying degrees of
simultaneous rigidity and flexibility as well as contradictions. For
instance, as the Armenian school problems were heating up around the
issue of language and religious teaching, in 1982 the Ministry of Post and
Telegraphs, along with Ershad, printed a stamp commemorating the
birth of Jesus Christ.[74] In another case, in late 1984 it was announced that
a person's religion would appear on their passport. At first this appeared
to be one of those pronouncements that would never materialize, but by
the end of the decade it had come into effect. However, instead of having
the religion stamped on the passport, the religious affiliation was included
in the questionnaire filled out by applicants for passports.[75]

Some rules and restrictions varied in their impact on different communities. Restrictions on employment in the military had more of an effect
on Zoroastrians than Armenians or Jews since traditionally more
Zoroastrians were hired in the military establishment. Restrictions on
language had a more dramatic impact on the Armenians and they, along
with Assyrians and Chaldeans, were more affected by the restrictions
placed on the importation and publication of the Bible compared to the
Jews, for example, who were still allowed to print the Torah unrestricted.
(Christian evangelism was a threat to the Islamic authorities but not
Jewish evangelism – they could not conceive of Muslims converting to
Judaism.) Considering the large exodus of Jews from Iran and the dis-
interest of the Jewish leftists in religion, the need for Torah dissipated.

The relationship between the RRMs and the Muslim community

varied based on the individuals involved, the nature of the situation, and the encounter. Overall, there were significantly fewer problems among the people compared to the number of problems in state–minority relations. In the 1990s, along with changes in all spheres of society and state, fewer problems have materialized and there has been a rejuvenation at the intellectual and cultural level. For example, an Iranian photography student set up an exhibit on Armenian life in Isfahan. Similarly, on the third anniversary of the death of Isayee Shajanian, an Isfahani Armenian painter and miniaturist, people gathered for an exhibit to commemorate his work.[76]

A brief look at the first and second parliaments helps to pinpoint further the structural and institutional operations of state–minority relations. Most of the decisions and practices were institutionalized by the end of the second parliament.

The first and the second Majlis: 1980–88

The nature of the two parliaments was very different. Between 1980 and 1984, the pro-Khomeini elements were in the process of consolidating their power. This era is marked by the start of the Iran–Iraq War, ethnic conflict, the rise and fall of President Bani Sadr and his supporters, armed struggle against the opposition (especially the Mojahedin-e Khalq), the bombs which killed Ayatollah Beheshti and many important pro-Khomeini supporters, the elimination of various leftist groups including the Tudeh Party, and deep factionalism. The mix of diverse voices, war, internal conflict, and attempts to purge perceived opponents and rebuild a new state and society make up the environmental context of the first Majlis.

The first Majlis was headed by Hashemi Rafsanjani, and it reflected inexperience as well as an unusually open forum of debate and discussion on a wide range of topics. Rafsanjani often advised the extremists, and several times called on Hezbollah to refrain from excesses. He acknowledged problems with the behavior of Hezbollah in their contacts with several deputies. The Majlis was also wrestling with procedural matters and the role of the Council of Guardians was debated openly.[77] Every issue was discussed at great length with varied pro and con arguments. For example, in a discussion about the election laws, even the issue of displaying posters of candidates was discussed, as well as whether it should be a crime if they were removed by unauthorized persons.[78] A range of small and large problems plaguing the country was debated candidly, such as shortage of paper, foreign sailors' entry visa problems, and the shortage of water for drinking and agriculture.[79] For instance, a discussion ensued over taxing cigarettes: those taking a pro-tax stand focused on the health hazards of smoking while those opposed to cigarette taxes viewed them as a punishment for farmers and workers of the country.[80]

The second Majlis began in 1984 at a time when the power of the pro-Khomeini faction was already thoroughly consolidated and the opposition had fled, been imprisoned, or eliminated. Here as with the first Majlis, certain slogans were frequently expressed; the most common recited by all deputies in unison was: "God is great, God is great, Khomeini is leader, death to those opposed to velayat-e faqih, salutations to the combatants of Islam, greetings to martyrs, death to the United States."[81] As with the first Majlis, deputies voiced acute problems afflicting the nation; some were unresolved old issues (such as water shortages), and others were new concerns (such as shortages of doctors, medical practitioners, and pharmaceuticals). In contrast to the first Majlis, there were no procedural debates. Although legislation was still seriously discussed, the nature of exchanges and debates was more restrained, controlled, and even calculated. There were fewer outbursts or flamboyant comments.[82] While harsh exchanges and accusations still took place, compared to the first Majlis the parliamentary debates were more restrained.[83] Rafsanjani, who was still the speaker of the Majlis, warned the deputies several times to pay attention to what they said because it was being heard in Iran and throughout the world. At one point, he remarked that "these problems are best left to private sessions."[84]

The speeches of the Majlis deputies were characterized by two distinct features. Ayatollah Khomeini's statements and speeches were often utilized to justify and/or rationalize a position for or against something or someone. On anything and everything he was quoted or paraphrased as rendering support. The two main factions on economic issues, those favoring privatization and those supporting state ownership, generously invoked the authority of the faqih.[85] The second feature was delivering lengthy speeches, more than two-thirds being rhetorical, and then making the point near the end.[86] Deputies of the RRMs followed the same pattern without exception throughout both Majlis sessions.

The RRM representatives' oath of office before assuming their duties was the same as the Muslims', replacing the Quran with their own religious text at the appropriate point. They swore to "protect the sanctuary of Islam" and to guard the gains of the Revolution and the foundations of the Islamic Republic.[87] The RRM deputies could serve on most house committees except those dealing with Islamic legislation such as the Judicial Committee; they were also forbidden from serving on the Foreign Affairs Committee.[88]

Tables 3 and 4 identify the elected deputies for recognized religious minorities by their birthplace, age, education, committee membership in the Majlis, total votes cast, and the percentage of votes received. The information is obtained from official sources of the Islamic Republic of Iran. These sources do not give any information on Sergen Bait Ushana, the Assyrian and Chaldean deputy in the first Majlis. The Zoroastrian deputy, Malekpoor, was reelected to the second Majlis but all the other minority representatives were replaced. In the elections for the third Majlis in 1988, all the incumbents of the second Majlis won, the only exception being Malekpoor who was replaced by Aflatoon Ziafat.[89]

As with the Muslim deputies, it is impossible to discern the precise political perspective and beliefs held by each RRM representative. One can only identify patterns based on a cumulative analysis of speeches and the messages they contain. RRM deputies in the first Majlis exhibited the same versatility as the Muslim deputies.

Some RRM members of the first Majlis were rumored to have been left sympathizers, left meaning a range of political and social views, many of which had become part of revolutionary slogans and clerical terminology. It is unclear whether these allegations, some advanced by members of their own community, were correct. What is clear is that their speeches and interviews reflected a worldview very similar to that of other deputies.

Sergen Bait Ushana, the Assyrian and Chaldean representative, did not serve his full term. He left for Britain and died there in 1988. Some suspect him to have been pro-Tudeh, since his departure coincided with the arrest of the party leadership and the subsequent dissolution of the Tudeh Party of Iran in early 1983.[90] Hratch Khachatourian, the southern Armenian deputy, was reelected to the second Majlis but the Council of Guardians (in charge of approving or disapproving the credentials of elected deputies) unexpectedly declared his seat void.[91] In the elections held a few months later, Artavaz Baghoomian was elected.

Again, it is unclear what sets of circumstances were at work, especially during the first Majlis. A strong left/revolutionary rhetoric was prevalent at all times. For instance, Parviz Malekpoor, the two-time Zoroastrian deputy who was also a member of the Budget Committee, strongly favored nationalizing foreign trade and "eliminating the profiteers," thereby guaranteeing economic independence for Iran. He argued that otherwise a group of profiteers would dominate through connections with the international capitalist network. He favored stronger state control over the economy and dismissed the need for merchants. He stated the commonly held view, often voiced in the Majlis, that counter-revolutionaries (zed-e enqelab) were active in the country and that one should be on the alert for conspirators in order to prevent Satanic forces

Table 3. Recognized religious minority (RRM) representatives in the first Majlis 1980–84

Name	RRM	Birthplace	Approximate age in 1980	Education	Commitees	Total votes cast for all candidates for seat	Number of votes received
Sergen Bait Ushana	Assyrians and Chaldeans						
Hratch Khachatourian	Armenians of the South	Isfahan	32	M.D. (general practice)	– agencies associated with Prime Ministry	4,706	2,494
Hrair Khalatian	Armenians of the North	Bakhtaran (Kermanshah)	53	Associate degree in accounting and banking	– Economics and Finance	20,352	11,064
Parviz Malekpoor	Zoroastrians	Rafsanjan	32	B.A. in electrical engineering M.A. in operational research Studied in the United States for one and a half years	– Plan and Budget – Industry and Mines – Commerce and Distribution	3,680	2,481
Khosrow Naqi	Jews	Tehran	35	B.A. in judicial law M.A. in private law	– Work, Social, Administrative, and Employment	9,418	7,225

Source: Negareshi be Avalin Dorehye Majlis-e Shoraye Islami (Tehran: Ravabet-e Omumi-ye Majlis, 1364 [1985/86]), pp. 232–35, 264–65, 268–69.

Table 4. *Recognized religious minority (RRM) representatives in the second Majlis 1984–88*

Name	RRM	Birthplace	Approximate Age in 1984	Education	Committees	Total votes cast for all candidates for seat	Number of votes received
Artavaz Baghoomian	Armenians of the South	Isfahan	31	B.A. in accounting	– Accounting	4,335	2,622
Artur Khonanshu	Assyrians and Chaldeans	Urmieh, Eastern Azerbaijan	43	B.A. in French Study of religious texts	– Inquiry	8,995	5,517
Manuchehr Kalimi Nikrooz	Jews	Isfahan	38	Doctor of Pharmaceutics	– Public Health and Welfare	8,636	6,549
Parviz Malekpoor (re-elected)	Zoroastrians	Rafsanjan	36	as in table 3	– Oil	8,682	8,546
Vartan Vartanian	Armenians of the North	Isfahan	42	M.A. in mechanical engineering Six years of Bible study	– Industry and Mines	31,464	20,628

Source: Moarefi-ye Nemayandegan-e Dovomin Dorehye Majlis-e Shoraye Islami (Tehran: Ravabet-e Omumi-ye Majlis, Mehr 1364 [September/October 1985], 2nd ed. 1366 [1987/88l], pp. 14, 38, 100, 114, and 127.

moving against the Revolution.[92] Malekpoor also raised important issues and suggested solutions to other national problems, such as the high rate of influx of rural migrants to the cities, especially Tehran. Despite housing shortages and high prices, the rural migrants were not willing to return to their villages. Even if they had land, water, roads, tractors, and other such necessities, as long as they were without seeds, they could not function. He urged the government to provide for the rural population.[93]

Focusing on the left rhetoric alone should not overshadow the continuous presence and the crosscutting impact of personalism in high politics. Not all particulars of personal contacts are known; however, it is known that Parviz Malekpoor and Hashemi Rafsanjani (house speaker in both Majlis sessions) were close friends. This might explain Malekpoor's reelection for a second term, the RRM deputies' propensity to select him as their speaker on many occasions, and his open and daring commentaries on the floor.

An overall review of most of the daily proceedings of the Majlis shows that the active and vocal participation of RRM deputies on the floor of the house was minimal.[94] Minority representatives rarely made comments on national issues but were almost always called upon to comment on subjects that concerned their own group or the RRMs in general. This was not a rule but one of those practices that became customary after frequent repetition.

RRMs did not always vote the same way. For example, during the first Majlis, after a long debate on the pros and cons of the confirmation vote for Mir-Hossein Musavi as minister of foreign affairs (no RRM spoke out), votes were cast. All the RRM deputies voted for him and with the majority.[95] In October 1985, President Seyyed Ali Khamenei appointed Musavi as prime minister. The RRM vote on Musavi's proposed new cabinet varied greatly; minority members voted differently from each other and they did not all necessarily side with the majority on each candidate. The overall voting pattern here shows much individualized preference and reasoning for each candidate.[96]

Several pieces of legislation, parts of which involved the minorities, were passed by the first Majlis. Yet, there were serious concerns for groups other than the recognized religious minorities. In the long discussions over a bill on activities of parties, political and professional societies and associations, and Islamic or officially recognized religious minority associations during the first Majlis, on almost every single article the major concern expressed by the majority of deputies was not over the RRMs but, rather, over leftist organizations, the Communists, and the Mojahedin. This reflects what the regime's supporters viewed as a more serious threat to the new system.[97]

Only Articles 4 and 5 of the bill dealt with the RRMs. Article 4 specified that religious minorities could form their own collectivities to address religious, cultural, social, and welfare issues specific to (vizheh-ye) their minority. Bait Ushana opposed the use of the word "specific" arguing that it limited the range of the RRM activities. He argued that RRMs could form their own groups already based on the constitution. These groups were entitled to express their views on all issues facing the nation. The use of the word "specific" meant that RRM assemblies should express their views only on matters of concern to the minorities. Bait Ushana asked for the elimination of the word "specific" from Article 4.

While some supported his interpretation, others disagreed. Opposition to the elimination was adamant on the use of "specific" because it determined the boundaries of organizational activity. Zavarehi, undersecretary of the Interior Ministry, argued that, if a Christian group was formed, their activities would be limited to the Christian faith. They would not set out to turn Muslims and/or Jews into Christians. Ushana's motion on elimination was put to a vote. Of 181 present, only 56 voted in favor of the motion to strike the word. Yet it set into motion other concerns. Deputy Imami Kashani suggested the elimination of "social and welfare" emphasizing the "religious" aspect of minority status. Deputy Mahalati opposed this, arguing that "social and welfare" was an extension of religious customs of a minority. Its inclusion allowed the RRMs to form benevolent societies and this was their right. Another deputy, Moadikhah, pointed out that the RRMs faced social problems of their own and needed their own societies to address them. Ushana also opposed Kashani's motion in strong terms and asked the Majlis not to vote on the motion, as it was a violation of the constitution and the basic rights of the RRMs. Of 180 present, only 14 sided with Kashani and the motion was defeated.[98]

These proceedings reveal the perpetual preoccupation of some deputies with the issue of conversion and religious proselytizing. In discussions on reform of another piece of legislation, the RRM issue was raised again in a bill on elections in the section on qualifications for running for elective office. It revolved around a sentence in the addendum which was presented by the Majlis committee responsible for drafting the legal language of the bill. The committee's version added the phrase "if the candidates [representing the religious minorities] were members of the religious minorities," implying that a Muslim candidate may run for office and be elected representing one of the RRMs. Malekpoor, speaking on behalf of all RRM deputies, opposed this addition and called it unconstitutional. The language of the Islamic constitution, he said, was clear on the point that members from minority communities would serve as deputies representing their minorities' interests. Deputy Khalkhali, in his usual outrageous manner of speech, saw no problem with Muslims representing Christians, Jews, or Zoroastrians. In a country where the RRMs' president, prime minister, and most deputies to the Majlis were Muslim, RRM deputies could also be Muslim. "It is certain that a Muslim can better represent the rights of a Christian than a Christian . . . a Muslim might be better in knowing the ins and outs of political events . . . this is up to them [the RRMs]. Why should we take this right away from them [the RRMs]?"[99]

Deputy Majid Ansari spoke in opposition to Khalkhali's position. He put forth several reasons why the RRM deputies should come from the RRMs' communities: (1) the spirit of the constitution strongly implied this by designating five seats to the RRMs; (2) a deputy should keep abreast of the conditions of her/his constituency, be involved in its religious and cultural affairs, and listen to the problems of its members – a Muslim could not do this within a Zoroastrian, Jewish, or Christian community; (3) the Majlis text on rules governing the oath of office clearly articulated that the RRM deputies should swear by their own religious book – therefore, a Muslim who represented them should swear on a religious book other than the Quran in violation of the constitution; and (4) it would reflect negatively abroad, since no one would believe that selecting a Muslim deputy was the RRMs' choice.[100]

Moezzi, undersecretary of the Interior Ministry, reiterated that the government had not made the addition; this was done by the Majlis committee. Therefore, the government did not object to its elimination. At this point, Mohediye Savaji, the committee spokesman, interjected that, even though the RRMs might not ever want to elect a Muslim to represent them, this clause gave them the option to do so in the future and the presence of the clause did no harm. Eventually, however, the phrase "if the candidates were from the minorities" was eliminated by a majority vote of the Majlis deputies.[101]

Two distinguishing features

Under the Islamic Republic, there were two radical departures that distinguished state–minority relations from those under the shah's regime. These were the inter-minority discourse and the localized nature of state–society relations in post-revolutionary Iran.

Since the inception of the Revolution, as was the case with majority Shii population and ethnic groups, the recognized religious minorities had revealed their diversity. The RRM communities were divided on social, political, and economic issues from the first day of the Revolution. Some of these divisions lingered from the shah's era; some were the result of a new consciousness on possible alternatives as citizens, and others were prompted by opportunism and personal desire for power. For example, the Association of Iranian Jewish Intellectuals, commonly known as Roshanfekran, a new group formed in 1979, held a different view from what can be termed as that representing Jewish mainstream businessmen and merchants. They were one of the first groups to support the Revolution. The Jewish deputy who had sat in the Assembly of Experts, Aziz Daneshrad, was affiliated with this group.[102] The association believed that the Jewish community could develop good relations with the new regime. Its activities were quite unorthodox by Iranian Jewish standards; for instance, it arranged a meeting with Hani al-Hassan, a representative of the Palestinian Liberation Organization in Tehran. Another group, the Jewish Council for Cultural and Social Advancement, began a series of seminars on diverse political groups to help develop a better understanding among all factions.[103] The Jewish leftist minority liberally condemned Israel and Zionism, yet in the early years did not have a major impact on the overall state–Jewish minority relations of the Islamic Republic.[104] Amnon Netzer, a scholar of Iranian Jewish affairs, has used the designations "radical intellectual" and "leftist and non-Zionist" to describe the post-revolutionary Jewish elements who replaced the "old Jewish oligarchy."[105] Elements from the left continued to endorse the regime in the post-Khomeini era and, with the departure of chief rabbis, major industrialists, and businessmen, they became the main spokesmen for the Jewish community.

Armenians were also divided along similar lines with one major exception. Compared to other RRMs their groups were much more cohesive. Under the shah's regime the pro-Dashnak elements had come to dominate much of the cultural life of the community.[106] This had been the traditional role of the Dashnak Party, which challenged pro-Communist, pro-leftist, or anti-Dashnak individuals and groups at every turn in all Armenian diasporas throughout the world. Its goal had always been to preserve and protect the Armenian cultural heritage in different cultural settings. The fall of the shah's regime bolstered its opposition and set off an intercommunity conflict. In 1979, reportedly, the Armenian Archbishop of Tehran, Artak Manukian, was held hostage for several hours, and an active member of Dashnak was almost stabbed to death.[107] The opposition to the Dashnak Party was an amalgam of diverse individuals who were not always unified. While politically they may be classified as left of center, they were motivated by ideological or personal dislike of Dashnak's past (or present) manipulation of political and social avenues

1, 2. Demonstration by Iranian Jews on the occasion of the Israeli air raids in Lebanon, Tehran, 1980 (Rahmat Rahimian).

of expression in the diaspora. In contrast to the Jewish case, however, the Armenian religious institution solidified the support of the community and never relinquished control and authority.

Founders of new minority groups were generally young professionals. Some saw themselves as intellectuals; some were actively involved in political causes; some had sympathy with various progressive and leftist forces; others were pro-Tudeh; and then there were always those whose motivations were personal. There were similar divisions and personal motivations among the Assyrians and the Zoroastrians. In fact, one of the most exciting features of the first Majlis was diversity of views within its RRM factions. Ideological diversity was played out on the floor of the Majlis where, for example, on some national issues the two Armenian deputies would vote on opposite sides of issues.[108]

All inter-RRM factions claimed strong loyalty to the Islamic Republic of Iran. In 1990 when the United Nations Human Rights envoy, Galindo Pohl, released its report on the status of religious minorities, one of these new associations, the National and Cultural Association of Armenians, was among the first groups to protest the report. In a letter to the UN bureau in Tehran, the group said that it owed its founding in 1979 to the Islamic regime and before the Revolution it could not operate freely. The association called the Pohl report "false" and asked that the UN respect the rights of Iranian citizens.[109]

The intensity of factionalism among the RRMs has subsided considerably since the early years. The competitive nature of politics, however, has been kept alive in the election of candidates to the Majlis. The latitude allowed to religious minorities in running for seats has been more liberal compared to the country's general elections for Muslims. Part of the reason is the open process in registering a candidate. Individuals who wish to challenge the status quo candidates can do so simply by placing their name in nomination. They do this through the government rather than their religious or community centers. Therefore, there is no communal control over the initial process of the elections. This allows an array of candidates at this stage. For example, in the nomination stage of the elections for the fourth Majlis in 1992, the Zoroastrians had some twelve candidates for one seat. As the date of the vote approached, the numbers dwindled to three.[110] A total of twenty-five candidates from religious minorities registered to run for parliamentary seats.[111] This picture is radically different from the highly controlled process of the Pahlavi era, and it makes the elections, at the very least, interesting. The process facilitates campaigning; pamphlets are distributed throughout the main cities with a significant minority population and candidates must lecture to various community associations in order to win their vote.

Why have the minorities been given such freedom while in other matters they have been restrained? As with other spheres of regime policy, it is difficult to assess whether something begins as a planned policy or simply evolves, with habitual repetition establishing a policy. Overall, the regime has shown an unusual mixture of restraint and flexibility. Also, the presence of factionalism and of a multitude of covert and overt groupings has been the rule rather than the exception in post-revolutionary Iran. The low numbers of the recognized religious minorities do not pose a serious threat to the regime. In other words, the theocratic regime has nothing to lose but may have everything to gain by allowing open elections. Open elections among the RRMs can be a useful barometer for the regime. Although it is not a traditional divide-and-rule tactic (since minority factionalism has been present for decades), it appears to be a tactical device nevertheless. By allowing free elections, the community reveals itself to the regime, exposing its power centers as well as its vulnerabilities. The process takes away the mystery and secretiveness of the minority communities and, ultimately, informs the authorities. And it does not hurt to have some level of suspicion and a bit of paranoia present among RRM circles. There have been bullies and informers who have manipulated the process, taking advantage of the fear and vulnerability of their community.

The second distinguishing feature of the new republic has been the localized nature of state–minority relations. The local element was obvious from the beginning. For example, in the city of Shiraz the minister of education and training issued a declaration barring religious minorities from teaching in schools.[112] But this sort of localized arbitrary practice affected the Shiis and Sunnis as well. In 1982, in the same city, for instance, a clergyman changed the prison sentences of several prisoners to the death penalty and had them executed. He had no jurisdiction and had not even read the records of the prisoners. The judge who had originally and legally made the ruling on behalf of the Shiraz court took the case to Khomeini, but to no avail. He eventually resigned his position.[113]

On some policies Tehran's wishes were implemented. For example, the insulation of the RRMs from Muslims (e.g., no Muslims were allowed in community gatherings or religious centers) was applied nationally. Variations appeared predominantly in those areas where local permission on an ad hoc basis was required. Variations also have appeared at the policy implementation level in part due to individual initiative and in part because policy was not being uniformly applied across the country. Several factors came to impinge upon local minority relations: the long history of communal contact with the RRMs (e.g., Zoroastrians in Yazd,

Armenians in Isfahan, Jews in Shiraz, Assyrians in Rezaiyeh, or Chaldeans in Ahvaz), the nature of the relationship between the high-ranking clerics and the religious leadership of the community in question, the character and clout of the RRM representative acting on behalf of his community, and the local authorities' overall attitude and willingness to adhere to Tehran's views.

The state offered the recognized religious minorities some rights (e.g., their own political representation, some freedom in their communal life and practice of religion, etc.), but rules, restrictions, and blatant discrimination (legal details and variations to be discussed in chapter 4) made them into inferior subordinates. Chapter 4 explores not only this subordination but also the dynamics of exclusion (aimed in particular at the Bahais and the Iranian Christian converts). State ideology provides the link between the subordinated and excluded communities and defines the parameters of political action.

4   Distinctions and designations as policy output

General policy in regard to recognized religious minorities (RRMs) can tell us only so much about the dynamics behind thought and action in a revolutionary regime. The behavior of state actors vis-à-vis the RRMs was characterized by factors that are relevant to other questions and issues. These can be answered only by delving into the larger picture of the meaning of the role of non-Muslim minorities. The widening of the analytical realm allows us to focus on the uniqueness of each group. As a result, it becomes possible to see why the Jews were treated more harshly than were other recognized religious minorities, and why the Bahais and Iranian Christian converts (especially the Protestants) were persecuted. What did each of the these three minorities mean to the revolutionaries and religious extremists (be they clerical or not), and what can such meaning tell us about the underlying components of the policy sphere? The purpose is not to blame, condemn, or sit in judgment but simply to understand the movement of one set of negatives (e.g., stereotyping) into the arena of policy or action.

From a psychological point of view, ethnic conflict has three major components: perception, motivation, and action.[1] The three combine to lead ultimately to full-blown conflict by the final breakdown of relations. Perception of the other is the first stage, involving stereotyping and prejudice that tend to cultivate group hostility. Stereotyping of the other has been prevalent in all cultures and nations and even in various localities among the same people. As long as it is harmless, focusing on a predominant characteristic of the people (e.g., the simplicity of the Rashtis or the notable mothering of boys among Sicilians), it can even be humorous and reflect some of the common characteristics of a community of people. Yet, it is the negative intensity of hostile stereotyping which becomes demeaning to the victim and in the long run demeaning to the victimizer.

Perception in and of itself cannot lead to action; it tends to stay dormant until there is a motivation. Motives "supply the energy necessary for action" and "the degree of violence in conflict situations is a function of intensity of motivation."[2] It is with the help of motivation (for power, economic gain, security, etc.) that perception leads to action. Action driven by stereotyping in its ultimate form is institutionalized violence. Perceptions come to guide the prejudicial actions of individuals, groups, and states but they need the force of motivation to be activated into a full-blown conflict.

Walter Zenner argues that the perception of the minority by the major-ity is extremely important in discussions of ethnic identity and its compo-nents.[3] An important component of this perception is prejudice. Benard and Khalilzad's thoughtful work on this topic in regard to Iran views prej-udice as "the social and political employment of certain patterns of sim-plified, overgeneralized, nonrational thinking. It can operate, as such, on different levels: to maintain the cohesiveness of the group, to maintain a certain order, to defend a power relationship or to challenge it."[4]

Prejudicial behavior directed at the minorities has been prevalent in Iran for a very long time. During the first few decades of the century many Armenians recall being called "Armani sag Armani, jarukesh-e jahanami [Armenian dog Armenian, the sweeper of the floor of Hell]"; Jews were labeled thieves, liars, cheats, and in some places openly harassed; Zoroastrians were referred to as "atash parast [fire-worshippers]," and in Yazd public accommodations were segregated between Muslims and Zoroastrians. At different periods of Iranian history the state dealt with such cases differently. For example, during the Reza Shah era the segrega-tion of accommodations in Yazd ceased, but it returned during his son's rule.[5] However, public references and name calling of religious minorities were considered impolite during the reign of Mohammad Reza Shah. It was unbecoming to a modernizing (nation-)state to have reverberations of this sort in public. Religious minorities were employed in government and the oil industry. Moreover, some rich minorities shared major busi-ness ventures with the shah.

Pretended Western modernization does not exonerate upper, middle, or lower classes of responsibility for their negative stereotyping of others. Understanding the causes behind prejudice and ways of dealing with it is complex. Non-Muslim minorities have always known, without vocalizing the issue, what constituted discriminatory behavior or insulting words addressed to them. They would choose to ignore these, or would dismiss them as the utterances of the ignorant, the traditional, the religious zealots, and the backward. The modernized secular nationalists, however, ignored their own stereotyping of minorities and blamed the religious ele-ments for prejudicial deeds against the non-Muslims.[6] Perhaps there was a difference between the prejudicial views of the various segments of the Shii population. For the nonreligious, it was only when their personal interest was at stake or when they were in competition with people from a minority group that the latter's "non-Muslimness" and "otherness" was raised. A cultural prejudice can acquire modern characteristics by adding Western/secular elements to the old ones. In the final analysis, however, prejudice remains an individual attitude and in this it knows no categories; members of all classes and sectors of society, whether religious, traditional, secular, modernized, Westernized, leftist, professional, or a combination thereof, may be prejudiced.

Prejudice ultimately is a way of saying we are better than you, and it is an easy way of bolstering one's own sense of identity and pride. Prejudice can be held by minorities as well, Armenians and Assyrians against Jews and Muslims, or Jews against Muslims and Christians. But it becomes threatening only when the dominant group with complete hold over political power maintains these views about the minority and can elevate them to become part of state ideology. It is here that the danger of moving from perception to action exists. In other words, "the image of the polity that is held by the ruling elite and the definition of the state that is reflected in the constitutions, laws, and policies"[7] can be menacing for minorities.

Under the Islamic theocracy prejudicial encounters between the majority and minorities became more overt. A Christian woman returning from the Republic of Armenia was searched carefully and interrogated as to whether she had brought pig meat with her from her visit to a Christian country.[8]

This author along with two other women hailed a taxi in front of an Assyrian church. After some typical bargaining (common practice in Iran), the taxi driver agreed on the price. The male passenger sitting next to the driver on the front seat turned to us: "Why did you bargain? You Assyrians are so rich you could easily pay him whatever he asked for." An Assyrian female companion responded immediately, disagreeing with his comment. The passenger persisted and then suddenly changed his tune and began cursing Shii Muslims, being one himself. The female passengers remained silent.

The author was at Harvard University searching for material on Zoroastrians, when an Iranian middle-aged woman who worked there unabashedly responded to the author's inquiry: "What is there to know about them [the Zoroastrians]? They are all rich and have no problems."

In a letter to the *Iran Times* a writer elaborated on the conspiratorial tendencies of Jews at length. The Jews, the author of the letter wrote, do not fall asleep like normal people. For hours after going to bed they think and plot how to deceive people the next day.[9]

Similar bold commentaries were also made on Iranian television and in the print media following the Revolution. In one television program, the commentator impudently declared: "A dog, a pig, and a non-Muslim are najess." Letters of protest were sent to the television management by the RRMs. Without recanting the commentary the management replied that everyone is respected in Islam,[10] a standard response voiced after any complaint or protest.

In 1992, in a children's television program, a story was told of a son who went to Imam Reza and told him that he had abandoned his mother because she was a non-Muslim. Imam Reza, being kind and generous, commanded the son to return to his mother and help her at any cost even though she was not a Muslim. The son obeyed. As he returned to help and serve his mother, the mother was deeply moved by the devotion of his son and the greatness of Imam Reza, saw the light, and converted to Islam.[11]

In a curious letter entitled "A Word with Iranian Jews," an individual calling himself Dr. Rohani claiming to be the son of a cleric took upon himself to advise the Jews. He expressed the hope that the Jews would learn from Zoroastrians without making it clear what there was to be learned. He emphasized that he hated no religious minority and went on to engage in generalizations and discussions of Israel, and concluded that anyone who raises the special status of the Jews or their miseries was promoting the aims of the international Zionist movement.[12] Throughout the article, the author cited English-language sources. If his self-identification is correct, the tone of the letter suggests an individual who was probably educated in the West without abandoning the prejudicial views of his father, "the Imam of the town." His letter simply tells the reader that, as he had come from a traditional religious family and had acquired upward mobility to travel abroad for education, his religious prejudice transfused into the modern Europeanized version of anti-Jewish sentiment with traces of Marxism. The prejudice here has three components: (1) traditional religious anti-Jewish prejudice (based on ritualistic uncleanliness and similar views), (2) European anti-semitism (reminiscent of the nineteenth and twentieth centuries), and (3) the political impact of the creation of the state of Israel.

In post-revolutionary Iran, no lip service was paid to the idea and concept of "a nation." The state institutions developed and advocated a schism along Muslim versus non-Muslim lines. As a non-Muslim woman confessed to the author: "Watching television, I often hear the comment 'our dear Muslim brothers and sisters' instead of 'our hamvatanan [fellow countrymen/countrywomen]'; and every time I am filled with disgust." Elevating societal cultural prejudice into the state domain was accomplished by the formulation and maintenance of a fundamentalist state ideology. Disguised under an ideological rubric, personal, political, and economic motivations were at play, prompting sporadic or preplanned

actions depending on the situation and the timing of the event. The severity increased or decreased depending on state and local authorities' use of
personal or political motivations in creating a mixed policy, while maintaining the separation of Muslim and non-Muslim was a central theme.
The end result was "the maintenance or intensification of stratification"
between the dominant and the subordinate.[13]

Three subordinate groups – the Jews, the Bahais, and the Iranian
Christian converts – exemplify the move from perception to motivation to
the most severe action. Each situation was different. The Jews were an
established recognized religious minority with one representative in the
Majlis. The Bahais were never recognized as a religious minority in Iran.
The Christians were recognized in Islam, and their ethnic elements (the
Armenians, the Assyrians and the Chaldeans) had representatives in the
Majlis. However, the Iranian Christian converts were the exception, and
were not recognized.

The severity of treatment of the Jews

Objective research into the treatment of the recognized religious minorities leaves no doubt that the Iranian Jews have received harsher treatment
than the other RRMs. Even members of other recognized religious
minorities are in agreement on this point. Before Ayatollah Khomeini's
return to Iran, contacts were made with his advisors regarding the situation of the Jews. Khomeini's companions, such as Sadeq Qotbzadeh, Bani
Sadr, and Mehdi Askari, reiterated that, while relations with Israel would
come to a halt, Iranian Jewry need not fear and would come to no harm.[14]
Yet, in the last few months before Khomeini's return, Jews received
threats in the form of telephone calls and notes asking them to leave the
country.[15] After a robbery at a major carpet store owned by a Jew, many
Jewish merchants removed merchandise from their stores.[16]

Anti-Zionist and anti-Israel sentiments were central to the revolutionaries' thinking and were part of the routine of leftist and fundamentalist
daily slogans. In a sweeping assault against the independent and progressive press, in August 1979, the popular newspaper, *Ayandegan*, was
ordered to shut down. Major demonstrations were held against it, and
slogans attacked *Ayandegan*, Zionism, and Israel; one Islamic organization called it "the loudspeaker of Zionism." The demonstrators marched
to the residence of Ayatollah Khomeini, who came out to greet them.[17]
Overall, despite a commonly held view that the ayatollah's speeches were
focused on Zionism and Israel and not on Jews, several scholars have
found this not to be entirely correct. According to these scholars, pre-revolutionary preaching made no distinctions among Israel, world Jewry,

and Jews as a religious minority. But, in the post-revolutionary period, an emphasis was placed on negative portrayals of Zionism and Israel.[18] In one of his messages in November 1979, Ayatollah Khomeini declared: "Jews are different from Zionists; if the Muslims overcome the Zionists, they will leave the Jews alone. They [the Jews] are a nation like other nations; their life continues on and they cannot be rejected by Muslims."[19]

The change in tone and message may have been prompted by the Jewish community's direct plea for protection to the supreme jurist and the genuine concern of some of the ayatollah's lieutenants about a negative backlash against the Jewish minority. But Ayatollah Khomeini and his lieutenants were also limited by the fundamental precepts of Islam, which give clear unequivocal recognition to the Jews. It was this restriction, ironically placed upon them by the religion they claimed to represent, that prevented them from persecuting the Jews more severely. In other words, Islam was the shield safeguarding the Jews against the fundamentalist impulse.

The fundamentalist ideologues (clerical and lay) compensated for the religious limitation placed upon them by making accusations of treason, conspiracy, and intrigue to justify persecution. The stereotype of the Jew as the facilitator of intrigue was clearly evident in reverting to mythical religious beliefs. In a pocket calendar published during the early 1980s, at the end where general information usually appears, there was a listing on the Prophet and the Twelve Shii Imams. Different columns gave summary information about their lives (name of mother or father, date of birth, etc.). The last column was entitled "the murderer," where the name and identity of the murderers of the Twelve Imams were given. Under the Prophet Mohammad's name it identified a "Jewish woman" as the murderer of the Prophet. A popular Shii religious myth (that a Jewish female companion had poisoned the Prophet causing his eventual death) became part of a calendar's "factual" information and was distributed among the public. Even worse, the subject also became one of the questions in the ideological test for entrance to the Teachers' Training College where the students were given a multiple-choice question in order to identify the instigator of the martyrdom of the Prophet Mohammad, the "correct" answer being "a Jewess."[20]

In contemporary times, charges of treason, conspiracy, and intrigue included the belief in the overwhelming influence of Israel on Iran's economy and politics during the shah's reign. During the first year of the Revolution, for example, those who advocated the outright dismissal of Jewish university professors referred to them as Zionist professors.[21] While regime officials reassured the community leaders that the government differentiated between Zionism and the Jewish minority, they also warned the latter that:

as long as Jews "behave themselves," i.e., do not associate with Israel and conduct their [economic] activity properly, they will not be harmed. A high-ranking religious leader who was present at that meeting used an expression which meant "execution" in case the Jews did not conduct themselves as recommended.[22]

Within a few months after the return of Ayatollah Khomeini to Iran, the event which most startled the Jewish community was the execution of Habib Elghanian, a multimillionaire businessman in May 1979. He was a renowned industrialist with close connections with Israel. The significance of his execution was that, along with another Muslim businessman, they were the first private individuals (as opposed to military and government officials) to go in front of the firing squad. Although the government denied that Elghanian was executed because he was a Jew, the charges brought against him alarmed Iranian Jews. The charges were: "friendship with the enemies of God and being an enemy of the friends of God," "corruption on earth," "warring with God and his emissaries," and "economic imperialism."[23] The news media reveled in this execution. In jubilation they rationalized Elghanian's killing by pointing to his meeting in the early 1960s with Abba Eban (then Israel's deputy prime minister) and Moshe Dayan (the former defense minister and foreign minister of Israel in 1979).[24] A radio commentary averred:

[Elghanian] was a disgrace to the Jews in this country. He was an individual who wished to equate Jewry with Zionism. The Iranian people will punish any xenophile and spy from whatever (?sect) . . . The mass of information he kept sending to Israel, his actions to achieve Israel's designs, the colossal sum of foreign exchange and funds he kept transferring to Israel; these are only samples of his antinational actions; these were the acts used to crush our Palestinian brethren. The Iranian Jews hate to have a spy like [Elghanian] as their symbol. Like the Iranian Muslims, they want to have the features of Iranian religious minorities pure and clean.[25]

In another radio broadcast, the commentator, referring to protests in the Israeli Knesset (parliament) and press, said: "The more clamorous this propaganda barrage becomes, the more it convinces the Iranian nation of the validity of its diagnosis, for it finds out more than before that this alien spy was of great value to his overlords."[26]

An Iranian Foreign Ministry statement denied that Elghanian's death had any relevance to him being a Jew, because the other businessman who was executed with him, Rahim-Ali Khorram, was a Muslim, and during the trial the accused were never asked about their religious affiliation.[27]

It was noticeable, however, that many more Jews, compared to other RRMs, were imprisoned, and by December 1980 seven known Jews were executed; by 1982 there were two more. Their charges were an array of spying for Israel and the United States, supporting Zionism, corruption, treason, and drug dealing.[28] There were other events that had a dramatic impact on Jewish fear and insecurity. In August 1980, Chief Rabbi Yedidiya Shofet left for Europe asking the Jews to leave Iran quickly.[29] In 1983, some 2,000 Jews were rounded up as they left a Tehran synagogue where they had gathered for a Friday night prayer. The Revolutionary Guards took them by bus to prison where they spent the night.[30] Jews were singled out, and families were prevented from traveling abroad as a group. If, for example, a husband had to travel abroad, the passport of the wife was detained to be picked up after his return. Also, in contrast to other Iranians and recognized religious minorities, the Jews were often denied multiple-exit visas and had to file a new application and pay another fee every time they planned a trip. Typical bureaucratic delays and bungling placed many at the mercy of the low-level bureaucrats who could easily put their personal biases to good use by claiming loss of the passport, postponement, and similar problems.[31] Manuchehr Nikrooz, the Jewish representative, raised this problem on the floor of the Majlis in 1986.[32]

The end result was a substantial drop in the number of Jews living in Iran. On the Jewish flight from Iran, conflicting reports abound but many are not reliable and are exaggerated. Alois Mock, foreign minister of Austria, disclosed in late 1987 that Austria had accepted thousands of Iranian Jews since July 1983, more than a quarter of them having arrived during the first eight months of 1987. He credited the "quiet cooperation" of the Islamic regime and the government of Pakistan for the exodus.[33] The closest accurate estimates are that, of 80,000 Iranian Jews in 1979, more than half have left Iran, uncertain and fearful about the future, reducing their numbers to around 30,000 by 1986.[34] Beginning in the late 1980s, a few merchants and industrialists returned to Iran, some finding new economic opportunities, but the majority being disgusted with the severity of treatment; and some, for fear of arrest, did not return.

David Menashri is correct in observing that "executions of members of the religious minorities were not out of proportion to their numerical strength in the former establishment."[35] (Bahais and Iranian Christian converts were the exception.) Yet, prejudicial sentiments can easily be pushed to action by a strong motivation. Sorour Soroudi saw economic rivalries involving the bazaaris (bazaar traders) as an important motivation for severe treatment of the Jews.[36] David Menashri agrees that the Jewish communities' economic position deteriorated significantly as a result of the post-revolutionary environment.[37]

Walter Zenner has presented a theory he calls "middleman minorities."

He argues that middleman "or 'trading' minorities are ethnic groups which are disproportionately represented in occupations related to commerce, especially in the small business sector."[38] Although they become affluent, the trading minorities are not part of the ruling elite; their lack of political power makes them vulnerable to violence. Zenner, of course, is addressing the linkages between motivation and action, especially the extreme action of genocide. Yet his conclusions appear very familiar not only for the Jews but also for the Bahais:

> Two elements combine in anti-middleman ideology. One is to view commerce, especially that engaged in by stranger-middlemen, as evil and as violating the rights of natives. In its extreme form, moneymaking is seen as diabolical. The second is to view the minority middlemen as foreign agents who are enemies of the nation, whether this is the Bolsheviks, the Pope, or the Japanese Empire. Both serve to dehumanize the minority middlemen; when combined they form a potent weapon to use against them, and this helps exacerbate the normal frictions between businessmen, their competitors, and their clients.[39]

Yet there must be political mobilization for anti-middleman sentiment to turn into systematic violence. It was this that was absent in post-revolutionary Iran. Though they were under suspicion, the status of the Jews as a recognized religious minority and their own unique form of response to the regime (to be discussed later) prevented escalation of conflict. Bahais, however, were not as fortunate.

The persecution of Bahais

From the beginning the clerical regime targeted the Bahai population of Iran. The Bahais had the option, of course, of converting to Islam and enjoying the same rights as the dominant group. The negative perception of the Bahais in pre-revolutionary Iran has already been discussed in chapter 1. The clergy and religious segments have always held a deep hostility against the Bahais. They were the true "infidels," in the strict application of the term, to be dealt with harshly and to be destroyed. As noted earlier, in pre-revolutionary Iran, some Bahais acceded to important positions and were on the average more educated and successful in business than the population in general. But they had been manipulated by the regime, which sacrificed them to the clerics to placate the latter in their efforts to rid the world of what they felt to be an enemy of Islam.

In the years before 1979, the Bahais' unceasing propagation of their faith did not help their situation, either. Not unlike Christian missionaries, despite their upper-class status and apparent secularism, the Bahais were viewed (by Muslims and non-Muslims alike) as trying to use personal relations to attract individuals to their order. Many avid Bahais may disagree, but this process was deeply agitating to other Iranians, including secularists. Yet the Iranian secularists as well as the left and the intellectuals entertained a negative view of the Bahais regardless of their evangelizing. Many believed that Bahaism was a fake movement founded in Iran by the British colonialists as an instrument of indirect rule in order to destroy Shiism and progressive movements.[40]

In the turmoil of the revolutionary period, the popular perception, the leftist and particularly the Tudeh Party's views and religious fundamentalist ideas on Bahaism perversely merged together. There was no introspection, no pondering of the personal and group responsibility for making generalized accusations. In an atmosphere of anti-imperialist xenophobia certain targets were easier to aim for, violation of the basic rights of some groups was more tolerable, and some "indiscriminate" acts of violence were conveniently ignored.[41] Of course, the more secular and progressive elements had little power in the government to move in any direction. Yet, Firuz Kazemzadeh was not too far off when he suggested that in the twentieth century attacking Bahaism on theological grounds lost its appeal. In an environment where nationalism became the "surrogate religion" of educated Iranian secularists, Bahais were viewed as "unpatriotic" and were continuously linked to an array of foreign elements.[42] Of course, further investigation is needed to reveal how strongly, if at all, these nationalist, secular, and educated elements believed and emphasized the human rights of all Iranian citizens to their life, property, security, and, more importantly, whether they practiced what they preached.

Despite the hopes of the Bahai community for a degree of protection, the Provisional Government of Mehdi Bazargan was of little help. It is important to reiterate the weak, highly disorganized, and anarchic nature of Bazargan's government as a definite variable affecting the outcome. None of the recognized religious minorities felt solace in this "knife without the blade."[43]

The members of the National Spiritual Assembly of the Bahais of Iran first privately then publicly voiced their fears and addressed point by point the allegations of the religious elements against them. They were accused of being political friends of the shah's regime, anti-Islamic, agents of Zionism, and of having profited financially from the Pahlavi rule and having engaged in a conspiracy with the United States and the British governments.[44] According to Bahai sources, not only did they receive no response to their rebuttal, but there was every indication that the Bazargan government approved of and collaborated with the anti-Bahai persecutions. Of course, in assessing this view, allowance must be made for the disjointed and anarchic nature of the environment in which the Provisional Government of Mehdi Bazargan operated, as well as his own frustration with various factions. The election of President Bani Sadr in January 1980 did not change the prevailing anti-Bahai sentiment; Bahaism was officially described as a political movement against the Revolution and Islam. Before the Revolution, Bani Sadr had equated the universalist message of Bahaism with Western colonialism.[45]

A relevant example here which reflects on the mood of the times as well as a deeper issue on minority–majority relations is the following event. Mansur Farhang, who had been a professor of politics in the United States before the Revolution, and who became the first Iranian ambassador to the United Nations after the Revolution, in an interview with the MacNeil–Lehrer Report, a US television news magazine, on 12 February 1980, denied the mistreatment of Bahais and repeated the clerics' charges that the Bahais were SAVAK (the Iranian Secret Police under the shah) torturers. Farhang broke with the regime in January 1982 and only then began to write publicly and speak on the issue of Bahai persecution.[46] From attempted justification to vehement condemnation of the regime seems a typical path for many educated Iranians. The main problem is not in recanting but never honestly addressing the reasons for such extreme shifts in one's personal opinions. And religious minorities have witnessed such incidents often enough to be weary of the dominant groups' endorsement of any political ideology.

Numerous and varied sources from the United Nations, Amnesty International, and other independent human rights organizations substantiate incidence of persecution of the Bahais. The Bahai international community has worked actively to document every case in Iran. Here the purpose is analysis of the significance of these persecutions rather than citing of atrocities as discrete actions. After Khomeini came to power, many Bahais were dismissed from their work places, and the leadership of the Bahai community throughout Iran was targeted and many were arrested and executed. On 21 August 1980, all nine members of the Bahai National Spiritual Assembly (NSA) of Iran were arrested by the Revolutionary Guards and subsequently disappeared. The authorities denied any knowledge of their whereabouts. They are presumed dead. Nine Bahais were elected to a new NSA; eight were arrested on 13 December 1981, and secretly executed two weeks later. As time passed the execution rates mounted and, by the end of 1984, according to Bahai sources, 177 had been killed. While the killings continued, the rate of executions decreased substantially between 1985 and 1988, and there were no reported executions from 1989 to 1991.[47]

The hostility against the Bahais was fueled by the energy of the Revolution and its ideological elements. For some persecutionists it was a quest for power and wealth and for others, those who saw themselves as

3. National Spiritual Assembly of the Bahais of Iran, 1981. The photograph shows the entire membership of the 1980 National Assembly (arrested and disappeared in 1980 and presumed dead), six members of the 1981 National Assembly (nine were elected and eight of them were arrested and secretly executed on 27 December 1981), and several other Bahais (National Spiritual Assembly of the Bahais of the United States).

God's appointees, the motive was to guarantee Islam's purity. One of the most brutal acts occurred in Shiraz, long one of the central bastions of hatred toward Bahais. The House of the Bab, one of the holiest Bahai shrines, was destroyed, and in June 1983, ten Bahai women were executed after being tortured.[48] A few months earlier Qazai, an Islamic judge and head of the Revolutionary Court of Shiraz in an interview with a Shiraz newspaper said:

The Iranian Nation has risen in accordance with Quranic teachings and by the Will of God has determined to establish the Government of God on earth. Therefore, it cannot tolerate the perverted Bahais who are the instruments of Satan and followers of the Devil and of the superpowers and their agents . . . It is absolutely certain that in the Islamic Republic of Iran there is no place whatsoever for Bahais and Bahaism . . . Before it is too late, the Bahais should recant Bahaism, which is condemned by reason and logic. Otherwise, the day will soon come when the Islamic Nation will deal with the Bahais in accordance with its religious obligations and will . . . God willing, fulfil the prayer of Noah, mentioned in the Quran, "and Noah said, Lord, leave not one single family of infidels on the earth."[49]

4, 5. Destruction of the House of Bab in Shiraz. One of the most holy sites in the Bahai world, it was destroyed by Revolutionary Guards in 1979 and razed by the government in May 1981 (National Spiritual Assembly of the Bahais of the United States).

Kidnapping, imprisonment, disappearances, mob attacks, being beaten and dragged into mosques in order to recant the Bahai faith, confiscation of property, looting and burning of houses and buildings owned by the Bahais, desecration of Bahai cemeteries, barring Bahai professors from teaching and students from being admitted to the universities, and dismissal of Bahai teachers and Bahai students from schools were some of the severe measures leveled against the Bahai community.[50] They were widespread and systematic.

In a 1983 interview, Iran's prosecutor general, Seyyed Hossein Musavi Tabrizi, denied that Bahais were being persecuted because of their religious belief. The executed were spies and it was the agitation, sabotage, and funneling of money outside the country which had placed some Bahais in jeopardy. He reiterated that, if they practiced their religion without inviting others to join, did not advertise, and did not form associations, then they "not only will not be persecuted but they will not be imprisoned either." He stated in clear terms that any organized Bahai activity was against the law.[51]

In a frank letter in response, the National Spiritual Assembly of the Bahais of Iran addressed the issues raised by Tabrizi point by point. Copies of the letter were sent to various government agencies and elites. The letter acknowledged the collection and transference of funds abroad, but this was the Bahais' contribution to shrines and holy places. The letter emphatically denied the allegations of agitation and espionage and demanded proof of the charges. It reiterated the Bahai doctrine of non-interference in politics. At the end of the letter, the NSA contended that, in compliance with government orders, it was dissolving all local spiritual assemblies and committees in order to establish the Bahais' "good intentions" and to show their "complete obedience" to the regime. The NSA asked, in exchange, for an end to persecutions, guarantees of personal safety, permission for Bahais to practice their religion, return of their property, and the overall lifting of restrictions in the social and economic areas.[52] Some in the Bahai community abroad hoped that the dissolution would help the informal legitimization of the Bahais in Iran.

In the complex web of clerical political maneuvering, it is still difficult to ascertain the level of active support by individual clergy for various aspects of Bahai persecutions. Religious leaders were taking positions on a variety of issues; publicly they were either silent or endorsed strict measures. In a June 1980 issue of the newspaper, *Jomhuri-ye Islami*, for example, Ayatollahs Rabani Shirazi, Dastgheib, and Mahalati endorsed the act of not paying pensions to Bahais. They reasoned that according to Islamic law it was haram for Bahais to receive pensions, and those who ignored this were themselves "khati [offenders]."[53]

It has been suggested that one of the main forces behind the Bahai persecutions were members of the Hojjatieh Society. The date of the founding of the organization is unclear; it seems to go back to 1955. The central
aim of the society has been to combat Bahaism. Its members were the
main instigators of attacks against Bahais in the 1950s. The Hojjatieh's
operations are apparently channeled through various committees and are
very secretive. It has favored a strong private sector and an economy
based on free enterprise. Thus, the society has been known as the
adamant supporter of the bazaar. Society members have been religious
fundamentalists with a strong anti-Bahai and anti-communist stand. Its
members, reportedly well educated, had penetrated the Bahai groups
throughout the country before the Revolution. The sweeping tide of
Bahai arrests, imprisonment, and executions is often attributed to the
Hojjatieh infiltrators' access to Bahai registration books and confidential
correspondence. (The SAVAK also possessed information on the Bahais
that fell into the regime's hands.) After the Revolution, the Ministry of
Education and Training became known as the locus of operations of the
Hojjatieh members. The minister of education, Mohammad-Ali Rajai,
who had been appointed by the Revolutionary Council after the collapse
of the Bazargan government in November 1979, was allegedly a Hojjatieh
member. In an edict not only did he dismiss all Bahai teachers, but he also
ordered them to repay all salaries they had received; other government
agencies followed suit.[54]

Many Iranians blame the persecution of the Bahais on the Hojjatieh
Society. However, the society would appear to have been only the most
visible anti-Bahai force. The majority cannot avoid personal and communal responsibility for the persecution of the Bahais in this extreme
manner. To provide tacit support, to remain silent, to favor a less severe
treatment, or to prefer deportation over execution do not excuse the
majority for the actions based on prejudice and hate against an Iranian
religious minority group. The Hojjatieh Society came under attack in
1983, and its overt activities ceased. Yet, it is doubtful that its advocates
have disappeared from the clandestine political scene. Even if its
members had played key roles in the execution of Bahais, still those non-
members who went along or those elements of the secular left who chose
to ignore the incidents remain just as responsible for fashioning anti-
Bahai perceptions, harboring anti-Bahai motivations, and being an
accomplice to, if not necessarily taking charge of, anti-Bahai actions.

The religious elements used terms like "purification" and "defilement"
to describe their actions against Bahais. The charges were, as usual, quite
vague – such as "crimes against God," "warring against God," "corruption on earth," and "Zionism."[55] In an official reply to the Human Rights

Commission of the United Nations, in February 1983, the Permanent Mission of the Islamic Republic provided the official view of the government in a twenty-page document. It blamed the Western industrial countries for a weak United Nations and international human rights machinery. Then, it plunged into a history of Palestine and the British occupation and the founding of Bahaism. While the British fostered Bahaism in Iran, the state of Israel became the implementer of colonial goals. Bahaism was not a religion but a political entity created by "anti-Islamic" and "colonial powers." Bahais "formed the most powerful wing of the [monarchical] ruling regime" and were responsible for violations of human rights.[56] The government's response was not satisfactory and the situation of the Bahais became a constant theme in reports on human rights violations in Iran throughout the 1980s and into the 1990s.

By 1991, positive signs were being detected. The Bahais could bury their dead in some cemeteries, passports were being issued to some, their children were permitted to attend grade school and high school, and there was a partial lifting of the ban on meetings.[57] What seemed to be emerging was a slow recognition of the Bahai presence without abandoning any of the official views about their identity. However, a secret memorandum from the Supreme Revolutionary Cultural Council prepared at the request of President Rafsanjani and Ayatollah Khamenei offered recommendations on the "Bahai question." While prohibiting their incarceration without reason, it laid out the overall regime policy. "A plan must be devised to confront and destroy their cultural roots outside the country"; and, the government must block "their progress and development." If Bahais who studied at schools or universities or were in employment admitted their religion, they would be fired or expelled. A note in the handwriting of Ayatollah Khamenei at the bottom of the document endorsed the policy. The Iranian government has called the document a forgery, but international human rights organizations and the United Nations have verified its authenticity.[58]

Despite some minor temporary improvements, institutionalized persecution of the Bahais continued into the late 1990s. Bahai marriage, divorce, and inheritance rights were not recognized, and they were denied entrance to the institutions of higher education. The property of many Bahais was confiscated or remained in the government's hands after previous confiscation. Discrimination remained blatant in the employment of professionals and in the private sector. Most of their administrative centers, holy places, and cemeteries, if not destroyed, remained confiscated by the state.[59] At least eight Bahais were in prison for their religious beliefs in 1996 and countless numbers were harassed and suffered temporary detention.[60] In July 1998, a Bahai, after ten months of imprisonment, was executed in Mashhad charged with having converted a Muslim woman to Bahaism; he had denied the charges.[61] In September of that year, as the Bahais in the world protested and various governments condemned the act, some 500 homes and several office buildings owned or rented by Bahais throughout Iran were raided by government security forces and scores of people were arrested. It was then revealed that Bahais were secretly operating an Institute of Higher Education for their youth. Since university education was denied to Bahai children, the Institute provided training to nearly 1,000 students. Bahais say that the operation of the university was never concealed and that the authorities had knowledge of it since the early 1990s. Even more baffling was that most of those arrested in the raid were later released and the university was permitted to continue its operations.[62] The timing of the raid coincided with President Khatami's visit to the United Nations and friendly overtures to the West, advancing three possible theories for the attack: (1) the act was the work of the radicals in order to embarrass the president, (2) Khatami, like previous leaders of Iran, was using the Bahais to placate the extremists, and (3) he was at one with the radical elements and the whole incident was preplanned. The truth may very well be a combination of all the above.[63] The clerical state (with all its factions) has survived by compromises, bargaining, criticism, confrontation, and a host of other deals and maneuvers never to be known.

Since 1979, the overall policy on the Bahais has been accompanied with personal arbitrary decisions and irregular and capricious actions similar to those the recognized religious minorities have been subjected to. Firuz Kazemzadeh, secretary of external affairs for the Bahais in United States, pointedly summarized the gist of the issue for the Bahais of Iran:

Whenever political leaders have felt a need to divert public attention from some economic, social, or political issue, they have found the Bahai community an easy target because of the senseless hostility and prejudice inculcated in the public by generations of ecclesiastical propaganda.[64]

As in the case of the Jews, middleman minority status and accusations of profiteering and being foreign agents plagued the Bahais as well. But they not only lacked the religious safety net of the status of People of the Book but were much worse off for having their spiritual genesis in Islam. According to the ideological Shii state, no religion could be born after or even from Islam, and Bahais were therefore apostates. Therefore the hatred and hostility generated against them far exceeded that of the Jews. Not only the solidarity of a group but also its "assimilatory trends" can reenforce xenophobia.[65] The Bahais were viewed as a unified whole whose Iranian assimilationist character intensified the motivation of their opponents. Their highly integrated status in Iranian society (unlike, for example, the Armenians, who were distinct) fueled bigger and grander conspiracy theories: they were the enemy within.

The troubled path of nonethnic Christian groups

In post-revolutionary Iran a number of Christian churches continued to function, some of which were Catholic but most of which were Protestant. The members of these churches were mostly Assyrian, Chaldean, Armenian, Persian, and foreign nationals. The Persian members had converted from Islam or had parents who had converted. The operation of these churches had not been without trouble in pre-revolutionary Iran; they were watched by both the SAVAK and local Islamic groups, each for different reasons. Their activities were often curtailed by authorities because of clerical opposition.[66] Most of these churches had a missionary purpose, and some were closely identified with a foreign country.

Therefore, not surprisingly, the first major attack in post-revolutionary Iran was directed at the Anglican Episcopal Church. As early as 19 February 1979, the pastor in charge of churches in the Fars Province was murdered in his office in Shiraz. A series of incidents followed; in 1979 alone they included the confiscation of the Christian hospitals in Shiraz and Isfahan; raids on and looting of the house of Bishop Dehqani Tafti and the diocesan offices of the church in Isfahan; illegal confiscation of church property, including a farm for the training of the blind; and an attempt on the life of the bishop and his wife. In his memoirs, Bishop Tafti asserts that the early attacks and confiscation of the hospitals were not centrally organized or the result of a policy aimed at nationalization but were led by local thugs and fanatics. The main culprit was the Islamic Propagation Society (Anjoman-e Tabliqat-e Islami), whose members had been harassing the members of the Anglican Church for years. One of their early demands, for example, was that the hospital should not purchase milk from a Jewish woman who had been the main provider for twenty years. Tafti's detailed account of the events in both Shiraz and Isfahan point to the society's preoccupation with securing the financial holdings of the church establishment through whatever means possible.[67]

In 1980, Tafti's son was murdered, and sporadic attacks on the church and arrests of its activists continued. Eventually, in February 1981, the Anglican Church was formally declared dysfunctional in Iran and all foreign missionaries (clergy, church workers, laymen, etc.) were expelled. The Italian, French, and other national missionary schools were taken over by the government. Yet, in the tradition of regular departures from policy, reportedly, St. Luke's Church in Isfahan continued to operate and never really closed down. Consecration of a new bishop took place in June 1986 and four bishops were given visas to enter Iran for the occasion. By the mid-1980s, the attitude of the authorities toward the Anglican Church seemed to be softening.[68]

In addition to the Anglican Church, there were churches belonging to different Protestant denominations as well as the Pentecostal Church and the Catholic Church. The Protestant churches suffered more severe treatment than the Catholic Church partially due to their tendency to proselytize, and also because many of their adherents were Persians. A long list of violations of the rights of these churches was prepared and submitted to Islamic authorities in the mid-1980s. These included the arrest of Mehdi Dibaj (a Muslim who had converted to Christianity in his youth and who was involved with the Presbyterian, Anglican, and Assembly of God Churches). In addition, the regime had issued a divorce to his wife accusing Dibaj of adultery. Other grievances included closing church bookstores in four cities; closing churches in Sari and Mashhad; limiting the activities of the Ahvaz church to Sundays only; arresting the caretaker of the Ahvaz church, incarcerating him for twenty-seven days on weapons charges, and then releasing him on condition that he serve as an informant. Also included in the list of violations were the arrest and the contingent release of the caretaker of a church in Mazendaran on similar charges; threats against and beating of church members for the purpose of obtaining information; threats directed at and interrogation of the president of the Council of Protestant Churches and general superintendent of the Assembly of God Churches, Bishop Haik Hovsepian-Mehr; refusal to grant permission for the formation of groups and societies; rude and vituperative behavior toward the leadership of the church in Ershad; threats to close down churches that admitted Muslims into their ceremonies; tight control on telephone calls and monitoring of letters and correspondence of priests; accusations of spying, fueled by contacts with churches outside Iran; disallowing the establishment of new churches; and trials of those who had been Muslims on charges of national or individual apostasy. Similar orders were issued by the police authorities in the province of Isfahan in the mid-1980s.[69]

Mehdi Dibaj, arrested in 1983, had been held in prison without trial for ten years. In 1994 he was brought to trial on charges of apostasy and insulting Islam, and condemned to death. Bishop Haik Hovsepian-Mehr began a tireless campaign to bring his case to international attention, which eventually succeeded. Protests from the United Nations, the Vatican, and Western countries brought about an immediate release of

Dibaj. The consequences were tragic: several days after his release Bishop Haik disappeared and his body was discovered with multiple stab wounds, and within months Mehdi Dibaj and Bishop Haik's successor, Reverend Tateos Mikaelian, disappeared and were discovered murdered. Mehdi Dibaj had converted to Christianity, but Bishop Haik Hovsepian-Mehr and Reverend Tateos Mikaelian had been Armenians of the Protestant faith. Dibaj was well known for his vigorous evangelical activities and, despite the sensitivity and clear objection of the Islamists, he could not bring himself to stop. In his written defense dated December 1993, his religious zeal was obvious: "They object to my evangelizing. But if one finds a blind person who is about to fall in a well and keeps silent then one has sinned. It is our religious duty, as long as the door of God's mercy is open, to convince evil doers to turn from their sinful ways and find refuge in Him in order to be saved."[70]

Reverend Mikaelian was senior pastor of the St. John Armenian Evangelical Church in Tehran and had succeeded Bishop Haik as the president of the Council of Evangelical Ministers. He was widely respected and liked by Muslims and non-Muslims alike for his courage in protesting the violations of human rights and for favoring open dialogue with Islamic authorities. The government reacted to the killing first by silence, "punctuated by suggestions that the Protestant leaders had political agendas."[71] Then they claimed that the Mojahedin Organization was responsible for the killings of Dibaj and Mikaelian, a charge the Mojahedin denied. Departing from the customary practice of secrecy, the authorities held a public trial for the accused killers of Reverend Mikaelian, assigned them lawyers, televised the proceedings, and invited Western observers to the trial. The sentences were also unusually lenient and serious inconsistencies in court and police reports were overlooked.[72]

The picture is grimmer for the 1990s compared to the 1980s. According to the Iranian Christian International Ministry, which is often very critical of the regime, twelve churches were active in different Iranian cities. Three churches closed down in 1988 and a few were closed during the 1990s, including the Bible Society in February 1990 and the Garden of Evangelism, a camp and training center, in July 1989.[73] It is significant, however, that the Bible Society, a training center, and many more churches were allowed to operate throughout the 1980s, demonstrating the convincing leadership of these operations as well as the flexibility of the system. Throughout the 1990s, there have been reports of detention, torture, and killing of pastors throughout Iran. By 1996 only two Protestant churches, one in Tehran and one in Rasht, were allowed to conduct their services in Persian; others preached in Armenian or Assyrian.[74]

6. Tateos Mikaelian, senior pastor of St. John's Armenian Evangelical Church in Tehran and president of the Council of Evangelical Ministers, assassinated in 1994.

Closings and the proliferation of persecutions in the post-Khomeini era may have been caused by an increase in the number of Muslims interested in a spiritual alternative to the distorted Islam of the clerical-led regime. The widespread and systematic nature of persecutions point to the Islamic state as the main culprit. Under the watchful eye of the world, the best way to deal with the situation was to assassinate visible leading pastors through "unofficial" clandestine operations. The persecutions may also have been an effort to placate the more radical elements in a political arena filled with intrigue and deal-making. In either case, the fulfillment of the regime's ideological design had accelerated in the mid- to late 1990s.

Particularities as the end product

As with the recognized religious minorities, there are gray areas in the comparative analysis of the most severely treated non-Muslim minorities. Perceptions of who they are or what they represent as a group have been fundamental in the transition from perception and motivation to action. No repression takes place in a vacuum. Motivated by power, monetary gains, or ideological purity, the state authorities have been trenchant persecutors. Even in the mid- to late 1990s state authorities did not hesitate to proclaim their ideological view that neither the Christian churches nor Bahaism were religious organizations. Christian churches were "political organizations,"[75] and Bahaism was "an organized espionage ring."[76]

State–minority relations involving the Jews, Bahais, and Christians show two patterns: the sporadic nature and the localism of these actions. Sporadic attacks were particularly evident during the first few years of the Revolution, a period when Khomeini's supporters were attempting to consolidate their power base. Yet, their conduct should not be taken lightly as far as the relationship between perception, motivation, and action are concerned, as well as the overall policy sphere. Regime officials can point to sporadic mob or Pasdaran attacks as being beyond their control and hence can scapegoat them to disclaim policy responsibility. More importantly, though, the "occasional attacks can be seen as a ritual to restore the proper deference."[77] The overall intent is to make the targets fearful, and to force them into obedience and servitude.

Localism has also characterized incidents against minorities since 1979, in that certain parts of the country have witnessed more "sporadic" attacks than others. The local clerics and Revolutionary Guards have issued a disproportionately large number of proclamations and overseen a disproportionately large number of executions. There is, for example, the treatment these minorities received in Shiraz. The name of the city appears quite regularly in reports on violations of the rights of non-Muslim minorities; Shiraz has had a long history of reactionary and intolerant behavior toward non-Muslims.

During the early years of the Revolution, the religious minorities were affected by the changing power of clerical leadership in different towns and cities. A combination of local clerical rivalry as well as the upward mobility of mid-level clerics to more influential positions (e.g., local revolutionary courts) undermined the influence of traditionally powerful higher-ranking local clergymen. This might have been the reason, for example, why a high-ranking ayatollah in Isfahan, despite his belief that St. Luke's Church was not an espionage center, could not prevent the attacks against the church.[78] It is significant that, while St. Luke's Church continued to operate in Isfahan, the Anglican church in Shiraz was closed down.

The regime's revolutionary ideology has had all the necessary elements for nurturing prejudicial tendencies: anti-Israeli and anti-Zionist feelings, anti-imperialism, anti-Westernism, and xenophobia. Consequently, espionage, conspiracy, sabotage, serving as agents of some perceived enemy became convenient accusations to be used against anyone for any reason. The revolutionaries reaffirmed that "the ideal devil is omnipotent and omnipresent" and "a foreigner." "To qualify as a devil," wrote Eric Hoffer, "a domestic enemy must be given a foreign ancestry."[79] Scapegoating as a feature of the Shii worldview[80] became the cornerstone of the ideological theocratic state.

Thugs and fanatics have acted in different capacities since the Revolution. In some instances they have been motivated by personal resentment, anger, or ambition; at other times they have acted as representatives of local leaders; and at still other times they have proceeded on the basis of the policy impulses of the new state. The multidimensional character of the motivations for their activities should not be dismissed.

The Jewish case is significant because Jews were seen as a separate group of people protected by Islam, whereas the existence of the state of Israel and its good relations with the previous regime conveniently linked them to the anti-foreign fixation of the revolutionaries. Their status as "People of the Book" saved them, but the links between them and Israel made their treatment, compared to other recognized minorities, much worse. In fact, the post-1979 shadowy dealings of the Islamic Republic with Israel have been associated on more than one occasion to the fate of the Iranian Jews. The flow of arms and ammunition into Iran seemed to correlate with a steady outflow of Jews.[81]

Separation and distinction have their pitfalls when the group in question is linked to another state entity. Armenians in Iran may face a similar problem, now that an independent Armenian state has come into existence.[82] Although as a community they have enjoyed a positive image and have been more trusted than other religious minorities, their loyalty, too, could be questioned when political situations change in inter-state relations. It is easy to question, accuse, and scapegoat a non-Muslim religious minority. When Mohammad Reza Shah died in exile, in July 1980, banners and graffiti appeared in the streets of Tehran proclaiming: "Armenians, your king is gone . . ." In a country of some 35 million Shii Muslims at the time, Mohammad Reza Shah had become king of the Armenians overnight. This is not to be dismissed lightly: an intensely hated deposed monarch was directly associated with a Christian minority. Scapegoating intensifies when the minority is tied to another country directly. All diasporic communities are vulnerable to exploitation by state entities. When loyalty is questioned, distinctiveness becomes a liability.

The Bahai and Iranian Christian convert cases have one dimension in common with the Jewish case, namely their transnational character; the Bahais were linked to ex-colonialists and Israel, and the nonethnic Christians were the byproduct of foreign missionaries. But, on another dimension, the former two and the latter have been on opposite sides. Instead of being perceived as separate, the Bahais and Christians have been viewed as assimilationist. Ultimately they were Iranians who abandoned the dominant Shii Islam in favor of another religious route. Both were apostates proselytizing their beliefs, clashing directly with the Shii religious forces in Iran. This has been the most powerful motivation, and it explains why their problems remain far from being resolved.

Limitations and the legal domain

The new state has shown an intense preoccupation with conversion of Muslims to other faiths and proselytizing among the Muslims. On any major piece of legislation (some discussed in the previous chapters) involving religious minorities, blunt comments on the floor of the Majlis by deputies as well as various cabinet ministers point to an unceasing fixation on the possibility of Muslim conversion. Many of the limits imposed on recognized religious minorities, such as erecting a wall separating the church from the school yard or forbidding the import or printing of religious books, are acts directed at preventing any possible outlet to the Muslims.

Writings and commentaries by religious personalities on a continuous basis throughout the 1980s point to a preoccupation with religious conversion, stemming from the core belief of the superiority of Muslims to others. Ayatollah Nuri, in his apparent attempt to explain the importance of fairness in Islamic justice, recounted a story about Imam Ali, the most significant religious figure for Shii Muslims. Reportedly, Imam Ali had lost his armor and a Christian citizen had it in his possession. Ali brought the case to the judge, and the Christian claimed the armor belonged to him (this element of the story, of course, implies that the Christian was lying). The judge asked if there were any witnesses; Ali said no and the judge ruled in favor of the Christian. The Christian, overwhelmed with the justice of Islamic law, claimed that such law could only come from a "Divine origin," and converted to Islam, giving the armor back to Imam Ali.[83]

In 1982, for example, Ayatollah Mohammadi Gilani, the judge of the Central Islamic Revolutionary Courts, in his writings and interviews, pointed out that the spilling of the blood of a person who has turned away from Islam "is permissible for anyone who hears of it." In addition to specifying that the criminal should lose his wife and property, Gilani added that in such cases repentance was not acceptable.[84] Gilani was violating an unambiguous textual stipulation in Islam.[85] Perhaps because of that, in practice, however, repentance sometimes could save Bahais and Christian converts.

Various publications warned Muslims to avoid close contact with adherents of other religions for fear of being seduced by them to convert. In 1986, a youth magazine's religious advisor, while answering questions, wrote: "For common people it is unlawful to go to church because going to church and having fellowship with Christians gradually puts the people under their influence."[86]

Not every commentary, interview, and statement made by clerics can be used as evidence of clear-cut policy commitments by the regime because, in the Islamic Republic of Iran, making irresponsible comments has become the norm. Yet, along with evidence presented in this chapter and the previous one, the findings reported above demonstrate the underlying obsession with conversion.

There is evidence that the system has looked on with pleasure and provided rewards to encourage conversion from other religions to Islam. The text on religion for non-Muslims forced on RRM children (discussed pp. 82–83) has many passages evangelizing Islam and is one of the earliest attempts by the clerical regime. Others were less systematic. Customarily, announcements would appear in newspapers announcing such conversions, including Zoroastrians, Armenians, and Assyrians. The following is one example:

In the Name of the Almighty, I, Khodadad Zartoshti Bakhtiari, the son of Rostam, the holder of identification card No. 405 issued in Kermanshah, who was born into a Zoroastrian family, after the victory of the Islamic Revolution of Iran, discovered that Islam is God's true Religion. And because of the guidance and enlightenment by Hazrat Ayatollah Allameh Noori, I, full of honour and glory, embraced Islam as the God's last and most complete religion and chose the name of Khodadad Mohammadi Bakhtiary.[87]

Some cases of conversion were complicated and the motivation was anything but spiritual. In one widely publicized case, for instance, two brothers were in conflict over their inheritance from their father. One converted to Islam and married a Muslim woman, thereby winning for himself the entire inheritance. After a long court battle, realizing that the Muslim brother would inherit everything, the other brother also converted, ending up with his half of the inheritance.[88]

The law of inheritance states that, if there is a Muslim in the family, he inherits the entire estate. This has the effect of indirectly encouraging conversion to Islam out of greed, if nothing else. The reverse is also true; non-Muslim relatives may not inherit from a Muslim.[89] No distinction is made between recognized and nonrecognized religious minorities. Ayatollah Khomeini in his pre-revolutionary work had written that a Muslim could inherit from a non-Muslim, but a non-Muslim, even if he was the son or the father of the dead Muslim, could not inherit from him.[90] Ayatollah Montazeri made the same point in his work.[91] Not only did this become the law of the land, but it was also a repeat of the "Law of Apostasy" which was in effect under the Safavid Dynasty four centuries ago.[92]

Gender bias is evident even in matters of conversion. When an ethnic Christian female marries an Iranian Muslim, for example, one could expect announcements stating how happy she is to have become a Muslim. But, there are rarely any announcements when Christian ethnic males marry Muslim women despite converting. Ethnic Christians perceived that the Islamic authorities did not like conversions by Christian males for the purpose of marrying Muslim women but tolerated it begrudgingly. The Civil Code of the Islamic Republic of Iran states that a Muslim man can marry a non-Muslim woman, but a Muslim woman cannot marry a non-Muslim man. It does not make any exception for the People of the Book.[93]

In discussing Islamic criminal laws, one writer explained that, in certain circumstances, it is licit to shed the blood of a wrongdoer. One such circumstance is that of a non-Muslim who is "officially at war with the Islamic state and the Muslims." Elsewhere, he added that the main issue is religious equality, and non-Muslims are simply not equal to Muslims. Therefore, if a non-Muslim kills a Muslim, he will be killed, but if a Muslim kills a non-Muslim he will not be killed but simply pay the non-Muslim's blood money.[94]

The writer was not presenting these arguments in a vacuum; the adherents of his views presented an Islamic penal code, the Layeheye Qesas

(Bill of Retribution), to the Majlis in 1981, and despite protests by the RRMs and various Iranian groups, the bill was approved in 1982.[95] Qesas means that punishment for murder and bodily harm should equal the crime committed. Therefore, crime becomes a violation of personal rights requiring retaliation of the same kind. (Certain kinds of sexual contact are also subject to qesas.) Its passage resulted in a spate of publications that attempted to justify the condition of the RRMs under Islam.[96]

Punishment depends on the type of crime committed and qesas is one of four types. Others include "hodud," the quantity/amount and the quality of which is determined in shariah (religious law); "diyat," financial compensation for the crime based on shariah; and "tazirat," those punishments not clearly stated in shariah which can be assessed by an Islamic judge (such as the duration of imprisonment or the number of lashes administered for a certain crime). Punishment in these cases cannot exceed whatever appears in "hodud."[97] All four types of punishments are solidly rooted in and based on religious law.

The Iranian penal code treats Muslims and non-Muslims differently. Laws reiterate the inequality between the two segments of the population. For instance, if a non-Muslim male engages in a sexual relationship with a Muslim woman, his penalty is death; for a Muslim man it is one hundred lashes.[98] This is directly derived from fiqh (Islamic jurisprudence), extensively discussed and written about by high-ranking Shii clerics. Ayatollah Montazeri reiterated the above provision in his writings. (The penalty for a Muslim man was only fifty lashes if he had intercourse with an animal.)[99] There is a hierarchical ranking in the punishment: the non-Muslim male is killed; the Muslim male receives one hundred lashes but only fifty lashes if the sexual partner is an animal instead of a Muslim woman. In a related instance, if a Muslim falsely accuses another Muslim of fornication, his penalty is eighty lashes, but, if he falsely accuses a non-Muslim of fornication, the Muslim accuser will receive anywhere from one to seventy-four lashes.[100]

Differentiation between Muslim and non-Muslim extends to punishment in homosexual contact as well. The law distinguishes between active (fael) and passive (maful) partners. In the case of sexual intercourse, if both are Muslim, their penalty is death. If intercourse has not taken place, both shall receive one hundred lashes. But, if the active partner is a non-Muslim and the passive partner is a Muslim, the non-Muslim is subject to death (instead of lashes).[101] Several points are significant in this distinction: (1) the hierarchical placing of the value of life between a Muslim and a non-Muslim, (2) the harsher treatment of the non-Muslim, and (3) the designation of active or passive partner, which has two implications – the non-Muslim can easily be identified as active either by the Muslim partner or the Islamic judge and put to death, and the connotation that even in the realm of homosexual intercourse the non-Muslim will not be allowed to act as the active (which implied aggressive) partner in contact with the Muslim. Religious superiority and inferiority are thus reflected in the most intimate private relations of human beings.

In another place, the law is clear that, when a Muslim is killed, the killer will be subject to qesas (which includes a non-Muslim killer), and if a non-Muslim kills another non-Muslim the penalty is death. Yet, the law is silent on the killing of a non-Muslim by a Muslim. Ayatollah Khomeini, however, had a specific penalty in such cases. If the Muslim was a habitual killer of non-Muslims, then he had to be killed. If he was not a habitual killer, then he had to pay financial compensation (blood money) to the non-Muslim's family.[102] In other words, a Muslim killer (as long as he was not a serial killer of non-Muslims) could not be put to death for killing a non-Muslim, but a non-Muslim would be put to death for killing a Muslim. In addition, the amount of the diyah (financial compensation) to be paid to the murdered non-Muslim's family does not appear in the law.[103] This raises two questions: (1) why does the blood price not appear in any of the articles of the penal code? And, (2) how is the blood price of the non-Muslim victim determined?

The Islamic Republic's civil and criminal laws are based on fiqh as defined, explained, and interpreted by Shii religious leaders. Certain segments were deemed embarrassing to be openly displayed in the written law. Also, variations in circumstances may have required a specific ruling. On any ambiguous issue, the courts refer to the books in Islamic jurisprudence. In fiqh an RRM (and therefore non-Muslim) male is worth half of that of a Muslim male and an RRM (non-Muslim) female is worth half of the male of her religion. Therefore, the value of the life of a woman belonging to the Christian, Jewish, or Zoroastrian faith is half of that of a male from the same faith. Her blood price is determined, accordingly; she is worth one-fourth of a Muslim male. This religiously determined equation is unchangeable; in other words, the diyah can never increase since it is always measured against the value of a Muslim man.

In practice this leads to absurdity. When a car or anything with some monetary value is damaged, experts are brought in to set a value on the damaged good. The price may end up being much higher than the value of a non-Muslim woman determined by fiqh. In one case a non-Muslim woman was killed in a car accident; the driver was a Muslim. He was not killed but was required to pay blood money (worth one-fourth of a Muslim man) to the family of the deceased. Shortly after the incident, in a different city, several cows were hit by a Muslim driver. The price of the cows was determined by specialists, the end result of which was that the driver paid more money for the cows he killed than the first driver paid for killing a non-Muslim woman.[104]

Under the penal code the lives of Iranian Christian converts and the Bahais have no value whatsoever. Many cases have been reported. In a case similar to the above a Bahai was killed in a car accident; although the driver was found guilty, the relatives of the victim were not entitled to financial compensation. The driver paid some financial retribution to the government.[105] In case after case involving the Bahais, the government has taken over their financial holdings.[106]

Another crucial point is that the penal code (based on Islamic law) takes precedence over the penal laws of the recognized non-Muslim minorities. If, for example, males and females are treated equally in Christian, Jewish, or Zoroastrian traditions and penal codes, they still abide by the rules of the Iranian penal code which assigns to their females half of the value of their males. They are subjects of Dar al-Islam, and Islamic laws take precedence over their own.

Up to the end of 1998, there had been no changes in the penal code or other discriminatory laws against non-Muslims. To circumvent the rigidity of legal distinctions, proponents of change argue that Islamic civil and criminal laws contradict the Iranian constitution and international human rights covenants. They recommend either bringing national laws closer to international laws, or withdrawing altogether from the United Nations.[107] There is also a movement to try to seek a softer and reformist approach to the interpretation of Islamic law. Yet as long as Islam is viewed by the Islamic jurists as the last revealed religion and the final salvation for adherents of other religions (including People of the Book), the self-perceived superiority of the Muslim faith makes it only logical to devise unequal laws in an Islamic state. In other words, the legal inequality of the non-Muslim is directly tied to the interpretation of Islam. Is Islam one of the major religions of the world? Or is Islam the final calling of God to all humanity?

Making a change in the practice of the law wherever convenient is deemed a more feasible option for some. The following quote shows how flexibility in the policy sphere can be repeated in the practice of law as well:

Under Islamic law one of the qualifications of a witness in a law suit or wherever the evidence of a witness is required by law is his belief in Islam. This rule is reflected in the procedural laws and [it] could, therefore, be concluded that the evidence of a non-Muslim should not be accepted. Although this is the logical conclusion of the word of the law, this is not the case in practice, as the evidence of non-Muslims is frequently accepted in courts and in connection with most law suits or legal documents.[108]

According to this view one should seek solace when laws remain in the books but are not fully implemented. The proponents of this view still feel that some laws must change; they base their selection on the rules of probability. It is less likely for a non-Muslim man to have sex with a Muslim woman than it is for a non-Muslim to die and have his kin lose his inheritance to a Muslim in the family. Therefore, the inheritance rules affect the minority communities more often and are in more dire need of change.[109] By any standard this remains a conservative argument, perhaps even somewhat self-serving. "Is money that much more important than life itself that inheritance should be addressed first?," asked another person familiar with the issue. "As long as the life of a Muslim and a non-Muslim are not treated as equally worthy, no other shortcut will do. Addressing inheritance (money and property value) before raising the preciousness of the breath of life itself is shortchanging the basic value of humanity."

The above quote captures the essence of the problem. Recognized religious minorities may point to the contradictions between civil and criminal laws and the Islamic constitution to argue for improvement and balance. Reformists may pick and choose which laws to make inoperable first or last. The subordinated minorities can cautiously maneuver when allowed, but the excluded Bahais and Iranian Christian converts have no recourse. How far can the advocates of change take the rights of all the citizens of the country?

5   Prevalent responses of recognized religious minorities

Various disciplines, in different time periods, have addressed the issue of minority response. At whom or what the response is directed has varied as widely as the techniques and the content of the responses. Minority responses have been discussed in relation to a dominant group, prejudice and discrimination, state power and coercion, and restrictive legal structures. The responses have often been categorized by scholars using similar specifications such as mobilization on ethnic or class terms, revolt or rebellion, aggression, avoidance, withdrawal, adjustment, conformity, submission, assimilation, and integration.

A number of responses by religious minorities have been discussed throughout the book. This section focuses solely on the form, style, and meaning of the RRMs' behavior in responding to and dealing with a wide range of commentaries, acts, decrees, and national policies of a theocratic state. The first part focuses on similar responses of all the groups. The second section analyzes the unique features of the response of each recognized religious minority in order to demonstrate that in changing circumstances marginal groups continue to act in a learned cultural tradition.

Similar responses

Official acknowledgment of the rights of recognized religious minorities in the Islamic constitution has provided a protective shield within the confines of state ideology. Conformity and acceptance have been the overall responses from the recognized groups. Five factors are believed to be responsible for conformity: perception of benefits, the process of cooptation, development of a fatalistic attitude, traditional segregation of communities, and fear of coercion.[1] It is clear, based on the previous chapters, that the last three factors, namely fatalism, segregation, and fear of coercion were part of the RRM response to the Islamic Republican regime. The first, perception of benefits, has motivated the minorities to secure their survival and even prosperity. Advantages such as earning a living and engaging in profitable business ventures make submission less of a negative and more of a practical response.

Yet the above sociological typology, while coming close to describing the general minority responses, is enriched by two intertwined elements in the Iranian case: (1) the historical natural resiliency of the religious minorities, and (2) their vocal defiance of overarching intrusions, the latter prompted by their legal protected status in Islam. Just as the state has enjoyed flexibility in its policies toward the minorities, their responses have been an imaginative and interesting mix of adaptability and riposte.

Unified acts of conformity

Halim Barakat once wrote: "Victims often learn the language of their oppressors and conduct their discourse within its strictly defined parameters."[2] While the word "victim" might be inappropriate and too strong for the recognized religious minorities, the rest of the statement accurately reflects their situation in Iran.

Reminiscent of the spirit of the old millet system, expressions of loyalty to and respect for Islamic authorities became a dominant feature of the post-revolutionary RRM–state relationship. Throughout the 1980s frequent meetings were arranged, some very public, between the authorities and the minority community leaders. Single group meetings were used to convey respect and adherence to the new regime and also to raise the concerns of the community. This pattern went into effect naturally and immediately. In May 1979, for example, less than a week after the execution of Habib Elghanian, the Iranian Jews met with Ayatollah Khomeini in Qom, congratulating him and expressing solidarity with the Revolution. They also reiterated that freedom and respect were bestowed upon Jews in Islam, asking him to emphasize this point to reduce discord. Ayatollah Khomeini reportedly had emphasized Islam's respect for the minorities and, directly addressing the Jews, had said: "We distinguish between the Jewish community and the Zionists. Zionism has nothing to do with religion. The Zionists do not follow religion, since their anti-people method is contrary to the revolutionary course laid down by Moses – peace be upon him."[3] Shortly after the meeting a decree was made public stating that there would be no more executions except in cases of murder.[4] While in practice the decree was not followed, at the time it was interpreted as an assurance to the Iranian Jews.

Throughout the 1980s meetings between representatives of the RRMs and the Islamic authorities were commonplace. At times it was necessary for the religious leadership of the minorities (as opposed to the Majlis deputies) to have private or public meetings with Ayatollah Khomeini, other religious leaders, or government authorities. For instance, in the midst of language and religious instruction problems, in 1983, the Armenian Archbishop Artak Manukian met with Prime Minister Mir-Hossein Musavi. As reported in the Iranian press, the archbishop expressed appreciation to Islamic authorities stating that the community had no religious, cultural, or social problems. In return, the prime minister conveyed the sincerity of the Iranian people toward the Armenians.[5]

Similarly, religious occasions were used to convey moralistic and, at times, politicized commentaries on the state of the nation, the war with Iraq, and the role of the United States. For example, Jesus Christ's message of peace and love and unity of all living creatures was reported as a struggle against the enemies, United States, and Zionism.[6] The distortion is so profound that love is literally lost in hate. But this politicization of the minorities' religious discourse, their prophets, and moral codes of conduct were expected and more easily understood by the regime. "Being against" was the fundamental motto of the state ideology and so profoundly ingrained that any positivistic message was at risk of casting doubts on group allegiance.

The language of the minority press was very similar to that of its Muslim counterparts in seeing enemies and intruders everywhere. As a Zoroastrian magazine put it: "evil powers of the world with all their might are determined to destroy our revolutionary republic," and "intrigues and satanic conspiracies" are present everywhere.[7] The same magazine blamed economic problems during the monarchy and in the period of the Islamic Republic on the United States, "anti-revolutionaries and imperialists," "landowning and capitalist" classes, and the "imposed war."[8] Again, like the national press, the penetration of leftist terminology (particularly with its Tudeh twist) was notable.

As stated earlier, the language of the RRM deputies was also in congruence with that of the rest of the Majlis. Comments were made individually or collectively, for instance, on the occasion of the 1982 Israeli invasion of Lebanon. The Armenian representative from the south made a speech on behalf of all the RRMs condemning the invasion in strongest terms. At the conclusion of his talk, the Muslim deputies chanted "Well done. Well done."[9]

Group meetings were arranged and coordinated by the Islamic authorities. The meeting with Ayatollah Khomeini in 1982, for example, drew more than 800 delegates representing RRMs from all over the country. The gathering was so extensive that it included not only the usual Majlis deputies and religious leadership but also minority organizations and councils and representatives from all the towns and cities with an RRM population. Bait Ushana, the Assyrian and Chaldean deputy in the

Majlis, made a statement on behalf of all those present. The eloquent speech is an example of conformity in all aspects of the existence of minorities; it is reminiscent of the speeches delivered on similar occasions to Mohammad Reza Shah:

We, the officially recognized religious minorities, have sincerely tried and will honestly and selflessly continue to walk on the path of Your wise leadership toward the realization of the goals of the Revolution and the Islamic Republic of Iran side by side and in step with our Moslem brothers. We are happy that the results of our efforts and hardships have been noticed by the Honorable Imam and the leaders of the country and that the Imam has turned his attention to us as a brother.

The officially recognized minorities have been living on this holy land for thousands of years; living together with Moslem brothers for 1,400 years has familiarized them with all the correct revolutionary and human laws of Islam. Consequently, the minorities have great confidence in the decisive leadership of the struggling spiritual authorities of Islam to realize their popular anticolonialist and anti-imperialist goals and to protect the rights of the oppressed, poor and deprived masses of the beloved country and the world as well.

After being subjected to 2,500 years of royal deprivation and tasting the bitter yoke of the oppressors and despotism, we realize the true value of the freedom, independence and justice bestowed upon us by the Islamic Republic.

Only the wounded truly realize the goodness of the medicine. Therefore, we consider it our religious and national duty to make any effort, bar none, toward the complete independence of Iran, the elimination of any form of dependence on others and the further development and better defense of the Islamic Republic. To that end, no amount of sacrifice and selflessness can be too great. The friends of the Islamic Republic of Iran and its people are our friends, and their enemies are our enemies.[10]

Despite the compliant content and spirit of the message, the protection of the rights and intercommunity freedom was stressed emphatically. The RRMs hoped that they would "be accorded all kinds of cultural, educational, social, financial and political facilities by the officials." Since there were clear guarantees in the Islamic constitution, "the minorities [did] not have any significant problem in their everyday life, and, if certain small difficulties [arose] as a result of incorrect actions by certain uninformed individuals, they [could] easily be [anticipated] and prevented."[11]

The exchange of obedience and service for communal rights and protection in these messages is direct, clearly understood by all sides, and in the Iranian context very normal. It is a process of humbling one's group with a thorough acceptance of marginality and in return receiving guarantees of life, communal liberty, and security. The text of Bait Ushana's speech could have been written hundreds of years ago without significant revisions. People of the Book were humble subjects, well aware of their marginal status and in need of the protection of the Islamic state. But they also knew that, despite the clarity of their rights under Islam, they were always at the mercy of the benevolent rulers.

The RRMs acted in unison on special occasions. Anniversaries of the Revolution provided for such opportunities. On the fourth anniversary of the Revolution in 1983, a formal committee was put together by the minority deputies in the Majlis for the purpose of overseeing an elaborate celebration. This seems to have been in response to the third anniversary celebrations, which had amounted to festivities for two days in Roodaki Auditorium, when crowds of people had reportedly turned up and there was not enough room for them all. This time the celebrations were extended for a week and the program comprised three parts: celebrations, advertising, and sports. The Assyrian and Armenian teams played volley-ball, a youth chorus of Zoroastrians, Jews, and Armenians sang, and formal lectures were delivered by the Zoroastrian priest, Rostam Shahzadi, on behalf of the religious leadership of the RRMs, and the Jewish deputy to the Majlis, Khosrow Naqi, on behalf of the RRM depu-ties. Posters and notices were displayed and congratulatory cards were printed and mailed to religious minorities and all government agencies and organs as part of the advertising portion of the program.[12]

In February 1989, to mark the occasion of the tenth anniversary of the Revolution, a two-day Congress on Minorities was convened in Tehran. The participants included academics, minority representatives, and government officials. All the lecturers spoke with one voice about the rights and special privileges accorded the RRMs in the Islamic Republic. At the end of the Congress, an eleven-point resolution was issued con-demning Zionism and declaring that Zionists had "trampled upon all monotheistic and human values and [had] violated the sanctity of the holy places of Muslims, Jews, and Christians." Religious minorities, the resolution declared, were "an inseparable part of the great nation of Iran," having the same interests as their Muslim countrymen. The resolution expressed common "hatred of and repulsion for" the way in which minor-ity rights in the Islamic Republic were questioned by imperialists and Zionists. Ayatollah Khomeini was praised and his words quoted. The res-olution was signed by the religious leadership of the recognized religious communities. The signatories were Archbishop Artak Manukian, Archbishop Yohannan Issayi, Rabbi Uriel Davoudi, and Priest Rostam Shahzadi.[13]

Interviews were conducted and printed widely in the Iranian press. In general, the commentaries were congruent with the contents of the reso-lution, but some views were particularly revealing. Rabbi Davoudi was quoted as saying: "Iranian Jews are solely Jews and only Iranians, and have no solidarity [hambastegi] with foreigners." Both Archbishop

7, 8. Religious leadership of recognized religious minorities, their Majlis deputies, and community members in celebrations marking the establishment of the Islamic Republic, Roodaki Auditorium, Tehran, 1981 and 1982 (Rahmat Rahimian).

Manukian and Issayi reflected on the advantages of the post-revolutionary era for their Christian communities. They saw less emphasis on materialism and more interest in spirituality and religious activities. They claimed that Assyrian youth had more interest in their community and religion, and that the Armenians were awakened to their overall religious precepts.[14]

These expressed views should be placed into two contexts. The first context is clearly and obviously one of conformity and adaptability in the extreme. The extent of conformity is evident especially if the RRM clerical comments are compared to the comments made by Ayatollah Montazeri to mark the tenth anniversary of the Revolution around the same time period. Reflecting on the nature of Iranian government, he saw it characterized by "unprofessionalism, extremism, selfishness, monopolism, group inclinations, injustices, ignoring the people and the genuine values of the Revolution, and the lack of real power in the hands of the people."[15] No member of the RRM would dare to speak in such terms about the consequences of the Revolution, at least not in public. This is one of the many dimensions of marginality in Iran; it is a behavior that separates the marginal from the dominant group. The latter, even in the most oppressive circumstances, can be critical of the system, though often not without some cost. The dominant Shii Muslim group feels more righteous in expressing pro or con views; they might be marginal in terms of their hold on political power but not in terms of their own perceived rights to judge their own harshly. Religious minorities shy away from overt critical expressions against the authorities.

The second context of the expressed views of the RRMs' religious leadership has an additional, more authentic dimension: that of the faithful wanting to keep their flock together. The mixture might be puzzling to those with a secularist view of the world; yet there are unique ideas and beliefs shared by the clerical segments of religious minorities. Therefore, both dynamics are simultaneously at work here: a cultural and traditional adjustment to regime views, and the preferences of the religious segments of the minority communities to see their own people unified in their faith. Unlike the situation under the previous regime, the Islamic theocracy had bestowed a special, privileged status upon its clerical counterparts among the recognized religious communities; their attention was focused and their legitimacy unquestioned. Regardless of differences in doctrinal beliefs, the clerical class of the religious minorities spoke a separate language and had its own rhythm and preferences; theirs was the discourse of believers deeply committed to the maintenance of the moral fabric of their communities. Therefore, in some ways, as men of the cloth, they were genuine in condemning the Western world; in their view, as with many preachers in the West, there had been a major collapse of spirituality and morality in the world. The two contexts were not contradictory but culturally complementary.

Underlying the united response and the "anti-other" sentiment were the debilitating eight years of war with Iraq. The revolutionary paranoia about enemies and conspirators was reenforced by the brutal war that had begun in 1980 and ended in 1988. Many RRM families, as was the case with the Muslims, decided to leave the country for fear of war and particularly of military service of their sons. Some only sent their sons abroad. For those who remained, much of the RRM response should be placed in the context of the impact of the double crisis on their daily lives. All donated money and material supplies to the war effort; the donations came not only from Tehran but all those cities with an RRM population. The provincial contributions were highlighted and instead of Tehran RRMs becoming the central donors, it was common to read about Zoroastrians of Kerman or Assyrians and Armenians of Urmieh making their own bid to help.[16]

All the recognized religious minorities with the exception of the Jews served at the battlefront. The Jews did fundraising and contributed tractors and heavy equipment. Only in 1986 did a directive from the authorities reportedly ask Jewish men to enlist in the army. The recruitment laws, binding on the Iranian population, were not binding on the Jews.[17] However, they did end up serving, but at a later date and in much smaller numbers than the Zoroastrians and Armenians.

After the flow of volunteers was reduced, soldiers were called up based on their date of birth, to serve for two years. Technicians were sent to serve for a fixed period of time at the battlefront. They served either as medical practitioners or experts in repairing machinery or heavy and light vehicles. The RRMs did seize the occasion to reiterate their loyalty and support for the regime and the defense of the territorial integrity of Iran. They spoke of their own martyrs fighting side by side next to their Muslim brethren. The Zoroastrians, Armenians, and Assyrians were sacrificing their youth to defend the Islamic regime, and this message was repeated over and over again, in the national press and television, in interviews, and in minority publications. "Martyrdom," a term so often used by Muslims, especially the Shii, was adopted by the RRMs for their own who were killed in the war. Pictures of minority martyrs were printed and eulogies and poems were written for their passing.[18] Not a moment was wasted in highlighting the sacrifices made for the Islamic government. Among these sacrifices were calls (by the RRM religious leadership) to downplay religious and cultural celebrations, not to be extravagant, and to donate as much as possible.[19]

Religious leaders often gave sermons on the subject, visited the areas affected by the war, and held religious services with Muslim authorities. And, as one Islamic official put it, "There was absolutely no discrimination on the battlefield, especially in the respect shown to martyrs."[20] Differences seemed insignificant in death.

Reactions to discrimination and negative portrayals

Words and acts of conformity should not be interpreted as meekness on the part of the recognized religious minorities. Rarely did a negative commentary on television, an article in magazines or newspapers, or an interviewee's unabashed views go unanswered. Responding was within the domain of their rights as protected People of the Book. Religious recognition and the theocratic nature of the regime had given minorities much room to maneuver. Their behavior, while encompassing many aspects of conformity, was in no way passive or withdrawn. Previous chapters clearly showed the interconnections among arbitrary actions, policy, and the RRM response in several cases. This interactive dynamic remains one of the most fascinating aspects of state–minority relations in the post-1979 period. The minorities' responses did not always change things in their favor, but it demonstrated that they were not mere victims on the receiving end of things.

The reactions took different forms. In major cases involving a routine practice or policy, formal communication was made with the authorities either orally by the leadership of the community or by writing official letters. This was the case, for example, when in a formal letter to Prime Minister Musavi the Council of Tehran Zoroastrians requested an end to job discrimination against the RRMs in government organs and the military. To make their point, they attached to their letter photocopies of employment advertisements appearing in newspapers indicating adherence to Islam as the prime criterion for employment. The letter argued that these actions were infringements upon the rights of the RRMs as stated in Articles 13 and 28 of the constitution.[21]

Reactions to negative comments about minorities in the Iranian press commonly appeared either in letters to the editor or in minority publications. As early as 1980, the newspaper *Kayhan* printed an interview with Fakhroldin Hejazi, a Majlis deputy from Tehran. In his interview the deputy praised himself, highlighting his revolutionary credentials; he boasted of turning down invitations from jewelers but lecturing to shoemakers' apprentices. He also commented that, with the exception of a few high-ranking prophets, he considered "Imam Khomeini to be superior to other prophets, and his accomplishment bigger than his excellency [jenab] Moses' defeat of Pharaoh [surname of Walid bin Mus'ab, the tyrant king of Egypt]." The Society of Iranian Jews wrote a letter to the newspaper protesting some of his comments on the status of the Prophet Moses in history as well as his reference to the Prophet as "excellency." Their letter argued that (1) religious references have been simply "Moshe [Moses]" and people called him a prophet, (2) Hejazi himself was sarcastically referred to as "jenab," and the complaint was made that his misleading comments on the Jews might attract followers and sympathizers, and (3) Ayatollah Khomeini was too humble to be fooled by such "comparisons and poetic exaggerations" and the misconstrued attempt to build a personality cult. Hejazi was given permission to write an article in response to the Jewish group's statement. He vehemently denied personality worship; unlike some religions whose followers consider "their prophet to be the son of God [a snide reference to Christianity]," Islam worshiped God alone. He praised Moses as a great man in history for saving the children of Israel from imperialism and corruption and went on to elaborate on the meaning of the word "excellency." Then he compared the struggles of Moses and Khomeini, trying to explain why one did miracles and the other did not. As he neared the end of his long article, he urged Jews to condemn Zionism and take care that it did not infiltrate their ranks. He warned them to watch for some Bahai spies who had been bred by Zionists to create divisiveness. He again referred to Moses as "excellency" and could not resist making a derogatory remark directed at the Jews: "I am a teacher and perhaps earn less than the apprentices in your antique stores."[22]

Drawing on quotations and commentaries by the high-ranking clerical elite on behalf of RRMs was an effective tactic in responding to negative imaging, biases, and misrepresentations. On the fourth anniversary of the Revolution, the Zoroastrian deputy to the Majlis, Parviz Malekpoor, devoted some 90 percent of his commentary on the meaning of "Imam" Khomeini's message, praising him and his vision. Then in the last paragraph he mentioned that a poem had been printed in the newspaper *Jomhuri-ye Islami* by an "opportunist poet" who ridiculed the Zoroastrians' sacred beliefs. Did the responsible authorities of the paper expect to receive an order from Ayatollah Khomeini instructing them how to respect the beliefs of others? In conclusion, he wished the ayatollah a long life so that no one would fear for the future of the Revolution.[23]

This was a very common practice and an effective one. It was used to critique writings which did not treat minorities favorably, as well as to challenge national and local newspapers for their negative portrayals. In addition to utilizing statements by the Shii religious leadership on the rights of minorities, RRM writers used the war with Iraq to remind everyone that the minorities were not fighting and dying to defend Islam in order to be offended by some at home. As the editor of *Cheesta*, Parviz Shahriari, once wrote in attacking a book written by a Muslim about Zoroastrians: "Do you obey the order of the Imam in this fashion? Have you aimed your pen at the United States or toward those who are fighting side by side with their Muslim brothers against America and its servants?"[24]

Armenians and Assyrians had less difficulty with the media. If articles were written attacking Christianity or the Christian world, neither group felt compelled to challenge certain notions on Christianity. The Christian world was so vast and diverse that anything was possible; both were more concerned about their own national Christianity within the borders of Iran than the outside world. In addition, the treatment of Armenians in the media was generally favorable,[25] and the Assyrians were too few to be addressed separately and frequently. But any reference to the Jews meant the Iranian Jews, and any mention of Zoroastrians directly entangled the Zoroastrian minority. None of the RRMs, however, refrained from the use of quotations and comments of high-ranking clergy or influential clerical elites to demonstrate their rights and legitimate status in Iran. These comments often addressed all the RRMs in general and asked for respect, recognition, and peaceful symbiotic relations.[26] In addition, minority publications were used to transmit messages; the Armenian and the Zoroastrian yearly calendars were ideal examples. They highlighted those articles in the Islamic constitution which directly addressed minority rights and published pictures and names (and at times biographies) of those martyred in the war.

The recognized religious minorities, having lived in a dominantly Muslim society, had learned not only to respond as a group but also how to react individually. These individualized reactions, often on the spur of the moment, were instinctive among the RRMs. Resiliency, amiability, and subterfuge were the norm in practical daily interactions. John Simpson gives the account of a Jewish carpet dealer who was driving home with alcoholic beverages in his car. He was stopped by a Revolutionary Guard who asked to see the drinks. The man responded that he was celebrating Ayatollah Khomeini's victory and was released.[27]

In addition, some from amongst the RRMs came to truly believe that the theocratic system was better for them. What some might call self-delusion or deception was often based on their personal/individualized experiences and familiarity with Iran. It was in this same spirit that one interviewee for this book, an elderly Armenian woman who had known the author since her teenage years in Iran, strongly defended the regime and was incessant in her support and allegiance. When asked what she saw to be so admirable, the woman responded that she saw it in her daily dealings with Muslim Iranians. During the war, Muslim neighbors would inform her if any fresh food items had shown up in the market. She enjoyed the company of Muslims in various recreational classes she shared with them, and she truly believed that the predominance of a religious discourse had made them more authentic. Similar views were expressed by Jewish businessmen, some of whom had returned from the West.

The elements of personalism and individualism were conversely utilized in dealing with specific problems arising from the violation of state laws in the country. When individual members of the RRMs committed acts unacceptable to the Islamic theocracy such as adultery with a Muslim or drinking in public, the community leaders simply argued that the individual person was at fault, not the community. The culprit was an unfortunate isolated case whose actions should not reflect on others. Communities were preciously guarded and preserved.

Discrimination and institutionalized segmentation, however, have a direct impact on minorities: "One cannot long discriminate against people without generating in them a sense of isolation and of persecution and without giving them a conception of themselves as more different from others than in fact they are."[28]

The official segmentation and public stereotyping of the RRMs reinforced their own sense of solidarity and religious identity. The sense of "we" (Muslims) versus "them" (non-Muslims) intensified the minority sense of cohesion and self-pride. The Zoroastrian youth showed an increased interest in priesthood as a profession and the moral values and teachings of their religion.[29] Christian truck drivers carved a cross on their vehicles to exhibit their religious affiliation with pride.[30]

Responses unique to each group

The recognized religious minorities had a great deal in common not only with each other but also with the larger Muslim community. Some of the traits held in common have already been discussed in the previous chapters in the context of a sense of nationhood, ideological divisions, and various cultural, moral, ethical, and behavioral characteristics. There is, however, no doubt that each saw its relationship to the state differently. Relying on their own words, this section explores differing responses and self-representations of each group, one of the most revealing and fascinating features of minority response.

While the theocratic system insisted on treating them as one unified whole, as the protected People of the Book, each group attempted to stand out. Self-identification was an immediate feature of all the RRMs from the first day of the Revolution. Every effort was made to introduce one's own community, its past, its present, and its adherence to the new system. Yet each self-identification had close relations to the unique responses of each group.

Realizing that most of the provincial clergy and religious laymen who had acquired upward mobility (because of the Revolution) were unfamiliar with the Armenians, Armenian community leaders first attempted to introduce themselves. On the floor of the Majlis or in comments by religious leaders, every effort was made to emphasize their separation from other Christians, especially Christian missionaries. This was evident in a lengthy lecture delivered by Hratch Khachatourian, the Armenian deputy from the south in the first Majlis. He introduced the community by explaining who they were and what their religious denomination was. He especially emphasized the differences between Armenians and Christian missionaries, explaining that the missionaries had also tried to convert the Armenians, along with the Muslims, but to no avail. The Armenian national character shaped by the Gregorian Church had the intertwined features of religion and language.[31] The links between the Armenian Apostolic Church and the Catholic and Protestant Churches were repeatedly and emphatically denied by the prelacy, despite the fact that a minority of Armenians belonged to these denominations.[32] Even as late as 1989, this separation was emphasized in the strongest terms possible.[33]

This conscious religious and linguistic separation was based on facts; it was not manufactured by the prelacy. The need to emphasize the separation over and over again was motivated as much by religious preference as a desire to stay out of the conflict between authorities and other Christian groups in the country. Yet this sensitivity was historical. The Armenian Apostolic Church always had, if not an antagonistic, a distant relationship with other denominations, and it had always guarded the language–religion connection avidly.[34]

Another part of this strong separatist Armenian identity was its anti-Turkish stand. Armenians have been allowed to commemorate 24 April, the recognized beginning day of the Armenian genocide of 1915. The commemoration has been extensive, taking place in those cities with a significant Armenian population.[35] Of course, Ayatollah Khomeini had a deep dislike for the modern Turkish state. The "evil Ataturk" was responsible for the banning of Islam from politics and the state.[36]

The Armenians often linked the genocide to the war with Iraq and the suffering of the Muslim people. In 1985, the Armenian deputy from the south, Artavaz Baghoomian, assailed the United States secretary of state for his reflection on the status of minorities in Iran. Defending minority rights in Iran, he condemned the Reagan administration for its refusal to

9. Armenian demonstrations commemorating the 24 April 1915 genocide of the Armenians by the Ottoman Turkish government in Tehran,
1992.

accept the Armenian genocide in order to maintain good relations with
Turkey.[37] As a people subjected to massacres, the Armenians understood
the pain in letting the victimizer go unpunished, the Isfahan Archbishop
Gorun Papian said in an interview in 1988.[38]

Separating themselves to a point of near insulation has been a traditional mechanism of survival. Therefore, in this case, segmentation has
not only been imposed by the theocratic system, but it has been self-per-
petuated and reenforced by the community. Serving the nation but being
allowed their own cultural freedom was the behavioral motto of a community which had mastered the art of adaptability.

The Armenians, however, have not been assailed by the new regime,
and the societal prejudice against them had never reached that against the
Jews. Colored by these realities, the Jewish response has been different.
The self-introduction was religious; they were the followers of the
Prophet Moses and ethnonationally Iranian, separate and distinct from
Zionism and Israel. On the eve of Passover in 1979, the Jewish representa-
tives expressed their pleasure with the Revolution and declared solidarity
with the Iranian people.[39] Since that day, they have seized every opportu-
nity to distance themselves from the Zionists. When, for example, the
Majlis was discussing the credentials of Khosrow Naqi, the Jewish repre-

sentative declared Israel an "appendage of imperialism" and rejected its right to exist.[40] In the following year, in a lengthy speech, Naqi accused Zionists of having lied to the world, the biggest lie being that Judaism was the same as Zionism. From time to time "spiteful enemies and negligent friends" were deceived by them. Therefore, the official representatives of Iranian Jewry were declaring to the world that their Judaism was different; under the protection of the Islamic Republic they were progressing and favored "neither East nor West." Israel's Judaism was similar to Iraq's and Saudi Arabia's Islamism. Throughout Naqi's speech, every time he mentioned Israel, Ayatollah Khalkhali interrupted by yelling: "Felestin [Palestine]" and once "Felestin – We have no Israel." Naqi continued and at the conclusion the Majlis deputies showed their pleasure by the expression: "Well done! Well done!" Again, Khalkhali would not let it go: "Greetings to Felestin, annihilation on Israel."[41] Naqi's successor, Manuchehr Nikrooz, was also adamant in anti-Israel and anti-Zionist commentaries, and Rabbi Uriel Davoudi, in various interviews and lectures, condemned Israel, saying at one point: "Israel is not part of us."[42]

The Jewish response historically has been shaped by a process of self-preservation and self-maintenance, a strong tendency to convince the majority and the authorities that the Jews were "all right" as a minority.[43] This tendency has led Iranian Jews to oversell their anti-Israel public stand. Having been under suspicion, innately being suspicious of others (including other religious minorities), out of necessity and historical conditioning, they have developed a public and a private position. Their responses have swung between two extremes: outright denial of Israel and quietism. This tragic duality had to be maintained if they were going to live in Iran. Interviews by the foreign press with unidentified Iranian Jews clearly show their dilemma. The following is an excellent example: "We hear the ayatollah say that Israel was cooperating with the Shah and SAVAK, and we would be fools to say we support Israel. So we just keep quiet about it . . . Maybe it will work out. Anyway, what can we do? This is our home."[44] Unable to practice quietism, many Iranian Jews left home for good.

The self-identification of Zoroastrians has been distinctly different from all other recognized religious minorities. Their connection is to the territory of Iran; they are the true natives of the ancient land. As Malekpoor, the two-time Zoroastrian deputy to the Majlis, put it: "I have always emphasized that the faith of Iranian Zoroastrians is not separate from the destiny of all Iranian people . . . Zoroastrians belong to this land, they have not emigrated from a different place, they do not constitute a separate nationality."[45] This message was delivered later by some members of the Shii clerical ruling elite in their defense and introduction of Zoroastrians to the rest of the population.[46]

Zoroastrians have been bold and direct in expressing their concerns and discontent. There are many examples in this study which point to this unique characteristic. The following is one more example. In an interview Parviz Malekpoor pointed to one of the school texts in which, in imitation of an Iranian king in the Sassanian era, the Zoroastrians are accused of marrying very close kin with whom marriage is prohibited. Assailing the authors of the text, he said:

Do you want me to name various Muslim kings who have committed vice and immorality [fesq va fojoor]? Do you want me to even mention Islamic caliphs whose crimes and perversity became universal? And, then, will you accept if from this evidence I conclude that in "Islam" vice and immorality is permitted and crime and perversion is free? If my knowledge of Islam is deduced based on today's rulers of Islamic countries from King Hossein and Saddam to Zia al-Haq . . . won't you laugh at me? How is it then that in a textbook, which officially has been distributed by the [Ministry of] Education and Training of our revolutionary republic, one has to submit to such meaningless reasoning? Wasn't the [Ministry of] Education and Training in possession of Gathas [Zoroaster's Hymns]?

Malekpoor added that the ministry should have sought the advice of the Zoroastrian clergy, community representatives, and true Muslim scholars, finally reflecting: "We Zoroastrians have learned to be patient."[47]

Zoroastrians have emphasized oneness, not only with Muslims but with religious minorities as well. This ability to embrace all the citizens of Iran has made it easy for them boldly and directly to criticize the Islamic extremists and forcefully, even righteously, to claim rights on behalf of other minorities. In most of their correspondence and speeches (even in those for the Zoroastrian community), they have spoken on behalf of all, calling to the attention of the authorities problems, contradictions, and violations of the constitution. This sentiment has been reflected even in their own community events. During the commemoration for the Zoroastrians killed in the war, one community leader commented: "When the enemy's bullet whistles and moves forward, it does not ask for a person's religion and denomination; it aims for the heart of an Iranian."[48]

This ability to project oneness, fearlessness, integrativeness, and wisdom has distinguished Zoroastrians from other RRMs. They have maintained good relations with everyone and had everyone's respect. In contrast to the insulated and cautious posture of the Armenians and the oversell and quietism of the Jews, the Zoroastrians have been confident and, more so than any other minority, they have acted like a majority.

It is more difficult to assess the nature of the response of the Chaldeans and Assyrians; not only has information been hard to come by, but their small numbers have made their situation somewhat precarious. Personal interviews by the author have revealed that Assyrians have often responded in terms similar to the Armenians such as during the protests on educational problems in the early 1980s. Yet, on several occasions Armenians refused to allow Assyrians and Chaldeans to join in with them, arguing that they should organize their own separate protests and not hide behind the name (or clout) of the larger numbers of Armenians. They argued that, if demonstrations bore fruit, the Assyrians would benefit but, if there was a backlash against the demonstrations, the Assyrians could disclaim any part in it. On this issue, of course, there was a difference of opinion in the Armenian community. Some believed that a solid united front in any form would have been more effective.[49]

The meaning of the response

The analysis of the overall responses of the recognized religious minorities reveals their resilience and an instinctive activation of historically ingrained survival techniques. The following comment captures the meaning of the RRMs' response to the Islamic theocracy:

> Response to the dominant world is not simply a matter of individual trial and error, for the culture of a minority group contains traditional adjustment techniques that are passed on, intentionally and unintentionally, to the oncoming generation. These techniques will vary from group to group.[50]

Each community has unique features and differing perceptions of self versus the Muslim majority. Even opposing forces may be present within each group; in the case of Iran's RRM communities, the leftists have had a strong presence and even leadership positions. Yet even internal dissent does not deflect attention from communal protection. The left within all religious minorities acted as avid supporters of the rights of their own community. The "ethnic boundary" was maintained by "complex organizational behavior"[51] on the part of the ethnic group, who knew that the nature of continuity of the ethnic unit depends on the maintenance of this boundary and that "different circumstances obviously favour different performances."[52] RRMs as a whole have mastered the art of accommodation so well that they often appear in sync with the regime, any regime. They take on the coloring of the state ideology whether the system is Islamic theocracy or autocratic monarchy, and within its framework press for their communal autonomy. The state ideology may change, as it has changed several times in twentieth-century Iran. What helps in this process of adjustment techniques is the overall connection that the minorities feel they have with the country. Since each in its own way has a special affinity to the land and the culture of Persia, consciously or unconsciously, the loyalty to the (nation-)state becomes a natural extension of that affinity, regardless of ideological filtering.

Conclusion: the perils of marginality

As this author sat in a telephone-dispatched taxi in Tehran, the taxi driver turned and looked at her: "You people are much better off than we are!" His voice was coarse. Taken aback, she asked: "Who is 'you people'?" Without hesitation he replied: "Shoma aqaliatin digeh [Aren't you a minority]?" A whole range of philosophical thoughts raced through her head. The ease and intensity with which he used the label "aqaliat" was new to her in Iran. This was the unique byproduct of the theocratic system. The "aqaliat" was "the other," "the marginal," "the separate from us": it was an institutionalized "otherness" which was disturbing and different. The taxi driver, unaware of the turmoil and shock he had caused, continued to repeat his question but also to respond to it. "You *are* a minority. Aren't you? With that name, of course you *are!*" Then, eventually, when she admitted to the classification, the driver sighed with an energetic cheeriness: "See . . . I knew it."

Religious minorities have been segmented in word, thought, and action. The reference to the label "aqaliat" was expressed with the same ease by those members of the political and economic elite of the previous regime who had remained in the country after the Revolution. This institutionalization of segmentation, this designation and labeling was minimal and definitely not as overt during the shah's reign, and it remains a unique byproduct of the new regime. Before 1979, everyone was an "Irani" albeit in pretense; after the Revolution, Irani was replaced by aqaliat, Bahai, and Sunni. "Hamvatan [fellow countryman/countrywoman]" was replaced by "Muslim sisters and brothers." These theocratic state designations were reflected in school textbooks, communal and national commentaries, and debates. The strong objections of the RRM deputies in the Assembly of Experts to the use of the word "aqaliat" in Article 13 of the Islamic constitution was not without foresight; they preferred the word "javame [communities]" in its place. But afterwards they used "aqaliat" to refer to themselves as well.

Compartmentalization followed through an overall policy on recognized religious minorities. The worst legal embodiments of theocratic

154

rule were the provisions of the penal code of qesas and the revival of the "Apostasy Law" where the RRMs' dhimma status as inferiors was institutionalized. Besides the laws institutionalizing inequality and separation, the ideological state exhibited an incredible arrogance, an arrogance of religious superiority that allowed the clergy and their followers to lecture the non-Muslims on the precepts of their religions (including writing a religious textbook for their children). The state ideology, as in centuries past, was a perversion of the meaning of Islam. The intensity of persecution and discrimination was in proportion to the combined perception of the association with the West and the intent to annihilate Islam. Therefore, the Bahais suffered the most, followed by Iranian Christian converts and then the Jews. Zoroastrians were ultimately the indigenous people gone astray with "fire worship." The Armenians' quick disassociation from the West (they had suffered the allegation in the past) and their active role in the war with Iraq turned them into "the indigenous Christians." (Assyrians and Chaldeans, very few in numbers, followed suit.)

The response of the RRMs were very much embedded in the familiar cultural milieu. They adjusted but also resisted, they bent but stood firm, they educated but realigned themselves with the new circumstances. Each group resorted to its own shrewd traditional patterns of subterfuge, reconciliation, negotiation, and show of obedience to deal with the regime. Despite early objections, they used their "aqaliat" position to ensure continuity and legitimacy, and when possible they pushed through the outer limits enlarging the spaces within which they could maneuver. They acted in accordance with a long tradition of minority communities in the area and remained generally skeptical and ambivalent toward outside interference. They knew their oppressor better than anyone else and were well adept at dealing with it carefully, patiently, and cleverly. With passing years, the flexibility and division of the theocratic state resulted in contradictions in practice.

Although it is beyond the scope of this work, the review of the literature, human rights reports, and eyewitness accounts reveal that the majority Shii polity was subject to extremely harsh treatment throughout the revolutionary regime. This was on a par with the imposition of a new Islamic identity (rigidly defined by the state) in order to shape appropriate citizenship. The nature of restrictions imposed upon the RRMs and the intentional subjugation of the Bahais were aimed at minimizing and destroying exposure to alternative ideas. Therefore, restrictions upon the minorities were imposed not only to control them politically, but more importantly for the social control (e.g., through exposure, recognition, and knowledge) of the Shii polity.

If, for analytical purposes, we divide the state into three levels (officials, institutions and policies, and ideology or definition of politics), the Iranian theocratic state has been firmly grounded in the third level.[1] Variations have appeared at the first and second levels. State officials, institutions, and state policies have been at times rigid, and at other times contradictory, but also impressively flexible. Yet, the state definition of Islamic ideology remained rigid for the most part (certainly until the death of Khomeini). After 1989, affected by economic exigency, and a louder internal voice of dissent, state ideology began a gradual decline in intensity and rigor, setting in motion opposing poles of conflict. It became more deceptive as it tried to appeal to the West.

Although expressions of coexistence and cooperation in the 1990s abound, changes in the condition of recognized religious minorities have been minimal. Pronouncements by minorities were orchestrated, and less discord appeared on the surface. The penal code remained unchanged. Discrimination in employment continued, sometimes even reflected in job advertisements.[2] The situation of the Bahais and Iranian Christian converts, after an initial easing of pressure, continued as before and even worsened.

Reports for the 1990s indicate harassment and arrest on charges of spying and being a Zionist as well as continued problems for the Iranian Jews with leaving the country.[3] Several Jews have been executed by government. While their numbers are very low both in terms of the proportion of the Jewish population and compared to the execution of Muslims, the charges against them are similar to the past: "associating with Zionism"[4] and "espionage and economic fraud."[5] Meanwhile, the Jewish deputies in the Majlis continued to shower the authorities with accolades. In March 1992, Manuchehr Nikrooz, the Jewish Majlis representative, expressed regret for the assassination of the secretary general of Hezbollah in Lebanon, referring to him as "the crusading scholar." The statement, as usual, condemned Zionism and distanced it from the Jewish community in Iran.[6] The Jewish deputy, Kuros Kaivani (elected in 1992), speaking in the same vein, invoked Khomeini's infamous quote "We make a distinction between Jewish society [community] and Zionists," ending his speech in this way: "Iranian Jews believe and have always believed that the banner of Islam and its exalted clergy is a safe haven for them."[7] Manuchehr Elyasi (elected in 1996), then the Jewish Majlis deputy, began one of his speeches with greetings to the "heavenly spirit" of the late Ayatollah Khomeini. He said that Khomeini's "prophet-like statements" were instrumental in encouraging Jews to join the 1979 Revolution.[8] As in the 1980s, stereotypical and derogatory comments against Jews appeared in the Iranian media and, like before, the Jewish leadership criticized them to no avail.[9] In a letter to President Khatami, the society (sometimes called the Association) of Iranian Jews of Tehran severely criticized the derision of Jews in a television serial and a weekly program. The letter suggested that combating Zionism in the Iranian media had become a provocation against Jews.[10]

The Zoroastrians also continued as in the past. They complained about the lack of sports clubs and libraries for their youth and the need for more community centers.[11] Parviz Ravani, the Zoroastrian deputy in the Majlis, raised the dire need for the renovation of schools and for the construction of a new middle school for girls in Tehran.[12] In 1993 and 1994, the Zoroastrian festival of Chaharshanbeh Soori was interrupted by security forces. (The celebrations, popular among Muslims and other religious minorities for years, involve lighting fires and jumping over them; to ancient Persians the act symbolized cleansing and preparation for the new year.) The celebrations were allowed for the first time since the Revolution in 1992 but, in 1993, authorities said it took place during the period of mourning for Imam Ali; hundreds who did take part were detained and released later. In 1994 battles broke out in certain neighborhoods of Tehran between celebrating youths and the security forces due to Ayatollah Khamenei's orders not to allow the "atheists' celebrations." Despite a media blackout, reports indicated that almost a dozen were killed and 500 wounded.[13] The Zoroastrians, while more candid about their and the nation's problems, also engaged in conformist showmanship with the authorities. The sixth International Congress of Zoroastrians was held in Tehran at the invitation of the Iranian government. It declared that a permanent secretariat would be established in Iran, the birthplace of the faith. The Congress emphasized the training of Zoroastrian priests for the future. Yet it was clear that serious issues, such as discrimination against Zoroastrians in Iran itself, were not discussed.[14]

Assyrians, like the Zoroastrians, also held two meetings of the World Assyrian Summit in Tehran; in the last meeting, held in November 1998, the newly elected President Khatami was declared Man of the Year by the summit.[15] The Assyrian leaders were also full of praise, as before. In a speech the Assyrian Majlis deputy, Shamshun Maqsudpur (elected in 1992), gave a glorious new version of Assyrian history tracing it back to 6,750 BC. He referred to "Muslim professors" as experts on the ancient Assyrians and reiterated that the Assyrians "are among the most loyal citizens of this land."[16]

Marked by the collapse of the Soviet Union, the formation of independent Muslim republics, especially Azerbaijan and the Armenian Republic, and the battle over the region of Nagorno-Karabakh, the Armenian community ended up in a peculiar situation. Iran's economic

relations with Armenia, its political role as mediator in the Karabakh conflict, and its attempts to address the rage of a significant and vocal Azeri
population in Iran (a rage which was manifested through religious rhetoric[17] and threats against the Armenians of Tabriz[18]) punctured the com-
fortable insular world of the community. The Armenian Embassy opened
in Tehran in December 1992, and several economic agreements were
signed initially on banking, transportation, and trade.[19] There has been
substantial expansion in economic relations between Iran and Armenia.
According to official Iranian estimates, by 1996, Iran had become
Armenia's biggest trading partner.[20] Iranians opened businesses in
Armenia and many Armenian professionals were allowed to work in Iran.
Details on Iran–Armenia–Azerbaijan and Iranian Azeri and Armenian
communities remain outside the scope of this work but offer an ideal
topic for future research.

The Armenian representatives have continued their praise of the government. On the eve of the upheaval over the murder of Protestant priests,
Vartan Vartanian, the northern Armenian deputy in the Majlis, made a
statement, a literal copy of the government's official stand, in which he
blamed the killings on the "hypocrite terrorists."[21] Artavaz Baghoomian,
the southern Armenian deputy, in a 1995 speech said: "The peaceful
coexistence of the Iranian nation and the followers of various religions in
the country should serve as a suitable model for other countries."[22] Every
time a human rights violation report on Iran is issued, all recognized religious minorities, and particularly the Armenians, hold a press conference,
resorting to the same commentary as before, and publicly recant and criticize the report.

The unexpected landslide victory of Seyyed Mohammad Khatami in
May 1997 has raised hopes for change. He was the minister of Ershad
during the most critical years in RRM–state relations 1982–92, yet hardly
anyone had heard of him. His name does not appear as a main player or a
sympathizer with the religious minorities. He was very young to acquire
such a high post (in his mid- to late thirties) but his father Ayatollah
Ruhollah Khatami was "a close associate" of Ayatollah Khomeini and
was his representative in Yazd.[23] During the 1980s Mohammad Khatami
was an important official emissary on several occasions, and before
assuming his ministerial post amid complaints against crackdowns on the
press, he had expressed a typical view, namely that the press should voice
the views of the people which "are identical to those of" Ayatollah
Khomeini.[24] In other words, he is the byproduct of the system of clerical
rule.

In a speech delivered to the Zoroastrians in 1982 he reflected that his
affection and respect for Zoroastrians stem not only from his religious

views but from being raised in Ardakan (a town near Yazd) where he came
to associate with Zoroastrians in the street, bazaar, and school, and even
to participate in Zoroastrian festivities. "We all want to see good
thoughts, good deeds, and good words rule the world"; this was the com-
monality among all religions. But he also attacked imperialism and urged
the Zoroastrians to fight "with more hatred and more anger."[25] The
content of his message was no different from what other clergy had to say.
His lecture differed mainly in tone and form of expression.

Reflecting on the condition of the Bahais in January 1998, Firuz
Kazemzadeh, secretary for external affairs of the Bahais in the United
States, said there had been no visible difference since Khatami's election.
His comment was made long before the major crackdown on the Bahais
late in the same year, which coincided with Khatami's visit to the United
Nations and was interpreted as the hardliners trying to undermine the
new president.[26] Yet the Bahai issue remains the ultimate test for anyone
with liberal and reformist claims on governance in Iran.

During the 1990s, the theocratic state has responded to international
criticism of its treatment of minorities by employing two main strategies.
The first has been to extend invitations to religious leaders from outside
Iran to visit the country. A host of Assyrian, Greek, and Armenian high-
ranking clergy have paid visits, receiving extended press coverage and
claiming publicly that RRMs are doing extremely well. There are even
reports that an invitation has been extended to one rabbi from Israel.[27]

The second strategy has been to disavow criticism aggressively and
publicly. This strategy has been pursued by employing three tactics. The
first tactic is to reiterate that religious minorities have complete liberty,
and that they are even better off than the Muslims. A comment by the
previous foreign minister Ali-Akbar Velayati is typical. Addressing the
United Nations envoy in 1995, he said: "Where on earth do you think
religious minorities are treated with such open-mindedness? . . . religious
minorities enjoy complete freedom, and on the basis of Islamic compas-
sion, in some cases they enjoy more privileges than the Muslims." He
singled out the Jews to elaborate that, despite their low numbers, Jews
have one deputy in the Majlis.[28] When Pope John Paul II met the Iranian
ambassador to the Vatican, he called on Iran to guarantee religious
freedom and respect for international law. Reacting strongly to this simple
comment, a Mashhad paper wrote that RRMs are much better off than
Muslims because they possess social facilities and have "freedom to
indulge in their special dietary and drinking requirements," none of
which are "provided to other citizens and the Muslims."[29]

The second tactic which often follows the first is to draw on what
officials perceive to be "comparative cases" in the West. State officials

regularly refer to Muslims in Europe and claim that they do not have the same rights or any rights in the West. A member of the Iranian mission to the UN expressed concern for discrimination and violence against Muslims; his evidence was based on computer websites that disseminate anti-Muslim propaganda. He asked international bodies to address this issue.[30] In response to condemnations of human rights abuses, Iranian officials declared that there are more churches in Iran than the total number of mosques in European countries.[31]

The third tactic has been to utilize two types of linguistic verbiage, either separately or in combination, aimed at confusing and distorting the main issue. Since many who work in the universities and some ministries, particularly the Foreign Ministry, are educated in the West, especially in the United States, they are familiar with academic lingo. Employing words and "ideas" used in American scholarly circles, Iran is presented as a modernist and reformed theocratic state. The borrowed phrases, however, are an attempt to legitimize the theocratic state. The favorite thus far have been drawn from the "civilizations" debate and the "culture" arguments. The Iranian foreign minister in 1997 delivered a lecture to the United Nations General Assembly which was typical of the first type of linguistic verbiage. He talked about the "clash of civilizations" concept, rejecting the idea that there was a clash, and replacing the clash with cooperation and dialogue. He identified the most fundamental rights to be "the right to life, the right to self-determination, and the right to development." He used terms such as "empowerment" and "civil society."[32]

The second type of linguistic verbiage comes from a more sophisticated source, the clergy. Borrowing from the language of erfan (Islamic mysticism),[33] general references are made to humanity and human values. To those unfamiliar with the sophisticated and layered character of Shii theology, the comments would sound universal and seem to be a major departure from the past. But they are not. In November 1998, the minister of Ershad, in his speech to the Assyrian summit, said:

Shariah of religion differs from the Truth of that religion because shariah is the picture adherents have of their own religion where in fact human tastes [salayeq] have been taken into account. Therefore, adherents of different religions should converse from the angle of the Truth of the religion in order to get close . . . the Truths of religions are not against each other and Islam more than other customs respects and magnifies religions which came before Islam, particularly Christianity.[34]

The question that needs to be asked of the minister is: "Does Islamic shariah recognize other religions' shariahs as equal to Islamic shariah?" As most are unfamiliar with subtleties of deception in religious lingo, very few would raise this crucial question. Even as early as 1989, in an address to religious minorities Interior Minister Ali-Akbar Mohtashemi said that according to the Quran "no one is superior to the other because of race, color, and tribe." Note the purposeful omission of the word *religion* which gives the impression that religion is also included.[35]

Islamic officials and their apologists have always repeated the statement appearing in Article 19 of the Islamic constitution: "People of Iran from every sect and tribe enjoy equal rights, and color, race, language, and the like shall not be cause for advantage." Note the absence of "religion" in this phrase as well as the deceptive inclusion of "the like" in the article. Uninformed readers may assume by seeing color and race that religion is also included or conveniently presume its inclusion in "the like" since there can really be many differentiating factors separating human beings. But for Islamic theocracy religion is left out on purpose because all religions are not equal, and "the like" does not include religion at all. This conscious omission is clear when Article 19 is compared to Article 38 of the labor law where "religion" is mentioned as a factor against discrimination in salaries.[36]

The perils

The Iranian landscape shows that the behavior of members of the polity may be influenced but cannot be forever coerced and controlled. Despite official severity, during the early years some Muslims offered their homes to safeguard the Jews.[37] A Muslim village chief protected the religious identity of a Bahai family, safeguarding them from the villagers and the revolutionary agents. Despite threats of setting his shop on fire and even pouring gasoline on its doorsteps, a Muslim shopkeeper refused to hand over an unveiled Christian woman who had taken refuge in his shop after being chased by the Revolutionary Guards. There were the truly devout whose identity will never be known who, working in various capacities in government offices, helped quietly. There were members of the RRM community who hired Bahais or did errands to protect them.[38] In a system where the state and society had always been at odds and far apart, the society took care of its own quietly and secretly. Taking individual initiatives has a long tradition in the Iranian community. Regardless of the nature of the political system and the presence of more than its share of fanatics, Iran has somehow harbored a significant collectivity of people (religious and secular) who have, albeit quietly, taken action as individuals of conscience. It is in their behavior and actions, and not in symbols and references to kings such as Cyrus the Great, that Iran as a country finds its redemption.

To be marginal is to be at the outer or lower limits; it is to be on the edge. The perils of marginalization take multitudinous forms. When Assyrians and Chaldeans, despite their mutually antagonistic histories, had to share one deputy in the Majlis; when, despite enduring the deaths of their sons in a futile war between Iran and Iraq, Armenians were denied the teaching of their religion in regular hours and limited in language instruction (guaranteed under the Islamic constitution); when, despite their Persian cultural roots, the Jews were treated with suspicion and viewed as agents of Israel, or when the Jews adamantly and hyperbolically had to express loyalty to the Islamic theocracy; when Bahais were displaced, imprisoned, and executed by their own countrymen; when the Zoroastrian natives were called "fire-worshippers" and denied access to government posts because of their religion: all were perils of marginality for non-Muslim minorities as a collectivity and as individuals.

But the Shii Muslim population was also marginalized by political repression, corruption, competitive and opportunistic interests, double-talk and deceit, duplicitous behavior, economic woes, gendered injustice, a wasteful war, demoralization, and dislocation. Yet, instead of looking within and at the historical political manipulation of the non-Muslims, some have chosen to compare themselves to the recognized religious minorities, echoing the familiar tune, again: "They are much better off than we are!"

The comment that the RRMs are better off was put to several activist members of the non-Muslim recognized religious minorities, leading to a range of responses. One brushed off the issue and called it ridiculous. Another interviewed for this book, agitated by the question, which he had heard before, responded: "They say that because they are obsessed with sex. They think we are better off because our men and women assemble together in one room, house, or community centers. This means 'better off' to them. This is all they see, all they can see! They cannot see beneath the surface."

It has been suggested that altrocentrism can become a substitute for ethnocentrism. Altrocentrism is defined as the ability to see events as they appear to others.[39] Yet, this is easier said than done in an environment where the state has become an intrusive machine.

For Iran two contradictory and forceful currents can be identified: a repetition of past mistakes and an almost altruistic notion of existence. The latter has fostered a deep cultural bond across the country, while the former has repeatedly struck at its roots. To appreciate the power of altruistic cultural notions, it is vital to place the plight of the non-Muslim minorities in the larger context. It is astonishing that, during the critical years (the early to mid-1980s), considering how widespread the support for the Revolution was and how strong and omnipotent its force, repression of religious minorities did not become any worse. The wisdom of flexibility, the traditional cultural unity, and the individual's ever-enduring suspicion of the state were instrumental in preventing the overescalation of conflict and persecution of minorities.

On the surface, economic and political sectors may change and undergo reform. New leaders will be cheered for their foresight. Grand overtures will be made to those labeled as devils and enemies. And, no doubt, as before the non-Muslim religious minorities will be asked to play a role (e.g., Iranian Jews in relation to Israel). But all would be a shallow venture if fundamental lessons were left unlearned.

"I have always been loath to hide . . . the weak points of the community, or to press for its rights without having purged it of its blemishes,"[40] wrote Mahatma Gandhi of his struggle for Indian independence from British rule. Scapegoating non-Muslim marginal groups has been a historical blemish for Iran, its version of Islam, and state politics. If a community or society does not admit its mistakes, it cannot address them realistically, and it is bound to repeat them again. Blaming others is the easiest way of denying personal responsibility. Unless mindsets are altered, no change is deserving of praise. In the end it is essential to contemplate the perils of marginality for those who experience them and those who cause them. Failure to contemplate the situation and change behavior will guarantee the mindless repetition of the patterns examined above in the not too distant future.

Notes

INTRODUCTION: AN OVERVIEW OF POLITICS AND SOCIETY

1. See, for example, Simeon Potter, *Language in the Modern World* (Baltimore: Penguin Books, 1960), p. 21.
2. R. A. Schermerhorn, *Comparative Ethnic Relations: A Framework for Theory and Research* (New York: Random House, 1970), p. 12.
3. Richard M. Burkey, *Ethnic and Racial Groups: The Dynamics of Dominance* (Reading, MA: Cummings, 1978), pp. 8–9, 12, 34.
4. *The Random House Dictionary of the English Language*, unabridged edn. (New York: Random House, 1983), p. 876.
5. Joseph Rothschild, *Ethnopolitics: A Conceptual Framework* (New York: Columbia University Press, 1981), pp. 8–9. See also Joseph Bram, "Change and Choice in Ethnic Identification," *Transactions of the New York Academy of Sciences* 28, ser. 2, no. 2 (December 1965), 242–48; Immanuel Wallerstein, "The Two Modes of Ethnic Consciousness," in Edward Allworth (ed.), *The Nationality Question in Soviet Central Asia* (New York: Praeger, 1973), pp. 168–75.
6. See Karl W. Deutsch, *Nationalism and Social Communication* (Cambridge, MA: MIT Press, 1953); Karl W. Deutsch and William J. Foltz (eds.), *Nation Building* (New York: Atherton Press, 1963); Leonard Binder, "National Integration and Political Development," *American Political Science Review* 58 (September 1964), 622–31; Philip E. Jacob and Henry Teune, "The Integrative Process: Guidelines for Analysis of the Bases of Political Community," in Jacob and James V. Toscano (eds.), *The Integration of Political Communities* (Philadelphia: J. B. Lippincott, 1964), pp. 1–45; James S. Coleman and Carl G. Rosberg, Jr. (eds.), *Political Parties and National Integration in Tropical Africa* (Berkeley: University of California Press, 1964); and Lucian Pye, *Politics, Personality and Nation-Building* (New Haven: Yale University Press, 1962).
7. See Alvin Rabushka and Kenneth A. Shepsle, *Politics in Plural Societies: A Theory of Democratic Instability* (Columbus, OH: Charles E. Merrill, 1972); Cynthia H. Enloe, *Ethnic Conflict and Political Development* (Boston: Little, Brown, 1973); Crawford Young, *The Politics of Cultural Pluralism* (Madison: University of Wisconsin Press, 1976).
8. Eric A. Nordlinger proposed six such techniques: a stable coalition, proportionality, mutual veto, depoliticization of certain types of issues, compromise, and concessions. See his *Conflict Regulation in Divided Societies*

(Cambridge, MA: Harvard University Center for International Affairs, Occasional Paper 29, 1972). Milton Esman pointed to the dissimilar countries of Bangladesh, Yugoslavia, Canada, Nigeria, and Belgium, and concluded that communal conflicts will be more salient than class conflict. To deal effectively with such scarcities, he identified four classes of regime objectives: institutionalized dominance, induced assimilation, syncretic integration, and balanced pluralism. See his "Management of Communal Conflict," *Public Policy* 21 (Winter 1973), 49–78.

9. Studies focusing on some form of conflict management were prevalent in the 1970s. See, for example, Donald Rothchild's review article, "Ethnicity and Conflict Resolution," *World Politics* 22, no. 4 (July 1970), 597–616; R. S. P. Elliot and John Hickie, *Ulster: A Case Study in Conflict Theory* (New York: St. Martin's Press, 1971); Donald E. Gelfand and Russell D. Lee (compils.), *Ethnic Conflicts and Power: A Cross-National Perspective* (New York: John Wiley & Sons, 1973).

10. Young, *Politics*, esp. pp. 505–28.

11. Donald L. Horowitz, "Three Dimensions of Ethnic Politics," *World Politics* 23, no. 2 (January 1971), 240. There is a qualifier to Horowitz's view; he adds that the process of modernization is by no means "unilinear or irreversible."

12. Samuel P. Huntington, foreword to Nordlinger's *Conflict Regulation*, p. ii.

13. Walker Connor offered an elaborate critic of Deutsch's *Nationalism*, and identified contradictions in his arguments. Deutsch had argued that modernization would bring about eventual assimilation ending ethnic conflict. See Walker Connor, "Nation-Building or Nation-Destroying?," *World Politics* 24, no. 3 (April 1972), 330–31; see also his "Ethnonationalism in the First World: The Present Historical Perspective," in Milton J. Esman (ed.), *Ethnic Conflict in the Western World* (Ithaca: Cornell University Press, 1977), p. 20.

14. Rothschild, *Ethnopolitics*, pp. 255–56.

15. Anthony D. Smith, *The Ethnic Revival* (Cambridge: Cambridge University Press, 1981), p. 4. For a good analysis of the dilemma of democratic-liberal ideology and ethnic politics, see Enloe, *Ethnic Conflict*, pp. 59–66.

16. For an elaborate discussion of this issue, especially as it relates to Third World nationalism as well as to the situation of black Americans, see Enloe, *Ethnic Conflict*, pp. 39–59; for a comprehensive and brilliant comparative study of the relationship between nationalism and Marxism, see Walker Connor, *The National Question in Marxist-Leninist Theory and Strategy* (Princeton: Princeton University Press, 1984). Among other issues, Connor concludes that Lenin viewed ethnic assimilation as an inevitable historical process but prohibited coercive actions to speed it up. Connor asserts, however, that in practice the line between coercion and persuasion is a very thin one (pp. 480–81).

17. Dov Ronen, *The Quest for Self-Determination* (New Haven: Yale University Press, 1979), pp. 8–9.

18. *Ibid.*, pp. 53–70, 86–89.

19. The list is inexhaustible. For some examples, see Paul R. Brass, "Ethnic Groups and the State," in Brass (ed.), *Ethnic Groups and the State* (Totowa,

NJ: Barnes & Noble, 1985), pp. 1–56; Cynthia Enloe, *Ethnic Soldiers: State Security in Divided Societies* (Athens: University of Georgia Press, 1980); Ernest Gellner, *Nations and Nationalism* (Oxford: Blackwell, 1983); Michael Haas, "Comparing Paradigms of Ethnic Politics in the United States: The Case of Hawaii," *Western Political Quarterly* 40 (December 1987), 647–72; Dan Horowitz, "Communal Armed Organizations," *Archives Européennes de Sociologie* 27 (1986), 85–101; Nelson Kasfir, "Explaining Ethnic Political Participation," *World Politics* 31, no. 3 (April 1979), 365–88; Neil Nevitte and Charles H. Kennedy (eds.), *Ethnic Preference and Public Policy in Developing States* (Boulder: Lynne Rienner, 1986); M. Catharine Newbury, "Colonialism, Ethnicity, and Rural Political Protest," *Comparative Politics* 15 (1983), 253–80; and Kathleen A. Staudt, "Sex, Ethnic and Class Consciousness in Western Kenya," *Comparative Politics* 14 (1982), 147–67.

20. Sue Ellen M. Charlton, Jana Everett, and Kathleen Staudt (eds.), *Women, the State, and Development* (Albany: State University of New York Press, 1989), pp. 13–16.

21. Milton J. Esman, *Ethnic Politics* (Ithaca: Cornell University Press, 1994), pp. 255–56. Esman gives as extreme examples Hitler's Germany and Bosnia in the 1990s. But the "classic approach" is encouraging assimilation such as Arabization or Russification; he argues that liberals and Marxists prefer this method for eliminating ethnic differences.

22. *Ibid.*, p. 256. The archetype for the policy of exclusion is the apartheid system in South Africa, and for subordination the case of the Malaysian Chinese.

23. *Ibid.*, p. 259. Esman draws a simple diagram where he separates methods of policy implementation. Genocide, expulsion or "cleansing," population transfers, forced assimilation, exclusion, and subordination fall under "coercion." Induced assimilation, federalism, cultural pluralism, power sharing, ethnic coalitions, and reducing political salience are consensual methods (p. 259).

24. Ian Lustick, "Stability in Deeply Divided Societies: Consociationalism Versus Control," *World Politics* 31, no. 3 (April 1979), 342.

25. Joel S. Migdal, "The State in Society: An Approach to Struggle for Domination," in Migdal, Atul Kohli, and Vivienne Shue (eds.), *State Power and Social Forces: Domination and Transformation in the Third World* (Cambridge: Cambridge University Press, 1994), p. 16.

26. Joel S. Migdal, *Strong Societies and Weak States: State–Society Relations and State Capabilities in the Third World* (Princeton: Princeton University Press, 1988), p. 241.

27. Sami Zubaida, "An Islamic State?: The Case of Iran," *Middle East Report* 153 (July–August 1988), 7.

28. Esman, *Ethnic Politics*, p. 250.

29. Fredrik Barth, "Introduction," in Barth (ed.), *Ethnic Groups and Boundaries: The Social Organization of Culture Difference* (London: George Allen & Unwin, 1969), p. 15.

30. *Ibid.*, pp. 25, 36.

31. Esman, *Ethnic Politics*, pp. 256–57.

32. Lois Beck, "Tribes and State in Nineteenth- and Twentieth-Century Iran,"

in Philip S. Khoury and Joseph Kostiner (eds.), *Tribes and State Formation in the Middle East* (Berkeley: University of California Press, 1990), p. 189.

33. Richard W. Cottam, *Nationalism in Iran* (Pittsburgh: University of Pittsburgh Press, 1979), p. 51.

34. Abdol-Hossein Saidian, *Sarzamin va Mardom-e Iran* (Tehran: Ilm va Zendegi, 1369 [1990/91]), p. 13. The number of Shiis versus Sunnis remains unclear; another source identified 91 percent Shii and 7.8 percent Sunni in Iran; see *Iran Yearbook '88*, 1st edn. (Bonn: Moini-Biontino Verlagsgesellschaft, 1988), p. 148.

35. The estimate of 67 million appears in *The World Almanac and Book of Facts 1998* (Mahwah, NJ: World Almanac Books, 1998), p. 775. Shiis are estimated to be 89 percent and Sunnis 10 percent of the population. According to Abbas-Ali Zali, head of the Statistics Center of Iran, on 30 October 1996 Iran's population was 58.3 million (IRNA, 31 December 1996); the Voice of the Islamic Republic of Iran, Tehran, in its 1 June 1997 broadcast quoting Zali, gave the number 60,055,488; and the Persian daily *Salam* in its 1 March 1997 issue gave 59.5 million, attributing it to Zali. None provides a clear number for the Sunnis.

36. "Tarh-e Sarshomari-ye Ejtemai – Eqtesadi-ye Ashayer-e Koochandeh – Marhaleye Aval 1364," in *Gozide-ye Mataleb-e Amari*, 3rd year, no. 15, p. 21. For a detailed estimate on the number of tribes, nomads, and clans at different historical periods, see Iraj Afshar (Sistani), *Moqadamehi bar Shenakht-e Ilha, Chadorneshinan va Tavayef-e Ashaeri-e Iran*, vol. I (Tehran: Homa, 1366 [1987]), pp. 31–33. The work extends to a second volume which contains maps and accounts of characteristics and lifestyles of each group.

37. *Iran Yearbook '88*, p. 20.

38. *World Almanac*, p. 775.

39. **Azeri Turks**

    David B. Nissman, *The Soviet Union and Iranian Azerbaijan: The Use of Nationalism for Political Penetration* (Boulder: Westview Press, 1987), cites one Soviet source and one Iranian Azeri source, pp. 7 and 23, n. 2. Harry W. Walsh, "Azeri," in Richard V. Weekes (rev. and ed.), *Muslim Peoples: A World Ethnographic Survey*, 2nd edn. (Westport, CT: Greenwood Press, 1984), vol. I, p. 64, cites an estimated 8.8 million for Iranian Azeris. Lack of a census, Azeri assimilation with Persians, and their numerical integration with other Turkish-speaking people have made accurate estimates impossible.

    Different assessments as to the nature of Khiabani's movement exist. Some state that it was backed by the Soviet Union; see Hooshang Amirahmadi, "A Theory of Ethnic Collective Movements and Its Application to Iran," *Ethnic and Racial Studies* 10, no. 4 (October 1987), 384. Others deny an active role by the Bolsheviks; see Cottam, *Nationalism*, pp. 122–24. For another brief description of Khiabani's activities, see Ervand Abrahamian, *Iran Between Two Revolutions* (Princeton: Princeton University Press, 1982), pp. 112–13. For the 1990s, see Human Rights Watch, *Iran: Religious and Ethnic Minorities, Discrimination in Law and Practice*, vol. 9, no. 7 (New York, September 1997), p. 27.

Kurds

Martin Short and Anthony McDermott, *The Kurds*, 4th rev. edn. (London: Minority Rights Group, Report 23, 1981), p. 5. Most information about the Simko uprising is from Martin van Bruinessen, "Kurdish Tribes and the State of Iran: The Case of Simko's Revolt," in Richard Tapper (ed.), *The Conflict of Tribe and State in Iran and Afghanistan* (London: Croom Helm, 1983), pp. 379–93. See also W. Eagleton, Jr., *The Kurdish Republic of 1946* (London: Oxford University Press, 1963). For an interesting observation on the Kurds and the Kurdish Mahabad Republic, see Cottam, *Nationalism*, pp. 65–74. The Kurdish political and military interconnectedness across the border is much stronger than that of other ethnic groups in Iran; see Nader Entessar, "The Kurds in Post-Revolutionary Iran and Iraq," *Third World Quarterly* 6 (October 1984), 911–33; Daniel G. Bates, "Kurd," in Weekes, *Muslim Peoples*, vol. I, p. 421. For the 1990s, see Human Rights Watch, *Iran*, p. 24.

Baluch

The Baluch numbers are taken from two sources: Robert G. Wirsing, *The Baluchis and Pathans* (London: Minority Rights Group, Report 48, 1981), p. 6; and Selig S. Harrison, *In Afghanistan's Shadow: Baluch Nationalism and Soviet Temptations* (New York: Carnegie Endowment for International Peace, 1981), pp. 1, 9. Harrison cites higher figures than the MRG report, but he admits that no accurate counts of the Iranian Baluch exist. Most of his sources are Pakistani or Baluch informants (p. 96). For an excellent analysis of Dost Mohammad and the 1930s breakdown and cooptation of tribal chiefs of the Yarahmadzai tribe, see Philip Carl Salzman, "Why Tribes Have Chiefs: A Case from Baluchistan," in Tapper, *Conflict of Tribe and State*, pp. 262–83. Mohammad Reza Shah's policy vis-à-vis the Iranian Baluch was meticulous and comprehensive; see Harrison, *Afghanistan's Shadow*, pp. 94–112; Philip C. Salzman, "The Proto-State in Iranian Baluchistan," in Ronald Cohen and Elman R. Service (eds.), *Origins of the State: An Anthropology of Political Evolution* (Philadelphia: Institute for the Study of Human Issues, 1978), pp. 125–40.

Qashqai

On Reza Shah's policy, see Paul Barker, "Tent Schools of the Qashqa'i: A Paradox of Local Initiative and State Control," in Michael E. Bonine and Nikki R. Keddie (eds.), *Continuity and Change in Modern Iran* (Albany: State University of New York, 1981), pp. 113–14; on Mohammad Reza Shah's policy, pp. 109–27; Lois Beck, *The Qashqa'i of Iran* (New Haven: Yale University Press, 1986), pp. 129–42, 271–86. See also Beck, "Nomads and Urbanites, Involuntary Hosts and Uninvited Guests," *Journal of Middle Eastern Studies* 18, no. 4 (1982), 426–44. Thanks to Lois Beck for the latest population figures.

Bakhtiari

David Brooks gives the number of 300,000 in "The Enemy Within: Limitations on Leadership in the Bakhtiari," in Tapper, *Conflict of Tribe and State*, p. 349; on elite integration, see p. 360. Gene R. Garthwaite estimates that some 500,000 Bakhtiari follow a traditional lifestyle; see his "Khans and Kings: The Dialectics of Power in Bakhtiyari History," in Bonine and

Keddie, *Continuity and Change*, p. 141. In another work, Garthwaite puts the total number of Bakhtiari at approximately 700,000; see his "Bakhtiari," in Weekes, *Muslim Peoples*, vol. I, p. 81. Sekandar Amanolahi (Baharvand), gives the largest number, 1 million, in *Kuchneshini dar Iran: Pazhuheshi Darbarehye Ashayer va Ilat* (Tehran: Bongah-e Tarjomeh va Nashr-e Ketab, 1360 [1981]), p. 200. On uprisings, see Abrahamian, *Iran*, p. 142.

Turkman
On Turkman numbers, see William G. Irons, "Turkmen," in Weekes, *Muslim Peoples*, vol. II, p. 804. On their revolts, see Hafez Farman Farmayan, "Turkoman Identity and Presence in Iran," *Journal of South Asian and Middle Eastern Studies* 4 (Summer 1981), 60. For details on the 1925 revolt, see Hassan Arfa, *Under Five Shahs* (London: William Morrow, 1964), pp. 166–85.

Arab
Lois Beck, "Revolutionary Iran and Its Tribal Peoples," *Middle East Research and Information Project* (May 1980), 16; Afshar, *Moqadamehi*, vol. I, p. 395; and for a long list of Arab tribes and nomads with number of households, see pp. 395–426. Rahmat Abad (a pseudonym) village was one example; see Grace E. Goodell, *The Elementary Structures of Political Life: Rural Development in Pahlavi Iran* (New York: Oxford University Press, 1986), p. 57. On uprisings, see Cottam, *Nationalism*, p. 115. Human Rights Watch, *Iran*, p. 31, states that 70 percent of the 3 million inhabitants of Khuzestan Province are Arab.

Shahsevan
Richard Tapper, "Shahsevan," in Weekes, *Muslim Peoples*, vol. II, p. 670. There are so many versions of the Shahsevan background that after an elaborate discussion Tapper concludes that the best answer to the question of "Who are the Shahsevan?" is: "depends on who is asked, when, for what purpose, and in what circumstances." See his "History and Identity Among the Shahsevan," *Iranian Studies* 21, nos. 3–4 (1988), 108. See also his *Frontier Nomads of Iran: A Political and Social History of the Shahsevan* (Cambridge: Cambridge University Press, 1997).

Lur:
Afshar, *Moqadamehi*, vol. I, p. 347, gives a mid-1980s estimate of 300,000, of whom 140,000 are migrant and semi-migrant nomads; Golamreza Fazel, "Lur," in Weekes, *Muslim Peoples*, vol. I, p. 446, gives the number 580,000 for the Lurs. For details on the Lurs, see Sekandar Amanolahi, "The Lurs of Iran," *Cultural Survival Quarterly* 9 (February 1985), 65–69.

40. Beck, "Revolutionary Iran," p. 16, states that they are evenly divided between Sunni and Shii. However, Human Rights Watch, *Iran*, p. 31, for the 1990s, writes that a great majority of Arabs are Shii.
41. Shaul Bakhash, "Center–Periphery Relations in Nineteenth-Century Iran," *Iranian Studies* 14, nos. 1–2 (Winter–Spring 1981), 29–51.
42. The usage of the term "(nation-)state" instead of "nation-state" is adopted from Ronen, *Quest*, p. xi. He uses this more unconventional expression because in most contemporary cases the nation and the state do not overlap.

    For a commentary on the meaning of the 1935 name change issue in diplomatic relations, see Ehsan Yarshater, "Communication," *Iranian Studies*

22, no. 1 (1989), 62–65; for a detailed analysis of the issue of dress codes, see Houchang E. Chehabi, "Staging the Emperor's New Clothes: Dress Codes and Nation-Building Under Reza Shah," *Iranian Studies* 26, nos. 3–4 (Summer–Fall 1993), 209–29.

43. For a brief list of altered place names, see Abrahamian, *Iran*, p. 143.

44. When reporting on the June 1990 earthquake in northwestern Iran, the *Los Angeles Times* correspondent focused on the village of Tarem, which was thoroughly destroyed. All its residents were identified as Kurds who were moved by Reza Shah from another area. There are small enclaves like this throughout Iran; see *Los Angeles Times*, 25 June 1990, p. A12.

45. Amanolahi, *Kuchneshini*, pp. 238–43.

46. Amanolahi, "Lurs of Iran," 69, and Harrison, *Afghanistan's Shadow*, pp. 93–126.

47. Richard F. Nyrop (ed.), *Iran: A Country Study* (Washington, DC: American University Press, 1978), p. 409.

48. *Ibid.*, p. 98.

49. Keith McLachlan, "The Iranian Economy, 1960–1976," in Hossein Amirsadeghi (ed.), *Twentieth-Century Iran* (New York: Holmes & Meier Publishers, 1977), pp. 129–69.

50. Cottam, *Nationalism*, p. 74; James Bill, "The Patterns of Elite Politics in Iran," in George Lenczowski (ed.), *Political Elites in the Middle East* (Washington, DC: American Enterprise Institute, 1975), p. 34.

51. Nikola B. Schahgaldian, *The Iranian Military Under the Islamic Republic* (Santa Monica, CA: Rand Corporation, 1987), p. 40.

52. Cheryl Benard and Zalmay Khalilzad, *The Government of God: Iran's Islamic Republic* (New York: Columbia University Press, 1984), p. 56.

53. *Surat-e Mashruh-e Mozakerat-e Majlis-e Barrasi-ye Nahaiye Qanun-e Asasiye Jomhuri-ye Islami-ye Iran* [hereafter *Proceedings*], 18th session (Tehran: Department of Cultural and Public Affairs of the Majlis, Azar 1364 [November/December 1985]), 25 Shahrivar 1358 [16 September 1979], pp. 454–72.

54. *Ibid.*, 26th session, 31 Shahrivar 1358 [22 September 1979], pp. 661–62. The specific reference was "Mazhab-e Haq."

55. H. E. Chehabi, "Ardabil Becomes a Province: Center–Periphery Relations in Iran," *International Journal of Middle East Studies* 29, no. 2 (May 1997), 249.

56. Hossein Bashiriyeh, *The State and Revolution in Iran, 1962–1982* (New York: St. Martin's Press, 1984); Nikki R. Keddie, "Islamic Revivalism Past and Present, with Emphasis on Iran," in Barry M. Rosen (ed.), *Iran Since the Revolution: Internal Dynamics, Regional Conflicts and the Superpowers* (New York: Brooklyn College Studies on Society in Change, Social Science Monographs 47, Boulder, distributed by Columbia University Press, 1985), pp. 11–12; see also Eliz Sanasarian, "Review Essay: Iran and the Revolution," *Iranian Studies* 19, nos. 3–4 (Summer–Autumn 1986), 285–87.

57. A. H. Hourani, *Minorities in the Arab World* (London: Oxford University Press, 1947), pp. 15–16.

58. See James A. Bill and Carl Leiden, *Politics in the Middle East*, 2nd edn. (Boston: Little, Brown & Co., 1984), pp. 38–73; Hourani, *Minorities*, pp.

15–32. For historical accounts, see A. J. Arberry (ed.), *Religion in the Middle East*, 2 vols. (Cambridge: Cambridge University Press, 1969); Sydney N. Fisher, *The Middle East: A History*, 3rd edn. (New York: Knopf, 1979); and Marshall G. S. Hodgson, *The Venture of Islam*, 3 vols. (Chicago: University of Chicago Press, 1974).

59. John L. Esposito, *Islam: The Straight Path* (Oxford: Oxford University Press, 1988), p. 15.

60. See the classic work of Fazlur Rahman, *Islam*, 2nd edn. (Chicago: University of Chicago Press, 1969). On women, see Leila Ahmed, *Women and Gender in Islam: Historical Roots of a Modern Debate* (New Haven: Yale University Press, 1992). On sunna (traditions of the Prophet), see Daniel W. Brown, *Rethinking Tradition in Modern Islamic Thought* (Cambridge: Cambridge University Press, 1996), esp. pp. 8–10.

61. H. A. R. Gibb and J. H. Kramers (eds.), *Shorter Encyclopaedia of Islam* (Ithaca: Cornell University Press, 1953), p. 17.

62. Some of the events that solidified these views were: the expulsion of the Jews from Arabia reportedly because the Prophet Mohammad did not want two religions in the area; the message from Abu Bakr, the first Rightful Caliph, to the Christians of Nadjran; and the treaty of Umar, the second Rightful Caliph, with the Christians of Jerusalem. Although the document – Ahd-e Umar – was developed later it bore Umar's name. See *ibid.*, pp. 16–17.

As to how Muslims see the corruption of the Torah and the New Testament by their adherents and an explanation for the expulsion of Jews from Arabia, see Esposito, *Islam*, pp. 21–22, 18.

63. Moojan Momen, *An Introduction to Shi'i Islam: The History and Doctrines of Twelver Shi'ism* (New Haven: Yale University Press, 1985), p. 177.

64. Maxime Rodinson, "The Notion of Minority in Islam," in Gerard Chaliand (ed.), *Minority Peoples in the Age of Nation-States* (London: Pluto Press, 1989), pp. 57–58.

65. Bat Ye'or, *The Dhimmi: Jews and Christians Under Islam*, transl. David Maisel, Paul Fenton, and David Littman (Toronto: Fairleigh Dickinson University Press, 1985), p. 155.

66. Abd al-Rahman Awang, "The Status of the Dhimmi in Islamic Law," Ph.D. thesis, University of Edinburgh (1988), pp. xvi, 1–16, 34, 120–22. This study is based on an elaborate review of old and new Islamic texts of law. The confusion over the term Ahl al-Ketab in one Islamic historian's work is explored by Herbert Berg, "Tabari's Exegesis of the Qur'anic Term 'Al-Kitab,'" *Journal of the American Academy of Religion* 63 (Winter 1995), 761–74.

67. Hourani, *Minorities*, p. 22.

68. Hamid Enayat, *Modern Islamic Political Thought* (Austin: University of Texas Press, 1982), p. 128.

69. Gibb and Kramers, *Shorter Encyclopaedia*, pp. 298–99.

70. Awang, "Status," p. 37.

71. Gibb and Kramers, *Shorter Encyclopaedia*, p. 300.

72. *Ibid.*, p. 298.

73. Enayat, *Modern*, pp. 25, 27–30.

74. Momen, *Introduction*, p. 233.

75. *Ibid.*, pp. 236–37 (quote on p. 237).

76. Enayat, *Modern*, p. 19.

77. See Enayat, *Modern*, p. 78; Albert Hourani, *Arabic Thought in the Liberal Age: 1798–1939* (Cambridge: Cambridge University Press, 1983), pp. 131–60. See also how Abduh used this method on women's issues: Muhammad Fadel, "Two Women, One Man: Knowledge, Power, and Gender in Medieval Sunni Legal Thought," *International Journal of Middle East Studies* 29 (May 1997), 187.

78. Ann Elizabeth Mayer, *Islam and Human Rights: Tradition and Politics* (Boulder: Westview Press, 1991), pp. 94–95.

79. Awang, "Status," p. 60.

80. *Ibid.*, pp. 59–66, 37, 40–48. Among the exemptions are: conversion, death, lapse of time, the state's inability to protect the non-Muslim minority, excusable difficulties such as poverty, old age, etc.

81. *Ibid.*, p. 330.

82. *Ibid.*, pp. 308–09.

83. Momen, *Introduction*, p. 116; Majlesi is covered on pp. 114–17. For a brief analysis of Majlesi's view on women, see Parvin Paidar, *Women and the Political Process in Twentieth-Century Iran* (Cambridge: Cambridge University Press, 1995), pp. 33–34.

84. Mohammad Baqer Majlesi, *Hilliyat al-Mottaqin* (n.p.: Elmieh-e Islamieh, n.d.), pp. 237–38.

85. Bernard Lewis, *The Jews of Islam* (Princeton: Princeton University Press, 1984), p. 85.

86. For a personal story of the use of codes of pollution against the Sunnis, see Muhammed Fazel, "The Politics of Passion: Growing Up Shia," *Iranian Studies* 21, nos. 3–4 (1988), pp. 37–51.

87. See the excellent work by Sorour Soroudi, "The Concept of Jewish Impurity and Its Reflection in Persian and Judeo-Persian Traditions," in Shaul Shaked and Amnon Netzer (eds.), *Irano-Judaica III* (Jerusalem: Ben-Zvi Institute, 1994), pp. 142–70.

88. Jamsheed K. Choksy, *Purity and Pollution in Zoroastrianism: Triumph over Evil* (Austin: University of Texas Press, 1989), p. 79.

89. *Ibid.*, p. 41.

90. Soroudi, "Concept," pp. 147–48.

91. *Ibid.*, p. 147; Soroudi provides examples of daily lives of Jews in Iran including personal experiences, variations, and exceptions to the rule. In concurrence with Soroudi, this author remembers that a weekly Muslim cleaning lady in her parents' residence in the city of Shiraz did not consider Christians to be najess but was fanatically insistent about the uncleanliness of the Jewish landlord. A fat woman, she would nevertheless always jump from the entrance door (downstairs) onto the first step leading to the second-floor apartment in order to avoid the tiny hallway between the outside door and the back door to the first floor, on which the residence of the Jewish family was located. The inhabitants of Fars province, particularly the residents of Jahrom and Shiraz, were obsessed with nejasat-consciousness; see Laurence D. Loeb, *Outcaste: Jewish Life in Southern Iran* (New York: Gordon & Breach Publishers, 1977).

92. Sultanhussein Tabandeh, *A Muslim Commentary on the Universal Declaration of Human Rights* (London: Goulding & Co., 1970), pp. x–xi. This book was brought to the author's attention during field work in Iran as the core ideological work upon which the Iranian government had based its non-Muslim policy.

93. *Ibid.*, pp. 13–14.

94. *Ibid.*, p. 4.

95. *Ibid.*, pp. 17–19.

96. *Ibid.*, p. 34. The comment is a reference to religions that worship through images such as Buddhism and Hinduism.

97. *Ibid.*, pp. 36–37.

98. *Ibid.*, p. 70.

99. *Ibid.*, pp. 70–71.

100. *Ibid.*, pp. 71–72 (quote on p. 72).

101. *Ibid.*, pp. 72–73.

102. *Ibid.*, p. 71.

103. Mayer, *Islam*, p. 152. She accurately reflects on the relationship in Tabandeh's views between the inferiority of the non-Muslim and women (pp. 150–52).

104. Morteza Motahhari, *Adl-e Elahi* (Tehran: Hosseinieh-ye Ershad, 1349 [1970/71]), quote on p. 202; comments on pp. 202–04.

105. *Ibid.*, pp. 240–41.

106. *Ibid.*, pp. 243, 247.

107. Hamid Dabashi, *Theology of Discontent: The Ideological Foundation of the Islamic Revolution in Iran* (New York: New York University Press, 1993), p. 331. He paraphrases from Mehdi Bazargan, *Az Khoda-Parasti ta Khod-Parasti* (Houston: Book Distribution Center, 1355 [1976]), p. 78.

108. Seyyed Mahmud Taleqani, *Partovi az Quran*, vol. I (Tehran: Sahami-ye Enteshar, 1358 [1979]), p. 260.

109. Ayatollah Ruhollah Khomeini, *Velayat-e Faqih va Jehad-e Akbar* (Tehran: Nasr Publishers, n.d.), pp. 95–96.

110. The overall content of the brief speech shows Khomeini's deep resentment for the Iraqi government: Khomeini, *Majmuehi az Maktoobat, Sokhanraniha, Payamha va Fatavi-ye Imam Khomeini az Nimeye Dovom 1341 ta Hejrat be Paris (14 Mehr 1357)* (Tehran: Chanchesh, 1360 [1981/82]), pp. 188–89.

111. Khomeini, *Imam dar Barabar-e Sayhonism: Majmueh-ye Didgahha va Sokhanan-e Imam Darbareh-ye Regim-e Eshqalgar-e Qods* (Tehran: Daftar-e Siasi-ye Sepah-e Pasdaran-e Enqelab-e Islami, 1361 [1982]), p. 18.

112. *Ibid.*, p. 20.

113. Khomeini, *Majmuehi*, p. 82.

114. *Ibid.*, p. 50. The speech shifts back and forth between Israel and the Jews; see p. 49.

115. *Ibid.*, p. 111.

116. *Ibid.*, p. 172.

117. *Ibid.*, p. 175.

118. *Ibid.*, pp. 176–77.

119. Imam Khomeini, *Resaleh-ye Ahkam* (Tehran: Ismailian, n.d.), pp. 26, 28.

120. Khomeini, *Imam dar Barabar-e*, p. 114.

121. Khomeini, *The Imam Versus Zionism* (Tehran: Ministry of Islamic Guidance, 1984), p. 51.
122. Khomeini, *Majmuehi*, p. 11.
123. Khomeini, *Resaleh-ye Ahkam*, p. 29.
124. Khomeini, *Majmuehi*, p. 277.
125. *Ibid.*, pp. 316–17, 279. The term "gabr" has various meanings; it was often a reference to ancient Persians. The word means a helmet but its use by the Shii clerical circles means infidel or pagan.
126. Khomeini, *Imam dar Barabar-e*, p. 13.
127. Ayatollah Allameh Nuri, *Hokumat-e Islami va Tahlili az Nehzat-e Hazer* (Tehran: Bonyad-e Elmi va Islami, 2nd edn., in English and Farsi, 1360 [1981/82]), pp. 30–31. (The book is a collection of interviews with Nuri.)
128. Ayatollah Yahya Noori [Nuri], "The Islamic Concept of State," *Hamdard Islamicus* 3, no. 3 (Autumn 1980), 85.
129. United Nations, Economic and Social Council, Commission on Human Rights, 47th session, Agenda Item 12, *Report on the Human Rights Situation in the Islamic Republic of Iran by the Special Representative of the Commission on Human Rights, Mr. Reynaldo Galindo Pohl, Pursuant to Commission Resolution 1990/79*, E/CN.4/1991/35, 13 February 1991, pp. 90–91.
130. For the Zoroastrian case, see International Solidarity Front for the Defense of the Iranian People's Democratic Rights (ISF-Iran), *The Crimes of Khomeini's Regime* (n.p.: ISF-Iran, May 1982), p. 50. Several prominent Zoroastrians categorically dismissed the occurrence of this event in Yazd or anywhere else in Iran. The latter case was reported in *Iran Times*, 7 December 1984, p. 15.
131. *Christian Mission to the Communist World, Inc.* reveled in such accounts; see particularly September 1988 and April 1989 issues.
132. H. H. Gerth and C. Wright Mills (eds.), *From Max Weber: Essays in Sociology* (New York: Oxford University Press, 1958), p. 233.
133. James A. Bill, *The Eagle and the Lion: The Tragedy of American–Iranian Relations* (New Haven: Yale University Press, 1988), p. 10.
134. Momen, *Introduction*, p. 194.
135. This issue is reiterated in different sections of Abrahamian's *Iran*. See also Abrahamian, "Communism and Communalism in Iran: The Tudeh and the Firqah-i Dimukrat," *International Journal of Middle East Studies* 1, no. 4 (October 1970), 291–316.
136. This was common knowledge; it was also pointed out in an editorial by Shireen T. Hunter, "Soviet Approach to Iran Outruns Complacent West," *Los Angeles Times*, 17 July 1989, Part II, p. 11.
137. See Homa Nategh, interview recorded by Zia Sedghi, 1 April 1984, Paris, France, tape 3, p. 13, Iranian Oral History Collection, Harvard University.

1 ETHNIC ANATOMY AND POLITICS OF NON-MUSLIM MINORITIES

1. See George A. Bournoutian, *Eastern Armenia in the Last Decades of Persian Rule, 1807–1828* (Malibu, CA: Undena Publications, 1982); Bournoutian, *A History of the Armenian People: Pre-History to 1500 AD* (Costa Mesa, CA: Mazda Publishers, 1994). For a brief account of the Armenian diaspora

worldwide, see David Marshall Lang and Christopher J. Walker, *The Armenians* (London: Minority Rights Group, Report 32, 1982).

2. For historical details, see Richard G. Hovannisian, *Armenia on the Road to Independence, 1918* (Berkeley: University of California Press, 1967); Hovannisian, *The Republic of Armenia, Vol. I: The First Year, 1918–1919* (Berkeley: University of California Press, 1971). Modern Armenian nationality is explored by Ronald Grigor Suny, *Looking Toward Ararat: Armenia in Modern History* (Bloomington: Indiana University Press, 1993).

3. James R. Russell, *Zoroastrianism in Armenia* (Cambridge, MA: Harvard University Press, 1987), pp. 3, 6. See also his "Christianity in Pre-Islamic Persia: Literary Sources," in *Encyclopaedia Iranica*, ed. Ehsan Yarshater (vols. I–IV, Boston: Routledge & Kegan Paul, 1985–90; vols. V–VIII, Costa Mesa, CA: Mazda Press, 1992–98), vol. V, pp. 523–28. For detailed accounts of each Persian dynasty and Armenia, see various subheadings under "Armenia and Iran," in *Encyclopaedia Iranica*, vol. II. For the close connection between the Persians and the Armenians during the Arsacid Dynasty, see Bournoutian, *History*.

4. For an interesting account of the origins, development, and numbers of Armenian residents in Persia in every city, town, and village, see H. L. Pahlavanian, *Iranahay Hamaynk: 1941–1979* (Erevan, Armenia: Khach Ga Publishers, 1989), pp. 20–41.

5. For a thorough account of the story of the forced migration and subsequent perils, see *Patmutiwn Nor Jughayi*, originally compiled by Harutiun T. Ter Hovhanyants in 1880 (Isfahan: New Julfa Vank, vol. I, 1980, vol. II, 1981); Vartan Gregorian, "Minorities of Isfahan: The Armenian Community of Isfahan, 1587–1722," *Iranian Studies* 7, nos. 3–4 (Summer–Autumn 1974), 652–80. See also Paul G. Forand, "Accounts of Western Travelers Concerning the Role of Armenians and Georgians in Sixteenth-Century Iran," *Muslim World* 65, no. 4 (October 1975), 266–67.

6. For an account of the conflicting sources and their significance, see Edmund M. Herzig, "The Deportation of the Armenians in 1604–1605 and Europe's Myth of Shah Abbas I," in Charles Melville (ed.), *Persian and Islamic Studies in Honor of P. W. Avery*, Pembroke Papers I (Cambridge: Cambridge University Press, 1990), pp. 59–71.

7. For eyewitness accounts, see Forand, "Accounts," 268–70.

8. Ismail Rain, *Iranian-e Armani* (Tehran: Tehran Publishers, 1949), p. 41.

9. Abrahamian, *Iran*, pp. 97–100, 110–11; Cosroe Chaqueri, "The Role and Impact of Armenian Intellectuals in Iranian Politics, 1905–1911," *Armenian Review* 41 (Summer 1988), 1–51. Chaqueri argues that, in comparison with other non-Muslim religious minorities, Armenians were more dynamic actors intellectually, politically, and militarily (pp. 48–49); see also Chaqueri, "Sultanzade: The Forgotten Revolutionary Theoretician of Iran: A Biographical Sketch," *Iranian Studies* 17, nos. 2–3 (Spring–Summer 1984), 215–35. The probable motivation behind the participation of some Armenians in the Constitutional Revolution of 1905–11 is discussed by Houri Berberian, "The Dashnaktsutiun and the Iranian Constitutional Revolution, 1905–1911," *Iranian Studies* 29, nos. 1–2 (Winter–Spring 1996), 7–33. For the Armenian role in the nationalist movement during

World War I, see Aram Arkun, "Armenians and the Jangalis," *Iranian Studies* 30, nos. 1–2 (Winter–Spring 1997), 25–52. For the role of Dashnak in the Constitutional Revolution, see Aram Arkun, "Dashnak," in *Encyclopaedia Iranica*, vol. VII, pp. 90–94. See also Janet Afary, *The Iranian Constitutional Revolution, 1906–1911: Grassroots Democracy, Social Democracy, and the Origins of Feminism* (New York: Columbia University Press, 1996), in which she explores the overall impact of all liberal and democratic groups in the formulation of the first constitution of Iran.

10. Pahlavanian, *Iranahay*, pp. 107, 111. He states that in 1909 for every 50,000 individuals there was one deputy; Armenians, numbering 100,000, asked for two deputies and were refused. Therefore, until the fifth Majlis (1925–27), they had only one deputy. See also "The Place of Islam in the Persian Constitution," *Muslim World* 1, no. 3 (July 1911), 341–42.

11. Abrahamian, *Iran*, p. 163.

12. Pahlavanian, *Iranahay*, p. 110.

13. Thanks to Ervand Abrahamian for this information.

14. Mohammad H. Faghfoory, "The Ulama–State Relations in Iran: 1921–1941," *International Journal of Middle East Studies* 19 (November 1987), 415 and 429, n. 4.

15. For a typical perspective on the Armenians, see the 15 January 1969 issue of the Tehran-based *Kayhan International*; the articles were reprinted in Amir Taheri, "Deep Roots in the Land," *Armenian Review* 22, no. 2 (Summer 1969), 45–48; and Edwin Leane, "The Second Renaissance," in the same issue, 48–50.

16. The only possible exception to this may be the Bahais. The number of Bahais in Iran is estimated to be between 150,000 and 300,000; see Roger Cooper, *The Bahais of Iran* (London: Minority Rights Group, Report 51, 1982), p. 7. While 300,000 may be an inflated figure, it is doubtful that the number of Bahais in Iran has increased since the Revolution and, in fact, it is likely that there has been a substantial decrease due to severe persecution and emigration. Official statistics put the estimated number of Armenians during the mid-1970s at 250,000; see *Iran Almanac 1977* (Tehran: Echo of Iran, 16th edn., 1977), p. 394.

17. *Iran Times*, 23 January 1987, p. 6, based on an interview with Archbishop Artak Manukian, prelate of the Armenian Apostolic Church. See also David Zenian, "The Islamic Revolution: A Blessing in Disguise for Iranian-Armenians," *AGBU [Armenian General Benevolent Union] News*, September 1991, 8–11.

18. This information is taken mainly from John Joseph's work on the Nestorians. For a comprehensive dissection of each of these groups and their relevance to ancient Assyrians, see John Joseph, *The Nestorians and Their Muslim Neighbors: A Study of Western Influence on Their Relations* (Princeton: Princeton University Press, 1961), pp. 3–18.

19. John Joseph, *Muslim–Christian Relations and Inter-Christian Rivalries in the Middle East: The Case of the Jacobites in an Age of Transition* (Albany: State University of New York Press, 1983), p. 150, n. 25.

20. Eden Naby, "The Iranian Frontier Nationalities: The Kurds, the Assyrians, the Baluchis, and the Turkmens," in William McCragg, Jr., and Brian Silver

(eds.), *Soviet Asian Frontiers* (New York: Pergamon Press, 1979), p. 84, n. (e).

21. Jay M. Rasooli and Cady H. Allen, *The Life Story of Dr. Sa'eed of Iran: Kurdish Physician to Princes and Peasants, Nobles and Nomads* (Pasadena, CA: William Carey Library, 1983), p. 23, n. 9.

22. Joseph Yacoub, *The Assyrian Question* (Chicago: Alpha Graphics, 1986), p. 5.

23. Arian Ishaya, "Family and Household Composition Among the Assyrians of Iran: The Past and the Present," in A. Fathi (ed.), *Women and the Family in Iran* (Leiden: E. J. Brill, 1985), p. 215. See also Ishaya, *The Role of Minorities in the State: History of the Assyrian Experience* (Winnipeg: University of Manitoba Anthropology Papers 19, 1977), p. 6. On p. 7, she provides estimates of Assyrian population throughout the world. In fact, here the present-day Assyrian national claim is that anyone whose mother tongue is Syriac and is referred as a "Syrian Christian" is an Assyrian. This expanded definition includes not only the Chaldeans but also the Jacobites, the Nestorians, and the Maronites who strongly reject it (pp. 10–15).

   A similar view was communicated to the author by Archbishop Yohannan Issayi in Tehran, in 1992. He explained that after 1918 many Chaldeans began to refer to themselves as Assyrians; therefore, today it can be said that among Assyrians there are Catholics, Protestants, and Nestorians. Yet, the author is aware that many Chaldeans will strongly disagree with this definition. With dwindling population, intermarriages with Armenians and other Christians, and migration out of the country, the issue of national identity remains a dubious one.

24. R. Macuch, "Assyrians in Iran: The Assyrian Community (Asurian) in Iran," in *Encyclopaedia Iranica*, vol. II, p. 820. He explains that sometimes, in order to magnify the concept and identity of Assyrians, their ethnic identity has been "overextended to all Oriental Christians, even to Ethiopians" (p. 819).

25. *Proceedings*, 61st session, 15 Aban 1358 [6 November 1979], pp. 1667–68.

26. Yacoub, *Assyrian Question*, p. 5.

27. Joseph, *Nestorians*, pp. 38–39.

28. *Ibid.*, pp. 120–29.

29. Richard Merrill Schwartz, *The Structure of Christian–Muslim Relations in Contemporary Iran*, Occasional Papers in Anthropology 13 (Halifax, Canada: Saint Mary's University, 1985), pp. 51–52.

30. Eden Naby, "The Assyrians of Iran: Reunification of a Millat, 1906–1914," *International Journal of Middle East Studies* 8, no. 2 (April 1977), 239–40, 245.

31. Macuch, "Assyrians," p. 820.

32. Using primary sources, Naby sets out to demonstrate these points in her "Assyrians." On the missionary influence, see Schwartz, *Structure*, pp. 45–46, 60. He states that, in contrast to Urmieh Christians, the missionaries did not keep a low profile and were extremely vocal (p. 63). See also Schwartz, "Missionaries on the Rezaiyeh Plain, Iran," *Muslim World* 69, no. 2 (April 1979), 77–100.

33. Compare differing accounts by Joseph, *Nestorians*, pp. 134–38, for the

Hakkari Nestorians, and pp. 138–44 for the Iranian Nestorians; and van Bruinessen, "Kurdish Tribes," pp. 384–86.

34. The killings intensified when the Kurdish group led by Simko and the local Azeris formed a coalition against Christians. At the instigation of the Tabriz Azeri governor, Simko invited the Nestorian patriarch for apparent peace talks, but killed him and his escorts. Shortly after this the Turkish army invaded the region and continued the massacre of Christians. Simko's forces joined with the Turks and killed many escaping Nestorians; see Schwartz, *Structure*, pp. 54–55; and Joseph, *Nestorians*, p. 144.

35. Joseph states that the delegation claimed most of northern Mesopotamia; see his *Nestorians*, pp. 153–55.

36. *Ibid.*, p. 158.

37. Naby indicates that their permanent settlement in the West had taken place as early as 1911: "Assyrians," 246, n. 48.

38. See Joseph, *Nestorians*, p. 225; and Schwartz, *Structure*, p. 85. For an indepth historical analysis of these events, see Husry's two articles, in which he argues that the Assyrians of the Hakkari region attempted to manipulate the British. The British tried to accommodate the Assyrians because of the support of the Archbishop of Canterbury. The massacre was the eventual outcome of the ambitious and inflexible Mar Shimun XXI who was educated in the seminary at Canterbury. He asked for temporal authority from the Iraqi government and refused the government's offer to recognize him as the spiritual head of the Nestorian Church in Iraq; see Khaldun S. Husry, "The Assyrian Affair of 1933 (I)," *International Journal of Middle East Studies* 5, no. 2 (April 1974), 161–76; and his "Assyrian Affair of 1933 (II)," *International Journal of Middle East Studies* 5, no. 3 (June 1974), 344–60.

39. According to personal communication to the author by Archbishop Yohannan Issayi in Tehran in 1992, one of the main causes of the reduction of the Assyrian and Chaldean population in villages was the major earthquake of 1930 that destroyed over one hundred villages.

40. Ishaya, "Family," p. 221; and *Iran Almanac 1977*, p. 394.

41. Communicated to the author by Archbishop Yohannan Issayi in Tehran in 1992.

42. A famous Chaldean developer, Aziz Georges Safiri (d. 1968), played an important role in the industrial development of Ahvaz. He built the first Chaldean church there and was the pope's official representative for the Christians of southern Iran. For a list of Christian churches by title, language, patriarchal seat, and religious offshoots in the Middle East, see Joseph, *Muslim–Christian*, pp. 144–46. In a 1992 interview, Joseph Habbi, a priest and dean of the Chaldean Philosophical and Theological College in Baghdad, estimated that there were some 700,000 Christians within the 18 million population of Iraq, the majority among them being Chaldeans; see Thalia Griffiths, "Iraqi Christians See Little Festive Cheer," Reuters, Baghdad, 20 December 1992.

43. For Christians and Christianity in Persia in pre-Islamic times, see Russell, "Christianity," pp. 523–28, and Werner Sundermann, "Christ in Manicheism," in *Encyclopaedia Iranica*, vol. V, pp. 535–39. For Christian missions, see Yahya Armajani, "Christians – Christian Missions in Persia,"

in *Encyclopaedia Iranica*, vol. V, pp. 544–47. For smaller missionary societies, see Robin E. Waterfield, *Christians in Persia: Assyrians, Armenians, Roman Catholics and Protestants* (London: George Allen & Unwin Ltd., 1973), pp. 175–76.

44. Waterfield, *Christians*, p. 165.
45. Joseph, *Muslim–Christian*, pp. 38–39.
46. Schwartz, "Missionaries," 81.
47. Waterfield, *Christians*, p. 169.
48. H. B. Dehqani Tafti, *Moshkel-e Eshq* (Newport Beach, CA: Gutenberg Press, 1364 [1985/86]), p. 28.
49. *Ibid.*, pp. 44–46.
50. *Armenian International Magazine [AIM]* 5 (August–September 1994), 16.
51. Shlomo Deshen and Walter P. Zenner (eds.), *Jewish Societies in the Middle East: Community, Culture and Authority* (Washington, DC: University Press of America, 1982), p. 3.
52. Young, *Politics*, p. 56.
53. Waterfield, *Christians*, p. 112; and Habib Levy, *Tarikh-e Yahood-e Iran*, vol. II, 2nd edn. (Beverly Hills, CA: Iranian Jewish Cultural Organization of California, 1984), pp. 211–12. Levy's work, despite being comprehensive and raising many important issues, is not considered an objective assessment of the history of Iranian Jewry. Yet the contribution is significant for its passionate oratory on the Jewish perils and its early publication date in Iran (1956 and 1960).
54. Amnon Netzer, "Persian Jewry and Literature: A Sociocultural View," in Harvey E. Goldberg (ed.), *Sephardi and Middle Eastern Jewries: History and Culture in the Modern Era* (Bloomington: Indiana University Press, 1996), pp. 240–55.
55. J. Lassner, "Abu Isa Esfahani," in *Encyclopaedia Iranica*, vol. I, p. 324.
56. This view was reenforced because of what followed the Safavid rule. Nader Shah Afshar (r. 1736–47), originally a Shii, declared himself a Sunni upon ascending to the throne. In return for turning all Persians into Sunnis, he tried to make Shiism another Sunni legal school (Jafari), to no avail. During his reign Jewish persecution was reduced and Christians and Jews were hired at his court. The impact of the Safavid dynasty and Shiism is discussed in several works; see Vera B. Moreen, "The Status of Religious Minorities in Safavid Iran 1617–1661," *Journal of Near Eastern Studies* 40 (April 1981), 119–34; Moreen, "The Persecution of Iranian Jews During the Reign of Shah 'Abbas II (1642–1666)," *Hebrew Union College Annual* 52 (1981), 275–309; Moreen, "The Downfall of Muhammad Ali Beg, Grand Vizier of Shah Abbas II (Reigned 1642–1666)," *Jewish Quarterly Review* 72 (October 1981), 81–99; Moreen, *Iranian Jewry's Hour of Peril and Heroism: A Study of Babai Ibn Lutf's Chronicle (1617–1662)* (Jerusalem: American Academy for Jewish Research, 1987); Amnon Netzer, "The Fate of the Jewish Community of Tabriz," in M. Sharon (ed.), *Studies in Islamic History and Civilization in Honour of Professor David Ayalon* (Leiden: E. J. Brill, 1986), pp. 412–13. See also Walter J. Fischel, "The Jews in Medieval Iran from the Sixteenth to the Eighteenth Centuries: Political, Economic, and Communal Aspects," in Shaul Shaked (ed.), *Irano-Judaica: Studies Relating to Jewish*

Contacts with Persian Culture (Jerusalem: Ben-Zvi Institute for the Study of Jewish Communities in the East, 1982), pp. 277–81, 287; he has a fascinating account about a disgruntled Jew who invented a badge and with the help of some local clergy had it enforced on his own Jewish community (pp. 275–76). See also Fischel, "Secret Jews of Persia: A Century-Old Marrano Community," *Commentary*, January 1949, 28–33; and Roger Savory, *Iran Under the Safavids* (Cambridge: Cambridge University Press, 1980), p. 231.

57. Bernard Lewis, "The Decline and Fall of Islamic Jewry," *Commentary* June 1984, 45.

58. *Ibid.*, 46, and extensive discussions in Bernard Lewis, *Semites and Anti-Semites: An Inquiry into Conflict and Prejudice* (New York: W. W. Norton & Company, 1986). In the case of Iran, after the pogroms of Tabriz Jews, the city ceased to become a Jewish stronghold: Netzer, "The Fate," pp. 411–16. Laurence D. Loeb emphasizes economic rivalry between Armenians and Jews in the cities of Isfahan and Shiraz, especially in wine-making and music. Their rivalry, he states, continued well into the nineteenth century, resulting in a victory for the Jews in Shiraz and the Armenians in Isfahan; see Loeb, "Dhimmi Status and Jewish Roles in Iranian Society," *Ethnic Groups* (December 1976), 104, n. 3.

59. Walter J. Fischel, "The Jews of Persia, 1795–1940," *Jewish Social Studies* 12, no. 2 (April 1950), 139–41. The protests of British officials led to reprimand by the king of the local religious leaders; see Mangol Bayat, *Iran's First Revolution: Shi'ism and the Constitutional Revolution of 1905–1909* (New York: Oxford University Press, 1991), p. 17. See also Michael M. Laskier, "Aspects of the Activities of the Alliance Israelite Universelle in the Jewish Communities of the Middle East and North Africa: 1860–1918," *Modern Judaism* 3, no. 3 (October 1983), 152–53; Avraham Cohen, "Iranian Jewry and the Educational Endeavors of the Alliance Israelite Universelle," *Jewish Social Studies* 48, no. 1 (Winter 1986), 15–44; Amnon Netzer, "Alliance Israelite Universelle," in *Encyclopaedia Iranica*, vol. I, p. 894.

60. Abrahamian, *Iran*, p. 105; Fischel, "Jews of Persia," 142–43. Levy states that there was a deputy named Azizolah Simani, but he lasted only a few days because of the hatred and disgust shown to him. Therefore, the Jews were represented by Hojat al-Islam Seyyed Abdollah Behbahani: Levy, *Tarikh-e*, vol. III, pp. 847–48. For details of events and the reaction of Jewish community, see Janet Afary, "Enqelab-e Mashruteh," in Homa Sarshar (ed.), *Yahudian-e Irani dar Tarikh-e Moaser*, vol. II (Beverly Hills: Center for Iranian Jewish Oral History, 1997), pp. 35–53.

61. Levy reports on anti-Jewish writings in the media by what he calls the pro-Hitler Iranians (*Tarikh-e*, vol. III, pp. 969–71); Abrahamian states that the Jewish deputy in the Majlis, Samuel Haim, was suddenly executed in 1931 (*Iran*, p. 163). Although Abrahamian provides no details, Haim's execution sheds light on the intercommunity rivalry during that time. There are two distinct views on Haim. Davoud Adhami's extensive research portrays him as a hero who cared deeply and worked relentlessly for the welfare of the Jewish community. He was undermined by his Jewish and Muslim enemies in government, especially Abdol-Hossein Taimurtash, Reza Shah's court minister. They spread the rumor that Haim was a British spy and involved in

a failed coup d'état against Reza Shah; see Adhami, *Besooye Kemal* (New York: Parkway Printing, 1996), pp. 149–341; on his execution, pp. 300–03. Levy, strongly pro-Pahlavi, is less enthusiastic about Haim; he admits his strong and courageous character and that he had enemies among conservative Jews, but justifies their enmity for fear of Haim's "extremism" and calls Haim's supporters "idealists." While Levy is circumspect on Haim's involvement in the coup plot, he praises Reza Shah for not holding the whole Jewish community responsible for the actions of one man: *Tarikh-e,* vol. III, pp. 947, 956.

62. Jaleh Pirnazar, "Jang-e Jahaniye Dovom va Jameeh-ye Yahud dar Iran," in Homa Sarshar (ed.), *Terua: Yahudian-e Irani dar Tarikh-e Moaser,* vol. I (Beverly Hills: Center for Iranian Jewish Oral History, 1996), pp. 99, 104–05.

63. Thanks to Mr. Fariar Nikbakht for sharing his research with me. Long before the arrival of the first group of Iraqi Jews in Iran, strong trade and family connections did exist between Jews of Hamadan, Kermanshah, and Baghdad.

64. Amnon Netzer, "Anjoman-e Kalimian," in *Encyclopaedia Iranica,* vol. II, p. 85. He states that 30,769 Jews or more than one-third of the Jewish population of Iran emigrated to Israel.

65. *Asnad-e Mohajerat-e Yahudian-e Iran be Felestin: 1300–1330 Hejrieh Shamsi,* compil. Marzieh Yazdani (Tehran: Entesharat-e Sazeman-e Asnad-e Melli-ye Iran, 1374 [1995/96]), pp. 100, 251.

66. Netzer, "Persian Jewry and Literature," p. 251. A short autobiographical piece by a Jewish girl clearly captures the Jewish identity issue; see Mehri Niknam, "A Jewish Childhood in Iran," *European Judaism* 28, no. 2 (Autumn 1995), 99–101. For further details on the lives of Iranian Jewish communities, see the memoirs of the Jewish deputy to the Majlis from 1975 to 1979, in Yousef Cohen, *Gozaresh va Khaterat-e Faaliethaye Siasi va Ejtemai* (Los Angeles: International Printing–Yousef Cohen Foundation, 1993).

67. David Sitton, *Sephardi Communities Today* (Jerusalem: Council of Sephardi and Oriental Communities, 1985), p. 184.

68. Heskel M. Haddad, *Jews of Arab and Islamic Countries* (New York: Shengold Publishers, Inc., 1984), p. 50.

69. Sitton, *Sephardi Communities,* p. 184.

70. Uri Bialer argues that, in order to help save the Iraqi Jews and to avert its political isolation, the newly founded state of Israel attempted to gain recognition from Iran, and, by bribing top-level officials, gained de facto recognition in 1950. See Bialer, "The Iranian Connection in Israel's Foreign Policy: 1948–1951," *Middle East Journal* 39 (Spring 1985), 292–315. See also Farhad Kazemi, "Iran, Israel, and the Arab–Israeli Balance," in Rosen, *Iran Since the Revolution,* pp. 83–95; and Rouhollah K. Ramazani, *Revolutionary Iran* (Baltimore: Johns Hopkins University Press, 1986), pp. 149–51.

71. *Iran Almanac 1977,* p. 394; *New York Times,* 13 May 1979, p. A9; 28 May 1979, p. A5; *The Economist,* 14 June 1980, p. 46.

72. *The Economist,* 7 February 1987, p. 40; John Simpson, "Along the Streets of Tehran: Life Under Khomeini," *Harper's Magazine,* January 1988, 36–45.

The latest reported number is 35,000; see *Iran Times*, 9 August 1996, p. 5. Several informed people have found 35,000 to be too high and an unrealistic figure considering the large exodus of Iranian Jews from the country. They suggest that the inflated size is concocted by the present leadership of the Jewish community in order to boost their own standing with the regime.

73. Ann Boyce believes Zarathushtra came to the scene when the Stone Age was giving way to the Bronze Age in Iran; see Boyce, *Zoroastrians: Their Religious Beliefs and Practices* (London: Routledge & Kegan Paul, 1979), pp. 1–2; for her explanation as to reasons for diversity in place and time of the existence of Zoroaster, see Boyce, *Textual Sources for the Study of Zoroastrianism* (Manchester: Manchester University Press, 1984), p. 15.

74. Boyce, *Zoroastrians*, pp. 1, 101–44; on various characteristics of Zoroastrianism and its dualism, such as the conflict between Truth and Falsehood, Matter and Spirit, Good and Evil, see William W. Malandra (ed. and transl.), *An Introduction to Ancient Iranian Religion: Readings from the Avesta and Achaemenid Inscriptions* (Minneapolis: University of Minnesota Press, 1983), pp. 19–23. For a religious interpretation of Zoroastrianism, see T. R. Sethna, *Amoozeshhaye Zarthosht: Payambar-e Iran*, trans. and commentary by Mobed Rostam Shahzadi (Karachi, Pakistan: Farhangarayi, 1975); and Mobed Bahram Shahzadi, *Message of Zarathushtra*, Religious Instruction, vol. I (Westminster: California Zoroastrian Center, 1986).

75. Jamsheed K. Choksy, "Zoroastrians in Muslim Iran: Selected Problems of Coexistence and Interaction During the Early Medieval Period," *Iranian Studies* 20, no. 1 (1987), 17–30.

76. Malandra, *Introduction*, p. 30.

77. Reports of such visits from India to Karaj, Shiraz, Kerman, Yazd, and Isfahan appear in *Cheesta*, 3rd year, no. 3, Azar 1364 [November 1985], p. 238.

78. Paul Ward English, "Nationalism, Secularism, and the Zoroastrians of Kerman: The Impact of Modern Forces on an Ancient Middle Eastern Minority," in Fred E. Dohrs and Lawrence M. Sommers (eds.), *Cultural Geography: Selected Readings* (New York: Thomas Y. Crowell, 1967), p. 277.

79. Jahangir Ashideri, *Tarikh-e Pahlavi va Zarthoshtian* (Tehran: Mahnameye Hokht, 2535 [1976]), pp. 437–39.

80. Shahrokh Shahrokh and Rashna Writer (eds. and transls.), *The Memoirs of Keikhosrow Shahrokh* (Lewiston, NY: Edwin Mellen Press, 1994), p. 51, n. 46.

81. Bayat, *Iran's First Revolution*, pp. 190–91. See also Ashideri, *Tarikh-e*, pp. 240–54.

82. Bayat, *Iran's First Revolution*, pp. 144–45. Her research credits the wealth and connections of Arbab Jamshid Bahman Jamshidian, successful merchant and the first Zoroastrian deputy to the Majlis. Lacking the same clout, the Armenians were represented by Mohammad Tabatabai and the Jews by Abdollah Behbahani. On Arbab Jamshid, see Shahrokh and Writer, *Memoirs of Keikhosrow*, pp. 57–60.

83. Malandra, *Introduction*, pp. 5–6; Abrahamian, *Iran*, p. 143. Boyce, *Zoroastrians*, pp. 220–21, states that an ardent Muslim-born nationalist, Ibrahim Poor-Davood, was the main instigator of this ideology. He bor-

rowed the suitable aspects from Zoroastrianism, and the community, having been treated poorly and having been marginalized for so long, naturally welcomed the attention and interest of the new state.

84. Abrahamian, in *Iran*, asserts that Keikhosrow "was gunned down in the street by the police in 1940 because his son in Germany, against his father's wishes, had broadcast a series of pro-Nazi speeches" (p. 163); Ashideri states that Keikhosrow died suddenly and mysteriously at sixty-six while returning from a wedding (*Tarikh-e*, p. 389).

85. Abrahamian writes about the Tudeh in Yazd and among the Zoroastrians (*Iran*, p. 302).

86. *Cheesta*, 4th year, no. 1, Shahrivar 1365 [September 1986], p. 15.

87. *Los Angeles Times*, 24 August 1985, Part II, p. 16.

88. *Iran Almanac 1977*, p. 394.

89. FBIS, 21 May 1993, p. 60.

90. See D. M. MacEoin, "Bab, Sayyed Ali Mohammad," pp. 278–84, "Babism," pp. 309–17, both in *Encyclopaedia Iranica*, vol. III; and in the same volume, Juan Cole, "Bahai Faith or Bahaism," p. 438; Peter Smith, *The Babi and Baha'i Religions: From Messianic Shi'ism to a World Religion* (New York: Cambridge University Press, 1987), pp. 5–71.

91. Abbas Amanat, *Resurrection and Renewal: The Making of the Babi Movement in Iran, 1844–1850* (Ithaca: Cornell University Press, 1989), p. 407.

92. Cole, "Bahai Faith," p. 439.

93. The clearest and simplest description as to the relationship between Bab and Bahaullah is provided by Fischel. He writes that Bahaullah "was looked upon as the real prophet, the Bab being considered only as his precursor and herald, whose relations to him were somewhat like those of John the Baptist to Jesus." See Fischel, "Jews of Persia," 152; for an excellent condensed account of Bahaullah's life, see Cole, "Baha-Allah," in *Encyclopaedia Iranica*, vol. III, pp. 422–29, and Cole, *Modernity and the Millennium: The Genesis of the Baha'i Faith in the Nineteenth-Century Middle East* (New York: Columbia University Press, 1998).

94. Cole, "Bahai Faith," pp. 440–41. Peter Smith presents a modern interpretation of the role of the Universal House of Justice today. He states that "the original charismatic power" of one has been "'routinized' in an elected institution." "Although regarded as providing infallible guidance for the development of the Bahai religion, the institution of the House of Justice comprises individual human beings who bear no divine afflatus." This "depersonalization of authority represents a further stage in a process of progressive routinization earlier exemplified by the 'humanization' of supreme authority in the person of Abdul-Baha and by its institutionalization in the Guardianship of Shoghi Effendi": Smith, *Babi and Baha'i*, pp. 133–34.

95. See, for example, Moojan Momen, *The Babi and Bahai Religions, 1844–1944: Some Contemporary Western Accounts* (Oxford: Oxford University Press, 1981); Peter Smith (ed.), *Studies in Babi and Baha'i History*, vol. III (Los Angeles: Kalimat Press, 1986); Mirza Abu'l-Fadl Gulpaygani, *Miracles and Metaphors*, trans. Juan R. Cole (Los Angeles: Kalimat Press, 1981).

96. For conversion of Zoroastrians to Bahaism, see Susan Stiles, "Early Zoroastrian Conversions to the Bahai Faith in Yazd, Iran," in Juan R. Cole and Moojan Momen (eds.), *From Iran East and West* (Los Angeles: Kalimat Press, 1984), pp. 67–93. Fischel cites various reasons as to why Jews converted to Bahaism; amongst them were the progressive and tolerant message of the movement, Bahaullah's claim that he was the messiah, and the connection of the movement to Palestine. The center of Bahai Jews was the city of Hamadan, but the number of converts was reduced after the activities of the Alliance in the area. See Fischel, "Jews of Persia," 151–56, and Fischel, "The Bahai Movement and Persian Jewry," *Jewish Review* 7 (1934), 47–55. The Bahai propagation among the Jews is also discussed in Levy, *Tarikh-e*, vol. III, pp. 871–74. Another scholar offers a similar explanation, arguing that Bahaullah's claim to be "the fulfillment of the messianic expectations" of Judaism, Christianity, and Zoroastrianism increased the religious appeal of Bahaism; see Momen, *Introduction*, p. 232. Smith writes on various appeals of Bahaism especially to the Jews and Zoroastrians in *Babi and Baha'i Religions*, pp. 93–97. Cole argues that in the 1880s the "openness and cosmopolitan attitude" of the Bahais attracted Jews and Zoroastrians to whom becoming a Bahai was like joining an "enlightened club." The first Zoroastrian converts were from Yazd; later, all Qazvin Zoroastrians became Bahais. Jews in Hamadan converted in significant numbers to Bahaism, and the trend continued until the 1930s. The establishment of Israel in 1948 ended Jewish conversions; see Cole, "Conversions: V. To Babism and Bahai Faith," in *Encyclopaedia Iranica*, vol. VI, pp. 236–38.
97. Cole, "Bahai Faith," p. 443.
98. *Ibid.*, p. 440.
99. Cooper, *Bahais*, p. 10.
100. Douglas Martin, citing the British consul in Shiraz, states that the killing of Bahais in April 1926 in the city of Jahrom in Fars province went unpunished. In *The Persecution of the Bahais of Iran, 1844–1984* (Ottawa: Association for Bahai Studies, 1984), p. 16, he asserts that the Reza Shah regime institutionalized the anti-Bahai prejudice in Iran; however, the book offers no solid evidence as to how a socioreligious prejudice is politicized and solidified by the state (pp. 18–20). See also William Sears, *A Cry from the Heart: The Bahais in Iran* (Oxford: George Ronald, 1982).
101. Cole, "Bahai Faith," p. 444.
102. For an excellent account of the anti-Bahai campaign, see Shahrough Akhavi, *Religion and Politics in Contemporary Iran: Clergy–State Relations in the Pahlavi Period* (Albany: State University of New York Press, 1980), pp. 76–90.
103. Martin, *Persecution*, p. 22.
104. D. M. MacEoin, "Bahai Faith: Bahai Persecutions," in *Encyclopaedia Iranica*, vol. III, p. 463.
105. It is often asserted that Amir Abbas Hoveida, prime minister of Iran, 1965–78, was a Bahai. Bahais deny this, stating that his paternal grandfather had been a Bahai but Hoveida's father had returned to Islam after being expelled from the community for his political activities. They admit that the shah's physician was a Bahai: Martin, *Persecution*, p. 24, n. 76.

106. Cole, "Bahai Faith," p. 441.

107. Martin, *Persecution*, pp. 26–29; he reports that the Bahai international community prepared a dossier of documents as evidence of their persecution under Mohammad Reza Shah's regime and submitted it to the Islamic Republic of Iran in 1980.

108. Smith, *Babi and Baha'i*, chronologies, pp. 222–23.

109. Peter Smith, "A Note on Babi and Baha'i Numbers in Iran," *Iranian Studies* 13, nos. 2–3 (Spring–Summer 1984), 295–96.

110. For 500,000, see *New York Times*, 14 January 1982, p. A12; for 450,000, see *Newsweek*, 24 March 1980, p. 61; for 300,000–350,000, see Smith, "Note," 297; for 150,000–300,000, see Cooper, *Bahais*, p. 7.

111. Bayat, *Iran's First Revolution*, pp. 16–17, quote on p. 17.

112. Abrahamian, *Iran*, p. 174. Faghfoory argues that the Reza Shah government publicized prejudiced and discriminatory measures against non-Muslim minorities, including the Zoroastrians, in order to portray the clergy as reactionary and backward; see "Ulama–State Relations," 427 and 431, n. 59.

113. Abrahamian, *Iran*, p. 163.

114. Esman, *Ethnic Politics*, p. 256.

115. Felix Aghayan, a member of the fifth and sixth sessions of the Senate (a constituent body of the pre-Revolution parliament) and a business associate of the shah, stated that delegating certain responsibilities to Bahais had a direct relevance to the shah's belief that they would be no threat to his regime. Aghayan, though an Armenian by birth, was not particularly revered by the Armenian community of Iran. Similar to other wealthy power elites in Iran, his attainment of influence and political position was simply due to his business connections with the shah. See Felix Aghayan, interview recorded by Habib Ladjevardi, 5 March 1986, Paris, France, tape 1, pp. 8–9, Iranian Oral History Collection, Harvard University.

116. The issue of intense "distrust" among Iranian political leadership has been raised in several studies; see Marvin Zonis, *The Political Elite of Iran* (Princeton: Princeton University Press, 1971). M. Reza Behnam focuses on authoritarianism and personalism, and the ensuing contradictions in social structure in *Cultural Foundations of Iranian Politics* (Salt Lake City: University of Utah Press, 1986). The views expressed were obtained during research on this topic.

2 THE ASSEMBLY OF EXPERTS: DEBUT IN THE YEAR OF DESTINY

1. Abdol-Ali Bazargan, *Masael va Moshkelat-e Nokhostin Sal-e Enqelab az Zaban-e Reis-e Dovlat-e Movaqat*, 2nd edn. (n.p.: author publication, 1362 [1983/84]), pp. 18, 189, 332, 362.

2. Shaul Bakhash, *The Reign of the Ayatollahs* (New York: Basic Books, 1984), pp. 74–75. For additional details, see H. E. Chehabi, *Iranian Politics and Religious Modernism* (Ithaca: Cornell University Press, 1990), pp. 264–66.

3. Founded in February 1979, the IRP was an umbrella organization that served to mobilize pro-Khomeini forces. It played an important role in the takeover of the American Embassy and the approval of the final draft of the constitution. Ayatollah Beheshti was in charge of all the main arteries of

the pro-Khomeini coalition as the secretary general of the party since its inception, the head of the Revolutionary Council, and the vice-chair of the Assembly of Experts. For an introduction to the complex nature of the party, see Eliz Sanasarian, "The Islamic Republican Party," in *Oxford Encyclopedia of the Modern Islamic World* (New York: Oxford University Press, 1995), pp. 312–15.

4. Bakhash, *Reign*, p. 81. See also "Introduction," in *Proceedings*, where seventy-two elected deputies are identified. The final public proceedings of the Assembly of Experts were published on the sixth-year anniversary of the founding of Islamic Republic in Iran with an introduction by Ayatollah Montazeri. The published proceedings consist of three volumes and cover sixty-seven sessions and are published unedited. More than 4,000 proposals were discussed in various committees in closed sessions. Whatever the shortcomings of this document, it reveals interesting points on the issue of political representation of religious minorities.

5. *Kayhan*, 17 Mordad 1358 [8 August 1979], p. 9.

6. *Dar Maktab-e Jomeh: Majmueh-ye Khotbehhaye Namaz-e Jomeh-ye Tehran*, vol. I, 1st to 25th week (Tehran: Vezarat-e Ershad-e Islami, Tir 1364 [July 1985]), pp. 3–4.

7. *Ibid.*, p. 26.

8. *Ibid.*, p. 27.

9. Mangol Bayat, "Mahmud Taleqani and the Iranian Revolution," in Martin Kramer (ed.), *Shi'ism, Resistance, and Revolution* (Boulder: Westview Press, 1987), p. 84.

10. *Dar Maktab-e Jomeh*, vol. I, pp. 68–69, 74, 94, 105.

11. *Ibid.*, p. 93.

12. *Ibid.*, p. 96.

13. *Proceedings*, 3rd session, 29 Mordad 1358 [20 August 1979], p. 37.

14. *Proceedings*, 10th session, 12 Shahrivar 1358 [3 September 1979], p. 227.

15. *Proceedings*, 5th session, 30 Mordad 1358 [21 August 1979], p. 111.

16. *Proceedings*, 9th session, 11 Shahrivar 1358 [2 September 1979], p. 223.

17. *Proceedings*, 32nd session, 5 Mehr 1358 [27 September 1979], p. 848.

18. *Proceedings*, 20th session, 27 Shahrivar 1358 [18 September 1979], p. 530.

19. For one example, see the exchange between Hojati Kermani and Musavi Tabrizi in *Proceedings*, 12th session, 14 Shahrivar 1358 [5 September 1979], p. 291.

20. *Proceedings*, 11th session, 13 Shahrivar 1358 [4 September 1979], pp. 257–59.

21. The author of Article 5, one of the key articles of the Islamic constitution, was Ayatollah Beheshti. The article designated the top leader of the country as the supreme jurist, an idea advocated in Khomeini's work. The supreme jurist possessed certain qualifications; he was "just and pious, aware of the [needs/requirements of the] times, courageous," and had good sense in administration and management. The top theologian had to be recognized by the majority of people. If a single jurist did not have majority support, a group of qualified jurists would assume responsibility for leadership.

When it came to the floor for debate, Beheshti delivered a strong speech in its defense. No one was prepared to oppose him publicly; a few voiced their objections but Beheshti maneuvered cleverly to block their comments and brought the article to a vote in which it won the usual clear majority.

It is the contention of this author that the wording of Article 5 was designed for him in contexts of both the "faqih" and "rahbar." Ayatollah Beheshti was carefully plotting his own ascent to the top leadership of the Islamic Republic. See *Proceedings*, 15th session, 21 Shahrivar 1358 [12 September 1979], pp. 373–84.

22. This is obvious, for instance, in the nature of debates involving Shoraye-Negahban (the Council of Guardians) in which no one questioned its existence. The debates revolved around the numbers and ratio of religious leaders and Muslim jurists, and whether it should be an elective or appointive office. Those in favor of an elected Council of Guardians argued that it would avoid dictatorship. See *Proceedings*, 36th session, 9 Mehr 1358 [1 October 1979], pp. 944–55.

23. Previously recognized religious minorities were required to vote only for one candidate; if they voted for more than one person, only the first vote would be counted: *Kayhan*, 9 Mordad 1358 [31 July 1979], p. 2.

24. See the text of the swearing-in in *Proceedings*, 6th session, 30 Mordad 1358 [21 August 1979], pp. 134–35; and the opening session, p. 10.

25. *Proceedings*, 3rd session, 29 Mordad 1358 [20 August 1979], p. 47.

26. *Proceedings*, 23rd session, 29 Shahrivar 1358 [20 September 1979], p. 597. A similar debate ensued over the selection of governors. Some argued that the governorship should be an elected office with local input. This view was defeated, and the governorship became a centrally appointed post. See *Proceedings*, 37th session, 10 Mehr 1358 [2 October 1979], p. 1004.

27. *Proceedings*, 37th session, 10 Mehr 1358 [2 October 1979], pp. 982–83. The whole speech appears on pp. 979–84.

28. *Proceedings*, 18th session, 25 Shahrivar 1358 [16 September 1979], pp. 454–72. Similar concerns were voiced to Prime Minister Bazargan; see Bazargan, *Masael*, p. 101. This issue refused to disappear. Later on during debates on qualifications for the presidency, similar rifts appeared; this time the debate focused more directly on the Sunni–Shii element. Some argued that adherence to Islam should be enough; this opened a lengthy and heated discussion on the Sunnis' right to the presidency. The original draft proposal (endorsing a Shii president) received a majority vote. See *Proceedings*, 64th session, 20 Aban 1358 [11 November 1979], pp. 1766–72 and 65th session, 20 Aban 1358, pp. 1796–97.

29. *Proceedings*, 8th session, 31 Mordad 1358 [22 August 1979], p. 184.

30. *Ibid.*, pp. 186–88; quote on p. 187.

31. *Ibid.*, p. 192.

32. *Proceedings*, 39th session, 14 Mehr 1358 [6 October 1979], p. 1045.

33. See comment by Qaemi in *Proceedings*, 26th session, 31 Shahrivar 1358 [22 September 1979], p. 669.

34. *Proceedings*, 28th session, 1 Mehr 1358 [23 September 1979], p. 722.

35. *Proceedings*, 41st session, 18 Mehr 1358 [10 October 1979], p. 1129, gives details of Deputy Tehrani's lecture. For Beheshti's response, see 42nd session, 19 Mehr 1358 [11 October 1979], pp. 1153–54.

36. *Proceedings*, 2nd session, 28 Mordad 1358 [19 August 1979], p. 21.
37. *Proceedings*, 3rd session, 29 Mordad 1358 [20 August 1979], p. 39.
38. *Proceedings*, 5th session, 30 Mordad 1358 [21 August 1979], p. 117.
39. *Proceedings*, 48th session, 26 Mehr 1358 [18 October 1979], p. 1310.
40. *Proceedings*, 67th session, 24 Aban 1358 [15 November 1979], p. 1836.
41. *Proceedings*, 19th session, 27 Shahrivar 1358 [18 September 1979], pp. 483–500.
42. *Ibid.*, p. 486.
43. *Ibid.*, pp. 486–87.
44. Many statements and comments on the part of both Muslim and non-Muslim deputies were made clearly for public consumption. The term "religious minorities" was often referred to in order to convey a general point about, for example, Islam, or the legislative power of the Assembly. In other words, not every reference was directly relevant to the situation or discussion of the rights of religious minorities; see *Proceedings*, 21st session, 28 Shahrivar 1358 [19 September 1979], pp. 544–45. RRM deputies in turn made similar remarks. For instance, at one point when the Assembly of Experts session was due to be closed for a commemorative demonstration, Bait Ushana announced that religious minorities too would be marching along with the Muslims. Beheshti, ever on cue, responded that no one expected anything less from them; see *Proceedings*, 52nd session, 3 Aban 1358 [25 October 1979], p. 1410.
45. *Proceedings*, 19th session, 27 Shahrivar 1358 [18 September 1979], p. 493.
46. *Ibid.*, pp. 489–90.
47. *Proceedings*, 4th session, 29 Mordad 1358 [20 August 1979], pp. 87–88.
48. *Proceedings*, 19th session, 27 Shahrivar 1358 [18 September 1979], pp. 490–91.
49. *Ibid.*, p. 500.
50. See comments by Priest Shahzadi in *Proceedings*, 56th session, 8 Aban 1358 [30 October 1979], pp. 1529–32.
51. *Proceedings*, 61st session, 15 Aban 1358 [6 November 1979], p. 1672.
52. *Ibid.*, p. 1666. This issue was raised again a few years later during the discussions on revision of election laws. This time, however, there was no controversy and the debates were focused on the clarity of expression; see *Mozakerat-e Majlis*, 27 Day 1362 [17 January 1984], meeting 562, p. 20. (For full citation of the latter, see ch. 3, n. 5.)
53. *Proceedings*, 61st session, 15 Aban 1358 [6 November 1979], pp. 1667–68.
54. *Ibid.*, p. 1672.
55. *Proceedings*, 56th session, 8 Aban 1358 [30 October 1979], p. 1531.
56. *Proceedings*, 65th session, 20 Aban 1358 [11 November 1979], p. 1780. His speech is on pp. 1779–80.
57. *Proceedings*, 39th session, 14 Mehr 1358 [6 October 1979], pp. 1043–45.
58. Bait Ushana commented on most issues that were discussed on the floor; he also had a tendency to raise issues that had already been discussed, ignored, or put aside in closed meetings. At one point, Beheshti directly asked him not to raise such issues again; see *Proceedings*, 17th session, 24 Shahrivar 1358 [15 September 1979], pp. 427, 435. For examples of his commentaries and questions, see 16th session, 22 Shahrivar 1358 [13 September 1979], p.

413; 37th session, 10 Mehr 1358 [2 October 1979], p. 1011; 43rd session, 21 Mehr 1358 [13 October 1979], p. 1167.

59. There are many press reports on this point; for two examples, see *Jewish Chronicle*, 18 May 1979, p. 1, and *Los Angeles Times*, 23 May 1979, p. 1.
60. *Proceedings*, 13th session, 15 Shahrivar 1358 [6 September 1979], pp. 331–32.
61. *Proceedings*, 67th session, 24 Aban 1358 [15 November 1979], p. 1836.
62. *Proceedings*, 56th session, 8 Aban 1358 [30 October 1979], pp. 1529–32, quote on p. 1530.
63. *Proceedings*, 65th session, 20 Aban 1358 [11 November 1979], pp. 1779–80. The discontent over the lack of equality with the Muslims lingered on and was voiced in Zoroastrian press; see *Cheesta*, 1st year, no. 3, Aban 1360 [November 1981], pp. 252–53.
64. During discussions on the issue of Iranian military involvement in other countries, especially in defending the rights of other Islamic ones, Priest Shahzadi commented that the first question should be whether it was in the interest of the nation; Iran's interests should come first. His comment triggered a long debate which eventually defeated the old version proposed by the subcommittee; see *Proceedings*, 51st session, 30 Mehr 1358 [22 October 1979], pp. 1387–92.
65. *Proceedings*, 4th session, 29 Mordad 1358 [20 August 1979], pp. 87–88.
66. *Proceedings*, 22nd session, 28 Shahrivar 1358 [19 September 1979], p. 582. Arabic was taught in schools during the shah's regime and Eshraqi's comment was factually incorrect.
67. See, for example, discussions which led to Article 100 on administrative councils: *Proceedings*, 15th session, 21 Shahrivar 1358 [12 September 1979], pp. 385–95; or discussions over Article 20, 27th session, 1 Mehr 1358 [23 September 1979], pp. 691–94. Ironically, the memoirs of Keikhosrow Shahrokh show similar trends and tendencies in the debates on minority rights in the convening of the constitution in 1906, some seventy-three years before; see Shahrokh and Writer, *Memoirs*, pp. 57–58.

3 POLICY SPHERE OF RECOGNIZED RELIGIOUS MINORITIES

1. George Eaton Simpson and J. Milton Yinger, *Racial and Cultural Minorities: An Analysis of Prejudice and Discrimination*, 3rd edn. (New York: Harper & Row Publishers, 1965), pp. 20–25.
2. *Ibid.*, p. 25.
3. *Ibid.*, p. 23.
4. *Ibid.*, p. 25.
5. The ministry was called Vezarat-e Ershad-e Islami (Ministry of Islamic Guidance) until its name change in the Majlis to Vezarat-e Farhang va Ershad-e Islami (Ministry of Culture and Islamic Guidance). Several agencies came under the authority of the ministry including haj (pilgrimage), tourism, printing and publications, and the news bureaus. Despite the official name change, in general conversation and correspondence, the ministry is still referred to as Vezarat-e Ershad. See *Mashruh-e Mozakerat-e Majlis-e Shoraye Islami* (Tehran: Majlis-e Shoraye Islami), 30 Azar 1365 [21

December 1986], meeting 352, p. 27. The proceedings also appear under the title *Ruznameye Rasmi: Mozakerat-e Jalaseye Alani-ye Shoraye Islami* (hereafter both will be referred to as *Mozakerat-e Majlis*).

6. Bishop Haik was assassinated in 1994; more on this in ch. 4 (see *Mojdeh* 15, nos. 1–2 [Spring–Summer 1994], 4).
7. Stated in the copy of a letter sent to the author. For the Armenian case, see *Mozakerat-e Majlis*, 9 Ordibehesht 1361 [29 April 1982], meeting 303, p. 15.
8. Communicated to the author by relatives and friends who were eyewitnesses.
9. The Abadan case was conveyed to the author by Armenians who, like the author, used to live there.
10. The author knows the individual in question.
11. The structure of the Iranian judicial system is complex. The system is divided into five types of courts: Special Civil Courts which deal with private cases and family law; General Courts which address civil issues; Penal Courts with two separate divisions, referred to as Penal Courts 1 and 2; Military Courts; and Islamic Revolutionary Courts.

    Amnesty International (AI) reports the existence of several other types of courts outside the judicial system. The two known to AI are: the Special Judicial Committees, which were established in 1989 by the Supreme Judicial Council, and the Special Courts for clerics, accountable to Velayat-e Faqih. The Supreme Court in Tehran, which has a branch in Qom, is supposed to play a role in adjudication process. See Amnesty International, *Iran: Violations of Human Rights 1987–1990* (New York: AI USA, December 1990), pp. 23–24. A law aimed at reorganizing the court system passed the Majlis in August 1994; for details as well as the problems of the legal system, see Human Rights Watch, *Human Rights Watch World Report 1995* (New York: Human Rights Watch, 1995), pp. 272–73.
12. The names of Bazargan, Beheshti, and Bahonar were often repeated by different individuals in conversations with the author. This positive sentiment was also clear in comments made, in public, by representatives of recognized religious minorities in the Majlis. See the comments on Beheshti by Parviz Malekpoor, the Zoroastrian deputy, in *Soroosh*, 3rd year, 17 Mordad 1360 [8 August 1981], 108, reprinted in *Cheesta*, 1st year, no. 10, Khordad 1361 [June 1982], p. 1163. See also the commentary in the Majlis by the Northern Armenian deputy, Hrair Khalatian, where he stresses that Bahonar had promised Armenians independence in their own affairs, placing the study of language and religion under the auspices of the church: *Mozakerat-e Majlis*, 12 Khordad 1362 [2 June 1983], meeting 473, p. 14.
13. Personal interviews, Tehran, 1992.
14. Personal interviews, Tehran, 1992.
15. *Chashm Andaaz* 57, September 1997, p. 80.
16. There was at least one reported case of the takeover of an Armenian school. The Artak Manukian Armenian School was forcibly confiscated and transformed into a Muslim school: see United Nations, E/CN.4/1991/35, p. 48. The Iranian government responded in 22 January 1991 stating that the school was placed at the disposal of other students because it did not have

enough Armenian students. This was said to have been done with the consent of the Armenian community and "they can restore it whenever it is deemed necessary" (p. 49). The Tehran Council of the Armenian Apostolic Church also responded to the report, calling it "high-handed," and saying that it treated "some persistent problems in a negative – even, on occasion, partial and biased – manner" (p. 50).

17. In response to the UN report by Reynaldo Galindo Pohl (*ibid.*), which mentioned the appointment of principals (p. 48), the Islamic Republic of Iran denied that the MET was forcing Muslim principals on recognized religious minorities: "the principals of these schools are appointed by them [the minorities] and in accordance with regulations of the Ministry of Education" (p. 49).

18. *Cheesta*, 1st year, no. 9, Ordibehesht 1361 [May 1982], p. 1033.

19. Communicated in a letter from the Parents and Teachers Association of Gohar school. A Persian copy of the letter is in *Nehzat*, no. 122, 14 Shahrivar 1364 [5 September 1985], p. 4. See also the comments attributed to Reverend Tateos Mikaelian, executive secretary of the Synod Council of the Evangelical Church of Iran, in *L'Express*, 6 September 1985, no. 1782, p. 12. Reverend Mikaelian denied being interviewed by the paper but acknowledged that most of the points raised in *L'Express* were correct.

20. See the comments of Artur Khonanshu, the Assyrian and Chaldean deputy in *Mozakerat-e Majlis*, 16 Day 1365 [6 January 1987], meeting 359, p. 18. See also the speech by Hrair Khalatian, the northern Armenian deputy, affirming similar practices in schools throughout the country. He mentions one (unnamed) school where, after protests, the principal was forced by the MET to resign; yet months had gone by and the principal refused to leave his post: *Mozakerat-e Majlis*, 12 Khordad 1362 [2 June 1983], meeting 473, p. 14.

21. This was first reported by the Soviet news agency Tass from what was then the Armenian Soviet Socialist Republic; see *Iran Times*, 4 December 1981, p. 6. The information was also confirmed by interviewees. The Ararat sports arena is an 80,000 m^2 fenced complex equipped with a variety of recreational facilities including an olympic-size soccer field and banquet rooms. For details and photographs, see Zenian, "Islamic Revolution," 8–9. For a case study of the Armenians, see Eliz Sanasarian, "State Dominance and Communal Perseverance: The Armenian Diaspora in the Islamic Republic of Iran, 1979–1989," *Diaspora* 4, no. 3 (Winter 1995), 243–65.

22. *Alik*, 19 January 1983, p. 2.

23. The letter was printed in *Alik*; it was summarized in *Iran Times*, 15 April 1983, p. 5.

24. *Mozakerat-e Majlis*, 9 Ordibehesht 1361 [29 April 1982], meeting 303, p. 15; 16 Shahrivar 1361 [7 September 1982], meeting 356, pp. 17–19; 12 Khordad 1362 [2 June 1983], meeting 473, p. 14.

25. This was obviously an excuse to rationalize the reduction or elimination of instruction in the Armenian language: no other plausible explanation exists as to why the minister suddenly became concerned about the overload, when the practice had existed for decades with the approval of the MET. See also *Iran Times*, 15 April 1983, p. 5.

26. Details of a long interview with Archbishop Manukian on this issue were published in *Alik*. Its translation appears in Persian in *Iran Times*, 2 September 1983, pp. 1, 6, 14. Many of the details of student protests were also confirmed by the participants, who recalled as children being frightened but determined. The author met some of them (as students) at the University of Southern California.

27. "Christians Protest in Iran," *Iran Liberation* 103, 6 January 1984, p. 1. This is a publication of the anti-government People's Mojahedin Organization and its information is often suspect. Yet the details of this particular report were confirmed by all recognized religious minorities.

28. Archbishop Manukian's interview in *Alik*, excerpts translated into English, in *Iran Times*, 27 April 1984, p. 15. The information was confirmed in interviews.

29. On the closing of the Mariam Catholic school and Nor Ani school in Majidieh, Tehran, see *Alik*, 3 May 1984, p. 1. The story of the closing of Armenian schools was also published in *Le Monde*, 2 June 1984; see *Iran Times*, 8 June 1984, p. 2.

30. *Iran Times*, 22 June 1984, p. 2.

31. Translated into English from *Alik*, in *Iran Times*, 6 July 1984, p. 16.

32. *Iran Times*, 6 July 1984, pp. 2, 16.

33. Communicated to the author by an individual present in these meetings.

34. Interview with Attorney Aida Avanessian, December 1996.

35. Personal interviews, Tehran and Isfahan, 1992.

36. The author has seen and read sections of the textbook.

37. Copies of letters of protest to the authorities were shown to the author. One letter raised the issue of Islamic proselytizing by referring to passages from a fifth-grade textbook: "In the Heavenly Book God says: we have not created you in vain; we have created you to live in this world and to do good deeds and to become worthy and complete"; "Then, we will take you from this world to the last invisible world where you could see the end result of your actions."

   In addition, see Artur Khonanshu's comments in *Mozakerat-e Majlis*, 16 Day 1365 [6 January 1987], meeting 359, p. 18.

38. Golnar Mehran, "Socialization of Schoolchildren in the Islamic Republic of Iran," *Iranian Studies* 22, no. 1 (1989), 35–50.

39. These problems were communicated to the author in discussions with religious minorities in Iran in 1992. See also the letter by Reverend Tateos Mikaelian to the northern Armenian deputy in the Majlis dated 18 Esfand 1361 [9 March 1983], where he protests the malicious act of the principal of his daughter's school. The principal purposefully lowered the enzebat grade for his daughter and others in school in order to destroy their chances of entering university. A copy of the letter is printed in *Nehzat* 123, 21 Shahrivar 1364 [12 September 1985], p. 9.

40. Middle East Watch, *Guardians of Thought: Limits on Freedom of Expression in Iran* (New York: Human Rights Watch, 1993), Appendix B, p. 136. For details of the experiences of several students, see pp. 136–40.

41. The author was told about this phenomenon. By accident, however, she ran into two non-Armenian men (one in a government office) who spoke fluent

Armenian. To her inquiry they responded that friends had taught them the language, but their Armenian was too refined to be the work of casual friends.

42. Information conveyed to the author in discussions and interviews in Iran and United States.
43. Shaykh Hossein-Ali Montazeri, *Resaleh-ye Towzih al-Masael* (Tehran: Tabliqat-e Islami, 1362 [1983/84]), p. 17.
44. *Ibid.*, pp. 20–21.
45. *Ibid.*, p. 21.
46. *Ibid.*, p. 373.
47. *Ibid.*, p. 21.
48. Soroudi, "Concept," p. 144, n. 4.
49. Khomeini, *Esteftaat az Mahzar-e Imam Khomeini*, vol. I (Qom: Entesharat-e Islami, 1366 [1987/88]), p. 102.
50. *Ibid.*, pp. 104, 121.
51. *Ibid.*, p. 109.
52. *Ibid.*, p. 103.
53. *Ibid.*, p. 104.
54. *Ibid.*, p. 107.
55. *Ibid.*, pp. 103–04.
56. The author is aware of several such cases, and this is also clear in a question put to Khomeini by a young girl. Her efforts in practicing the rituals of purity invited criticism from her religiously devout parents who accused her of being too fussy and whimsical. She asked whether she was responsible for the cleansing of the household. The answer was no: *ibid.*, p. 112.
57. The author witnessed these during her stay in Iran in 1992. Different applications of the practice was conveyed to the author by the RRMs. Similar points were also reported in US Department of State, *Country Reports on Human Rights Practices for 1984* (Washington, DC: Government Printing Office, 1985), p. 1241.
58. The author has always been aware of the discrepancy between rhetoric and practice. But this specific information on top clerics in Iran was conveyed to the author by two individuals who had continuous close and private contacts with them. They described a myriad of encounters, all indicating nonadherence (in private behavior) to the principles of nejasat. The author was asked not to use the stories of the encounters, the description of which would easily facilitate the recognition of the individuals and the high-ranking clerics in question.
59. *Cheesta*, 1st year, no. 2, Mehr 1360 [October 1981], pp. 160–61; no. 3, Aban 1360 [November 1981], p. 299.
60. *Mozakerat-e Majlis*, 9 Ordibehesht 1361 [29 April 1982], meeting 303, pp. 14–15; and *Cheesta*, 1st year, no. 9, Ordibehesht 1361 [May 1982], p. 1033.
61. Details of the discussion appear in *Cheesta*, 5th year, no. 2, Mehr 1366 [October 1987], pp. 97–100. The debate took place in 22 Ordibehesht 1366, in meeting 404, regulations of the armed forces, Tarh-e Qanuni-ye Artesh-e Jomhuri-ye Islami.
   A Zoroastrian who had reached a mid-level position in the military during the shah's reign told the author that those RRMs who remained in

the military were denied promotion. The military's excuse was that the minorities were unable to pass a required examination on Islam. Yet, for the very few who stayed, it became obvious that Muslims were sent out on regular and special assignments. He also admitted that for the professional military listening to a mullah's lecture on military affairs was an arduous task.

Concomitantly, in post-Khomeini Iran, an Armenian dentist was granted the highest honorary rank ever to be bestowed on an RRM since the Revolution. He was promoted to brigadier general (sartip). Yet, other sources state that since the Revolution the non-Muslims have not been able to hold positions of power. Non-Muslims who remained served mainly in a technical capacity. The trend has been to exclude the non-Shii Muslims as well; see Schahgaldian, *Iranian Military*, pp. 39–40.

62. The convening of the meeting was confirmed in interviews. For details of the meeting, see *Iran Times*, 15 October 1982, pp. 5, 11. According to the US Department of State, *Country Reports on Human Rights Practices for 1982* (Washington, DC: Government Printing Office, 1983), the main issue in 1981–82 was whether minority social clubs were to be classified as private or public (see p. 1142).

63. *Iran Times*, 15 October 1982, pp. 5, 11.

64. *Ibid.*, 24 December 1982, p. 5.

65. In a speech delivered by Musavi Ardabili, head of the Supreme Court, elimination of jazieh was attributed to changes in society since the times of the Prophet Mohammad; see *Iran Times*, 3 July 1987, p. 5. See also the discussion on the interpretation of the concept of jazieh in the Introduction, pp. 22–23.

66. See *The Times* (London), 11 July 1980, p. 8; US Department of State, *Country Reports on Human Rights Practices for 1983* (Washington, DC: Government Printing Office, 1984), p. 1262; *Cheesta*, 2nd year, no. 3, Aban 1361 [November 1982], pp. 386–88; United Nations, E/CN.4/1991/35, p. 48. The above information was confirmed in interviews with women in Tehran, 1992.

67. *Iran Times*, 12 September 1986, p. 14.

68. United Nations, E/CN.4/1991/35, p. 49. In an official response, the Iranian government admitted the arrest of some members "for their immoral offences." This was done "according to the decision of the judicial authorities and they were convicted by the court" (p. 50).

69. The author was told many stories by Muslims and non-Muslims. In one case during the early 1980s, a non-Muslim wedding, despite having received an official permit, was interrupted by the Revolutionary Guards breaking and jumping through the windows. Despite being presented with the official permit, they stayed for over an hour. When they left, the guests were so shaken and demoralized that the celebrations came to a halt.

70. *Iran Times*, 3 July 1987, p. 1.

71. The author has read the letter.

72. The author is in possession of a copy of the invitation given to her by H. E. Chehabi.

73. *Asbarez*, 14 May 1988, p. 8; *Cheesta*, 1st year, no. 10, Khordad 1361 [June

1982], p. 1198; 3rd year, no. 4, Day 1364 [December 1985], p. 320; 4th year, no. 1, Shahrivar 1365 [September 1986]; *Iran Times*, 27 April 1984, p. 2.

74. *Mozakerat-e Majlis*, 9 Ordibehesht 1361 [29 April 1982], meeting 303, p. 15.
75. This information has come from members of the RRMs who have regularly traveled abroad since 1987. The original announcement appeared in *Iran Times*, 7 December 1984, p. 1.
76. *Gardoon*, 1st year, no. 3, 1 Day 1362 [22 December 1990], p. 3.
77. *Mozakerat-e Majlis*, 10 Tir 1360 [1 July 1981], meeting 173, pp. 22–23, 24–41, 49–51.
78. *Mozakerat-e Majlis*, 16 Bahman 1362 [5 February 1984], meeting 572; 17 Bahman 1362 [6 February 1984], meeting 573 (the entire session).
79. See, for example, *Mozakerat-e Majlis*, 21 Tir 1360 [12 July 1981], meeting 180, p. 69; 5 Khordad 1362 [26 May 1983], meeting 470, pp. 29–30.
80. *Mozakerat-e Majlis*, 23 Esfand 1362 [13 March 1984], meeting 598, pp. 17–19.
81. This slogan is repeated frequently; see from the first Majlis, *Mozakerat-e Majlis*, 10 Tir 1360 [1 July 1981], meeting 173, pp. 3–4.
82. For a typical outburst ending up in a physical fight on the house floor during the first Majlis, see *Mozakerat-e Majlis*, 10 Aban 1362 [1 November 1983], meeting 524, p. 14. During the second Majlis such incidents were rare.
83. For one example, see *Mozakerat-e Majlis*, 9 Day 1365 [30 December 1986], meeting 356, p. 24.
84. *Mozakerat-e Majlis*, 14 Azar 1364 [5 December 1985], meeting 202, p. 21.
85. See, for example, Haerizadeh, a deputy from Birjand, who begins his speech by criticizing those who always use the imam's name; he then does the same. Haerizadeh was against privatization and favored a strong public sector. His circular critique, however, is an exercise in perverse logic: *Mozakerat-e Majlis*, 13 Mehr 1365 [5 October 1986], meeting 321, p. 19.
86. See, for example, *Mozakerat-e Majlis*, 19 Azar 1364 [10 December 1985], meeting 204, pp. 17–18.
87. For an example of the RRM oath of office, see the ceremonial swearing-in to the second Majlis of Baghoomian, the southern Armenian deputy: *Mozakerat-e Majlis*, 24 Mehr 1363 [16 October 1984], meeting 41, p. 28. For an example of the oath of Muslim deputies, see *Mozakerat-e Majlis*, 10 Tir 1360 [1 July 1981], meeting 173, pp. 24–25.
88. This information is from individuals who had intimate knowledge of the workings of parliament.
89. *Resalat*, 26 Ordibehesht 1367 [16 May 1988], no. 680, p. 5.
90. The Tudeh Party was officially dissolved in May 1983. The information was conveyed to the author by two individuals who were familiar with Mr. Ushana but who did not know each other. Sergen Bait Ushana's death was reported in *Cheesta*, 6th year, nos. 3–4, Azar–Day 1367 [December–January 1989].
91. Information obtained from interviews. See also *Iran Times*, 29 June 1984, p. 16.
92. Interview with *Kayhan*, 7 Shahrivar 1360 [29 August 1981], reprinted in

Cheesta, 1st year, no. 9, Ordibehesht 1361 [May 1982], pp. 1025–29.

93. Speech delivered in the Majlis on 23 Esfand 1360 [14 March 1982], reprinted in *Cheesta*, 1st year, no. 9, Ordibehesht 1361 [May 1982], pp. 1029–32.

94. In a rare commentary on the floor of the Majlis, Vartan Vartanian, the northern Armenian deputy, addressed the economic repercussions if oil were allowed to dominate other exports. He was a member of the House Committee on Industry and Mines. See *Mozakerat-e Majlis*, 25 Esfand 1365 [16 March 1987], meeting 386, pp. 39–40.

95. *Mozakerat-e Majlis*, 14 Tir 1360 [5 July 1981], meeting 174, p. 41. For another example of the RRM representatives voting in unison and with the majority, see 26 Mehr 1363 [18 October 1984], meeting 42.

96. The table gives some examples of how the RRM representatives voted on Musavi's proposed cabinet. See *Mozakerat-e Majlis*, 6 Aban 1364 [28 October 1985], meeting 186, pp. 41–55.

	For Akrami as minister of education and training	For Mohtashemi as minister of interior	For Aqazadeh as minister of oil	For Nili as minister of mines
Baghoomian	against	abstained	abstained	against
Khonanshu	against	abstained	against	for
Malekpoor	for	for	for	against
Nikrooz	abstained	abstained	for	for
TOTAL	192 for 32 against 34 abstentions	163 for 32 against 63 abstentions	146 for 65 against 47 abstentions	126 for 83 against 49 abstentions (rejected by the Majlis, falling short by 4 votes)

97. *Mozakerat-e Majlis*, 16 Tir 1360 [7 July 1981], meeting 176, pp. 22–25. For detailed discussions on other aspects of the bill, see also meetings 175 and 177.

98. *Mozakerat-e Majlis*, 7 Tir 1360 [28 June 1981], meeting 172, pp. 19–45. For the final outcome of this legislation, see *Majmueh-ye Qavanin-e Avalin Dorehye Majlis-e Shoraye Islami 7 Khordad 1359 ta 6 Khordad 1363* (Tehran: Edareh-ye Kol-e Omur-e Farhangi va Ravabet-e Omumi, Majlis-e Shoraye Islami, 1st printing 1363 [1984/85], 2nd printing 1366 [1987/88]), pp. 82–85.

99. *Mozakerat-e Majlis*, 9 Bahman 1362 [29 January 1984], meeting 568, p. 19.

100. *Ibid.*, pp. 19–20.

101. For the whole discussion, see *ibid.*, pp. 18–20, 22. For the election legislation

and its revisions in the final form, see *Majmueh-ye Qavanin-e*, pp. 563, 568–69, 644–45.

102. Yousef Cohen, Jewish deputy in the shah's Majlis (1975–79), writes in his memoirs that Rabbi Uriel Davoudi had serious disagreements with Aziz Daneshrad's views; see Cohen, *Gozaresh*, p. 317.

103. *New York Times*, 12 April 1979, p. A9, and *Los Angeles Times*, 27 February 1979, p. 1.

104. Sorour Soroudi, "Jews in Islamic Iran," *Jewish Quarterly* 21 (Fall 1981), 114. Her main source for this information is Amnon Netzer, "Iranian Jews, Israel, and the Islamic Republic of Iran" (in Hebrew), *Gesher* nos. 1–2 (Spring–Summer 1980), 47–50.

105. Netzer, "Anjoman-e Kalimian," p. 85.

106. Dashnak is short for Hye Heghapokhagan Dashnaktsutiun or Armenian Revolutionary Federation (ARF). Historically, the second Armenian political party (founded in 1890), and politically by far the most significant of these parties for the diaspora, it led Armenian resistance to Ottoman misrule, emerged as the governing party of the first Armenian Republic (1918–20), and after Sovietization remained the dominant political force of the Armenian diaspora. Since the emergence of the post-Soviet Armenian Republic (1991), the party's fortunes have declined. For a concise account, see Arkun, "Dashnak," pp. 90–94.

107. On the occupation of the church grounds in Tehran, see the whole issues of *Alik*, 18 and 19 December 1979. Although the report should not be viewed as entirely objective, it does present the events and the point of view of the Dashnak Party. On the second event, the author knows the people in question.

108. This information was obtained in interviews with an individual who had intimate knowledge of the cases, Tehran, 1992.

109. THR016–BBC report from IRNA, 6 March 1990.

110. The author was in Iran during the 1992 elections for the fourth Majlis. The information is obtained from Zoroastrian interviewees. For details of the 1992 Majlis elections, see David Menashri, "Iran," in Ami Ayalon (ed.), *Middle East Contemporary Survey*, vol. XVI (Boulder: Westview Press, 1992), pp. 400–15.

111. FBIS, 25 March 1992, p. 36.

112. *Proceedings*, 56th session, 8 Aban 1358 [30 October 1979], p. 1531.

113. Farhang Mehr, "The Impact of Religion on Contemporary Politics: The Case of Iran," in Richard L. Rubenstein (ed.), *Spirit Matters: The Worldwide Impact of Religion on Contemporary Politics* (New York: Paragon House Publishers, 1987), p. 154.

4 DISTINCTIONS AND DESIGNATIONS AS POLICY OUTPUT

1. Ross Stagner, "Foreword," in Jerry Boucher, Dan Landis, and Karen Arnold Clark (eds.), *Ethnic Conflict and International Perspectives* (Beverly Hills, CA: Sage Publishers, 1987), pp. 9–11. The basic structure is suggested by Stagner, but the additions, policy interpretations, and analysis are the author's.

2. *Ibid.*, p. 10.
3. Walter P. Zenner, "Middleman Minorities and Genocide," in Isidor Walliman and Michael N. Dobkowski (eds.), *Genocide and the Modern Age: Etiology and Case Studies of Mass Death* (New York: Greenwood Press, 1987), p. 257.
4. Benard and Khalilzad, *Government of God*, p. 74. For a detailed discussion, see p. 207, n. 12.
5. Conveyed to the author by Zoroastrians from Yazd.
6. Iranian secular nationalists are defensive about this topic. The following two real-life events may help in the understanding of this issue.

   One of the hairdressers of Empress Farah Diba was an Armenian. When he first met the queen's nanny (apparently a lower-class illiterate woman who had accompanied her mistress to the palace after her marriage to the monarch), he extended his hand to shake hers. She stepped back murmuring: "Don't touch me. You're najess!"

   A group of émigré medical doctors used to meet and socialize on a regular basis in a major city in United States. Among them only one couple were Jewish; the rest were Iranian Shii Muslims, none of whom practiced any aspect of the religion or attended mosque. At a social occasion, out of the blue, a group of them began a conversation about the "johoodha [a reference to the Jews]" and their conspiracies, deceits, and lies. A friend of the author, present in the gathering, turned to the Jewish couple: "How can you stand this? Say something!" "No," responded the couple, "we are used to it. Don't say anything!" My friend, unable to hold back, reminded the chatterers that they had Jews in their midst. They changed their tune immediately; addressing the Jewish couple, one of them sighed: "Khoda margam bedeh [God strike me dead – a colloquial expression]. We hope you don't think we were talking about you. We are speaking in generalities in which we know you'll agree with us." The Jewish couple remained silent and my friend walked out of the party in disgust.
7. Esman, *Ethnic Politics*, p. 250.
8. The incident was communicated to the author, Tehran, 1992.
9. *Iran Times*, 19 July 1991, p. 9. For a rebuttal by an individual who identifies himself as a Muslim, see 20 September 1991, p. 9.
10. The incident was communicated to the author during her field trip to Iran. Soroudi presents an elaborate discussion of the dog as a source of pollution in Shii Islam, particularly among the Shii. Jews were also called "sag-johood [Jew-dog]"; see Soroudi, "Concept," p. 155.
11. The author heard this story while watching the program during her stay in Tehran in 1992.
12. *Cheesta*, 1st year, no. 7, Esfand 1360 [March 1982], pp. 819–28.
13. Burkey, *Ethnic and Racial Groups*, p. 101.
14. FBIS, 24 January 1979, p. R15.
15. *New York Times*, 12 April 1979, p. A9.
16. *New York Times*, 1 February 1979, p. A10.
17. FBIS, 15 August 1979, pp. R5–R6.
18. David Menashri, *Iran: A Decade of War and Revolution* (New York: Holmes & Meier, 1990), p. 237, and Soroudi, "Jews in Islamic Iran," 113.

19. Khomeini, *Imam Versus Zionism*, p. 42.
20. Communicated to the author by two Jewish individuals, one of whom was in possession of the pocket calendar.
21. *Kayhan*, 27 August 1979, p. 10.
22. Soroudi, "Jews in Islamic Iran," 113–14. She cites private communication on the last point.
23. *New York Times*, 10 May 1979, pp. A1, A3.
24. *Ibid.*, p. A3, and 13 May 1979, p. A9.
25. FBIS, 16 May 1979, pp. R4–R5. Square brackets are the author's.
26. *Ibid.*, 15 May 1979, p. R5. For protests in Israel, see 5 June 1980, p. N4; 10 May 1979, p. N2.
27. *Ibid.*, 30 May 1979, p. R14.
28. Menashri, *Iran*, p. 238; "The Martyrdom of Seven Iranian Jews," *Israel Horizons* (March–April 1981), 9, 13.
29. FBIS, 21 August 1980, p. N7.
30. *The Economist*, 7 February 1987, p. 40.
31. US Department of State, *Country Reports on Human Rights Practices for 1991* (Washington, DC: Government Printing Office, 1992), p. 1414; *Iran Times*, 5 July 1985, p. 5; 9 May 1986, p. 6; and 31 October 1986, p. 13.
32. Nikrooz was arrested by orders of the Tehran public prosecutor and charged with moral turpitude. Judicial authorities declared that he was using his house as a care place for the elderly but was having immoral sexual relations with young men and women who worked there. Shortly after this incident he was released and all charges were dropped. Typically for many events in Iran, information on this incident is scarce. There may have been personal business dealings which led to Nikrooz's arrest and the arrest may have been justified. What distinguishes it from other arrests is the way it was handled by the judicial authorities. The charges were announced in the Majlis and then suddenly dropped, allowing the deputy to return to his work; see *Iran Times*, 5 December 1986, pp. 1, 14.
33. *Los Angeles Times*, 3 October 1987, p. 9.
34. Menashri, *Iran*, p. 237, and *New York Times*, 17 November 1986, p. A1. General estimates vary between 25,000 and 40,000.
35. Menashri, *Iran*, p. 237.
36. Soroudi, "Jews in Islamic Iran," 110.
37. Menashri, *Iran*, p. 238.
38. Zenner, "Middleman Minorities," p. 253.
39. *Ibid.*, p. 259.
40. See Nategh, tape 1, pp. 13–15. In fairness to Nategh, she did not see the Bahais as spies, foreign agents, or SAVAK assistants.
41. The author was naively surprised when in 1979 a self-declared progressive/secularist/leftist told her that if Bahais were to be persecuted it was because they had been up to something. In the same breath, he added, the forced veiling of women would do no harm.
42. Firuz Kazemzadeh, "For Bahais in Iran, A Threat of Extinction," *Congressional Record* 127: no. 127–E4201, 15 September 1981, 97th Congress, 1st session, Congressman Derwinski on Bahais in Iran, p. 20683. The editorial was originally published in the *New York Times*, 6 August 1981.

43. An excellent term coined by Prime Minister Mehdi Bazargan to describe the lack of authority of his Provisional Government; see Bakhash, *Reign*, pp. 52–70. See also a detailed account in Chehabi, *Iranian Politics*, ch. 7.
44. Martin, *Persecution*, p. 40.
45. Abol-Hasan Bani Sadr, *Moqeiyyat-e Iran va Naqsh-e Modarres*, vol. I (n.p.: Entesharat-e Modarres, 1356 [1977]), p. 57.
46. Martin, *Persecution*, pp. 41–43, 57–58.
47. *The Bahai Question: Iran's Secret Blueprint for the Destruction of a Religious Community* (New York: Bahai International Community Publications, 1993), Appendix I (list of Bahais killed or executed), pp. 44–47.
48. *Ibid.*, p. 18. See also *Newsweek*, 18 June 1984, p. 57, and editorial by Roy Mottahedeh, "Why Does Iran Kill Bahais," *New York Times*, 22 June 1983, p. A27.
49. *Khabar-e Jonub* 782, 22 February 1983, translated with an illustration of the paper in Martin, *Persecution*, pp. 65–66.
50. Persecution of Bahais was widely reported in a variety of sources: see US Department of State, *Country Reports on Human Rights Practices for 1983*, pp. 1262–63; United Nations, General Assembly, 45th Session, Agenda Item 12, *Report of the Economic and Social Council: Situation of Human Rights in the Islamic Republic of Iran – Note by the Secretary General*, A/45/697, 6 November 1990, Part III, pp. 31–36 (contains details of both trips of Professor Reynaldo Galindo Pohl of El Salvador, Special Representative of the Commission on Human Rights); and Cooper, *Bahais*.
51. *Kayhan (Havai)*, 21 September 1983, p. 9, cited with illustration of the paper and commentary in Martin, *Persecution*, pp. 79–80.
52. National Spiritual Assembly of the Bahais of Iran, *The Banning of Bahai Religious Institutions in Iran: An Open Letter* (translated from Persian), 12 Shahrivar 1362 [3 September 1983]. See also *Iran Times*, 23 September 1983, pp. 1, 12.
53. *Jomhuri-ye Islami*, 30 June 1980, with illustration in Martin, *Persecution*, p. 48.
54. Very little reliable information exists about the Hojjatieh Society; see "Hojjatieh Society, Past and Present – Conclusion," *Iran Press Digest*, 16 April 1985, pp. 5–8; Nikola B. Schahgaldian, *The Clerical Establishment in Iran* (Santa Monica, CA: Rand Corporation, 1989), pp. 61–65; *Christian Science Monitor*, 14 July 1983, p. 24; and Martin, *Persecution*, pp. 46–47 (which includes an illustration of the edict by the Ministry of Education and Training), pp. 60–63.
55. See comments by Imami Kashani, a member of the first Majlis: *Mozakerat-e Majlis*, 7 Shahrivar 1360 [29 August 1981], meeting 207, p. 23; *Kayhan*, 30 Day 1360 [20 January 1982], p. 15; US Department of State, *Country Reports on Human Rights Practices for 1984*, p. 1241.
56. United Nations, Economic and Social Council, Commission on Human Rights, 39th Session, *Annex II: Note Verbale Dated 3 February 1983 from the Permanent Mission of the Islamic Republic of Iran*, pp. 1–20, quotes from p. 15, and *Annex III: Statement Submitted by the Bahai International Community*, both E/CN.4/1983/19, 13 January–11 March 1983, pp. 1–4.
57. United Nations, E/CN.4/1991/35, pp. 52–60, and the Iranian government

reply, p. 89; United Nations, General Assembly, 43rd Session, Agenda Item 12, *Situation of Human Rights in the Islamic Republic of Iran*, A/RES/43/137, 31 January 1989, p. 2; US Department of State, *Country Reports on Human Rights Practices for 1991*, p. 1413. For human rights problems in general, see Amnesty International, *Iran Briefing* (London: Amnesty International Publications, 1987); and Amnesty International, *Iran*.

58. One copy of the original document with an English translation was given to the author by the National Spiritual Assembly of the Bahais of the United States. See also Human Rights Watch, *Iran*, p. 14. The note read, "In the name of God: the decision of the Supreme Revolutionary Cultural Council seems sufficient. I thank you gentlemen for your attention and efforts," and Khamenei's signature followed.

59. United Nations, 51st session, Agenda Item 12, *Question of the Violation of Human Rights and Fundamental Freedoms in Any Part of the World, with Particular Reference to Colonial and Other Dependent Countries and Territories*, E/CN.4/1995/55, 16 January 1995, p. 9.

60. Human Rights Watch, *Iran*, p. 13.

61. *Iran Times*, 31 July 1998, pp. 1, 10.

62. *New York Times*, 29 October 1998, p. A9; *Kayhan* (London), 8 October 1998, p. 4, provides names of the cities where raids occurred, showing that the act was systematic and purposeful.

63. Personal interview with Dr. Firuz Kazemzadeh, February 1999.

64. *Iran Times* (in English), 26 June 1998, p. 4.

65. These issues have had a long history of debate among ethnic politics scholars; see Zenner, "Middleman Minorities," p. 257.

66. Tafti, *Moshkel-e Eshq*, pp. 44–45.

67. Bishop Dehqani Tafti listed all the incidents in a letter to Ayatollah Khomeini from his exile in Britain in September 1980, receiving no reply; see John Simpson, *Inside Iran: Life Under Khomeini's Regime* (New York: St. Martin's Press, 1988), pp. 315–16; and Tafti, *Moshkel-e Eshq*, pp. 50–57.

68. For further details, see *Time*, 26 May 1980, p. 62; *The Times* (London), 21 August 1980, p. 1; and *New York Times*, 24 February 1981, p. A3. For the softening of attitudes toward St. Luke's Church, see Simpson, *Inside Iran*, pp. 317–18.

69. A copy of the letter, in Persian, sent to Islamic authorities was shown to the author by Reverend Tateos Mikaelian. A copy of the official Isfahan ordinance is in the author's possession.

70. *Mojdeh* (published by Iranian Christian International, Inc.) 15, nos. 1–2 (Spring–Summer 1994), 12.

71. Human Rights Watch, *Iran*, p. 17.

72. For reports of these incidents, see *Iran Times*, 21 January 1994, p. 1; 8 July 1994, p. 1; *New York Times*, 6 February 1994, p. A10; *Mojdeh* 15, nos. 1–2 (Spring–Summer 1994), 3–6. See also Human Rights Watch, *Human Rights Watch World Report 1996* (New York: Human Rights Watch, 1996), p. 279; Human Rights Watch, *Iran*, pp. 15–17; United Nations, E/CN.4/1995/55, p. 8. For the Mojahedin Organization view, see *Iran Zamin*, 7 July 1994, no. 7, p. 1; 14 July 1994, no. 8, p. 1.

73. *Mojdeh* 15, nos. 1–2 (Spring–Summer 1994), 5; United Nations,

E/CN.4/1991/35, p. 48. In a letter, the Iranian government maintained that the closing of the Bible Society was temporary, for failing to respect the laws and regulations of the Islamic Republic. The case was to be considered by the courts (p. 49). For other problems faced by Christian Iranians in select cities, see pp. 51–52.

74. Human Rights Watch, *Iran*, pp. 18–19.

75. United Nations, E/CN.4/1995/55, p. 8. The comment was made by Jarad Zarif, deputy minister for foreign affairs, in August 1994.

76. United Nations, General Assembly, 51st session, Agenda Item 110 (c), *Human Rights Questions: Human Rights Situations and Reports of Special Rapporteurs and Representatives. Situation of Human Rights in Iran*, A/51/479, 11 October 1996, p. 9. The comment was attributed to Ayatollah Yazdi in May 1996.

77. Zenner, "Middleman Minorities," p. 260.

78. Simpson, *Inside Iran*, pp. 314–15.

79. Eric Hoffer, *The True Believer: Thoughts on the Nature of Mass Movements* (New York: Harper Perennial, 1989), p. 93.

80. Momen, *Introduction*, p. 237.

81. See *Christian Science Monitor*, 21 November 1986, p. 11; FBIS/NES, September 22, 1987, pp. 26–27; September 24, 1987, p. 4; 28 September 1987, p. 5; February 16, 1988, p. 70. See also Sammy Segev, *The Iranian Triangle: The Untold Story of Israel's Role in the Iran–Contra Affair* (New York: Free Press, 1988); Ari Ben-Menashe, *Profits of War: Inside the US–Israel Arms Network* (New York: Sheridan Square Press, 1992).

82. Privately, it was conveyed to the author that in one situation, in a government office, an Armenian was asked point blank whom s/he identified with, Iran or Armenia. Taken by surprise, the person used religious metaphor to reply.

Houchang Chehabi reported that, when the Iranian policy of neutrality on Armenian–Azerbaijan conflict became unpopular in Iranian Azerbaijan, Ayatollah Khamenei visited the area and in Azeri issued a warning to the Armenian Republic. He also reported that death threats had been received by Armenians of Tabriz. The problem subsided when the Armenian religious leadership in Tehran issued a statement condemning Armenian advances against Azerbaijan and supporting the Iranian government; see Chehabi, "Ardabil Becomes a Province," 246, 253, n. 92. This author has been informed by sources in Iran that, in private meetings between Ayatollah Khamenei and Azerbaijan clerics, he warned them not to agitate the populace against the Armenians.

83. Noori [Nuri], "Islamic Concept of State," 79.

84. *Iran Times*, 31 December 1982, p. 13.

85. Thanks to Shahrough Akhavi for raising this point.

86. Translation from *Youth Magazine* (Tehran), March 1986, given to the author by Reverend Mikaelian.

87. This piece was translated from *Iran News*, 3 January 1982, p. 1, by Rustam Guiv Dareh-Mehr for the California Zoroastrian Center. One copy was mailed to the author by Iranian Christians International, Inc.

88. Details were conveyed to the author by several people who knew the two brothers, including Reverend Mikaelian.

89. Shirin Ebadi, *Tarikhche va Asnad-e Hoquq-e Bashar dar Iran* (Tehran: Roshangaran, 1373 [1994/95]), pp. 94–95, explains the inherent contradictions in the revised civil law Article 881.

90. Imam Khomeini, *Towzih al-Masael* (n.p., n.d.), problem 2783, p. 572.

91. Montazeri, *Resaleh-ye*, p. 553, on problems 3001 and 3002, and p. 537, problem 2930.

92. For a similar account in the past, see Fischel, "Jews in Medieval Iran," pp. 277–28.

93. Ebadi, *Tarikhche*, p. 120.

94. Ali-Akbar Hasani, *Nazari be Qavanin-e Jazai-ye Islam* (Tehran: Ettela'at-Iranchap, 1360 [1981/82]), pp. 57, 97.

95. For specific rules pertaining to qesas, see *Majmueh-ye Qavanin-e*, pp. 235–50.

96. For a typical work, see Ayatollah Abbas-Ali Amid Zanjani, *Hoquq-e Aqaliatha* (Tehran: Nashr-e Farhang-e Islami, 1362 [1983/84]).

97. *Majmueh-ye Qavanin-e*, pp. 265–66.

98. See Articles 88 and 82 in Ebadi, *Tarikhche*, pp. 92–93. See also Article 99J in *Majmueh-ye Qavanin-e*, p. 243.

99. Montazeri, *Resaleh-ye*, p. 556 on problems 3010 and 3011; p. 558 on problem 3018.

100. Ebadi, *Tarikhche*, p. 94 (see the last segment of Article 147).

101. *Ibid.*, p. 93. Ebadi refers to Articles 109, 110, and 121 of the penal code.

102. *Ibid.*, pp. 81–83.

103. *Ibid.*, p. 88.

104. Conveyed to the author by several people familiar with this and other cases involving recognized religious minorities.

105. United Nations, A/51/479, p. 9. For a similar case involving a motorcycle accident, see Human Rights Watch, *Iran*, p. 15.

106. Human Rights Watch, *Iran*, p. 14.

107. Ebadi is an advocate of this point of view; see *Tarikhche*, p. 14.

108. Aida Avanessian, "Armenian Community in Iran: Social and Legal Status," paper presented at the Middle East Studies Association Annual Meeting, 1996, pp. 5–6.

109. Interview with Attorney Aida Avanessian, Los Angeles, 1996.

5 PREVALENT RESPONSES OF RECOGNIZED RELIGIOUS MINORITIES

1. Burkey, *Ethnic and Racial Groups*, pp. 103–04.

2. Halim Barakat, "Liberation or Terrorism: Refuting the Language of the Oppressor," *Arab Studies Quarterly* 9, no. 2 (Spring 1987), 133.

3. FBIS, 15 May 1979, p. R1; Khomeini's quote is in 16 May 1979, p. R2. See also "Jews Are Our Brothers: Down with Zionism," *Review of Iranian Political Economy and History* 3, no. 2 (Fall 1979), 52–54. Yousef Cohen writes that the Jews were asked to meet with Ayatollah Khomeini two days after Elghanian's execution. He urged the community leaders to boycott the meeting to no avail; see Yousef Cohen, *Gozaresh*, p. 317.

4. *New York Times*, 16 May 1979, p. A11.

5. *Kayhan*, 20 Ordibehesht 1362 [10 May 1983], p. 2.

6. See, for example, the article printed at Christmastime in *Resalat*, 10 Day 1366 [31 December 1987], no. 576, pp. 1, 10.
7. *Cheesta*, 1st year, no. 7, Esfand 1360 [March 1982], p. 737.
8. *Ibid.*, no. 6, Bahman 1360 [February 1982], p. 624.
9. *Mozakerat-e Majlis*, 30 Aban 1361 [21 November 1982], meeting 378, p. 16.
10. Excerpts from "Khomeyni Receives Delegates of Religious Minorities," JPRS 82749, p. 63 (text of the entire speech, pp. 62–64), translated from *Alik*, 20 November 1982, pp. 1, 6. Details of Ushana's speech were also printed in *Cheesta*, 2nd year, no. 4, Azar 1361 [December 1982], pp. 527–28.
11. JPRS 82749, pp. 63–64.
12. For details, see *Cheesta*, 2nd year, no. 5, Day 1361 [January 1983], p. 640; nos. 7–8, Noruz 1362 [April 1983], pp. 936–43. See also "Minorities Celebrate Revolution Anniversary," JPRS 83083, p. 141.
13. *Ettela'at* 18684, 18 Bahman 1367 [7 February 1989], p. 18; and SWB/BBC, ME/0380 9 February 1989, p. A3, taken from IRNA in English 7 February 1989.
14. *Resalat* 899, 18 Bahman 1367 [7 February 1989], pp. 1–2; for a brief account of the Congress and interview excerpts, see *Iran Times*, 24 February 1989, pp. 1, 14.
15. *Iran Times*, 10 February 1989, p. 15.
16. "Christians Pray for Victory," JPRS 77324, p. 46, taken from *Kayhan International*, 3 January 1981, p. 2.
17. FBIS (taken from Hadashot in Hebrew, 3 July 1986), 7 July 1986, p. I7.
18. Armenian and Zoroastrian yearly calendars during the war years gave details on their recruits including the injured and those who had disappeared. The location of their death was also identified. Group photos were taken often next to a tank. For reports on the recruits, see FBIS, 4 August 1986, p. 13; 8 December 1987, p. 57; *Asbarez*, 10 June 1987, p. 5; 24 June 1987, p. 5; *Cheesta*, 1st year, no. 8, Farvardin 1361 [April 1982], pp. 992–93; 2nd year, no. 2, Mehr 1361 [October 1982], pp. 261–63; and Aban 1361 [November 1982], p. 392, which states that, by November 1982, seven Zoroastrians had been killed in the war.
19. "Armenian Support," JPRS 77324, p. 49, taken from *Kayhan International*, 3 January 1981, p. 2; and *Cheesta*, 1st year, no. 10, Khordad 1361 [June 1982], p. 1200.
20. In 1987, the Armenians donated a gilded chandelier to the mosque of Behesht-e Zahra cemetery and held Christian religious services for the Muslim martyrs. The comment was made by a government official present in the ceremonies; see *Hye Giank Weekly* (in Armenian), 24 July 1987, p. 13.
21. *Cheesta*, 2nd year, no. 6, Bahman 1361 [February 1983], pp. 764–65.
22. Original interview in *Kayhan*, 14 Ordibehesht 1359 [4 May 1980], p. 10; the response of the Jewish Society of Tehran appears in *Kayhan*, 23 Ordibehesht 1359 [13 May 1980], p. 2; response in *Kayhan*, 6 Khordad 1359 [27 May 1980], pp. 10–11. See also "Rights of Religious Minorities," JPRS 75967, 1 July 1980, pp. 79–83.
23. Parviz Malekpoor, "Payam-e Imam," in *Cheesta*, 2nd year, no. 6, Bahman 1361 [February 1983], pp. 641–44.
24. *Cheesta*, 1st year, no. 7, Esfand 1360 [March 1982], pp. 737–40; the quota-

tion appears on p. 740. For a similar critique where references are made to publications in *Kayhan* and *Saf* magazine in Kerman, see 2nd year, no. 5, Day 1361 [January 1983], pp. 529–33.

25. See article in *Asbarez*, 14 May 1988, p. 8.
26. Comments of the clerical elite were posted on placards or posters during special occasions including the RRM religious ceremonies. They would also appear in minority publications; see, for example, a comment to *Kayhan* by Ayatollah Mohammadi Gilani about respecting the human dignity of recognized non-Muslim minorities, highlighted in *Cheesta*, 2nd year, no. 6, Bahman 1361 [February 1983], p. 669; or 2nd year, no. 5, Day 1361 [January 1983], pp. 529–33.
27. Simpson, *Inside Iran*, pp. 42–43.
28. Louis Wirth, "The Problem of Minority Groups," in Minako Kurokawa (ed.), *Minority Responses: Comparative Views of Reactions to Subordination* (New York: Random House, 1970), p. 35.
29. Shahin Bekhradnia, "Decline of the Iranian Zoroastrian Priesthood: Its Effect on the Iranian Zoroastrian Community in the Twentieth Century," *BRISMES [British Society for Middle Eastern Studies] Proceedings 1991* (Exeter: Brismes, 1991), pp. 449–57.
30. The author was witness to this while traveling between cities during her visit to Iran in 1992.
31. *Mozakerat-e Majlis*, 16 Shahrivar 1361, meeting 356, pp. 17–19.
32. See the announcement from the Armenian Churches Association of Isfahan and Southern Iran in January 1981 denying any links with the Protestant and Catholic churches in "Armenian Support," JPRS 77324, p. 49.
33. See the interview with Archbishop Artak Manukian on the occasion of 1989 New Year celebrations in which he is quoted as saying: "The Armenian church in Iran has no connection to any Christian religious authority and power and Armenians should not be viewed as part of the Catholic Church or the Vatican" (*Resalat*, 12 Day 1367 [2 January 1989], p. 2).
34. This sensitivity caused a change of plans on the eve of the celebrations of 2,500 years of monarchy in 1971. All churches in Iran were asked to participate in celebrations together. It was the first time that the Armenian, Assyrian, Eastern, Catholic, Protestant, and Anglican Churches were to engage in a collective ceremony. The languages used were going to be Armenian, Assyrian, English, and Persian. The location was going to be the Armenian church in Tehran, yet the Armenians objected because they would not allow Christian sermons in Persian in their church. At the invitation of the Catholics, the sermons were moved to a Catholic church; see Tafti, *Moshkel-e Eshq*, pp. 42–43.
35. The 24 April genocide commemorations could involve demonstrations, vigils in front of the Turkish Embassy or the United Nations office, and church and school ceremonies. See *Iran Times*, 13 May 1983, p. 5; *Asbarez* (in Armenian), 28 April 1990, pp. 1, 14, and in English, p. 25.
36. Khomeini, *Majmuehi*, p. 99. In the same speech, he had praised the military might of the "Islamic" Ottoman Empire who were responsible for the Armenian genocide. Khomeini associated Ataturk with Reza Shah; see, for another speech, p. 287.

37. *Mozakerat-e Majlis*, 3 Ordibehesht 1364 [23 April 1985], meeting 123, pp. 19–20.
38. *Asbarez*, 13 February 1988, p. 8.
39. FBIS, 12 April 1979, p. R2.
40. Menashri, *Iran*, p. 238; taken from *Ettela'at*, 22 February 1982.
41. *Mozakerat-e Majlis*, 27 Day 1362 [17 January 1984], meeting 562, pp. 17–18. See also "Jews Declare," JPRS 83083, p. 142.
42. Menashri, *Iran*, p. 238; see p. 257, n. 129; see also a similar comment by the chief rabbi in "Jewish Clergy Support Elections," JPRS 82511, p. 57; *Iran Times*, 8 May 1987, p. 5.
43. This issue has been raised regarding the Jewish minority in Morton Borden, *Jews, Turks, and Infidels* (Chapel Hill: University of North Carolina, 1984); and Zenner, "Middleman Minorities," p. 259.
44. *Los Angeles Times*, 27 February 1979, p. 6. For similar views, see *New York Times*, 12 April 1979, p. A1; 28 May 1979, p. A5.
45. Lecture delivered to the Society of Kerman Zoroastrians; see *Cheesta*, 2nd year, no. 3, Aban 1361 [November 1982], p. 265.
46. Rafsanjani emphasized the "Iranian roots" of Zoroastrians; see *ibid.*, no. 5, Day 1361 [January 1983], p. 531.
47. The interview is with the weekly *Soroosh* published 22 Farvardin 1360 [11 April 1981]; it is reprinted in *Cheesta*, 2nd year, no. 2, Mehr 1361 [October 1982], p. 132.
48. *Cheesta*, 3rd year, no. 2, Mehr 1364 [October 1985], p. 157.
49. Communicated to the author in interviews in Iran, 1992.
50. Simpson and Yinger, *Racial and Cultural Minorities*, p. 158.
51. Barth, "Introduction," p. 15.
52. *Ibid.*, p. 25.

CONCLUSION: THE PERILS OF MARGINALITY

1. Charlton, Everett, and Staudt, *Women, the State, and Development*.
2. Any employment dealing with the armed forces and the military clearly asked for adherence to Islam; see the job advertisement for physicians for the Public Health Department of the armed forces in *Kayhan*, 15 Khordad 1377 [5 June 1998], p. 10. Some ads have a more convoluted language; the ad for a factory in Zanjan asks for "religious people and those bound to the foundations of the Islamic Republic of Iran"; see *Kayhan*, 27 Mordad 1377 [18 August 1998], p. 12. Some ads do mention, among conditions of employment, adherence to one of the recognized religions: see *Kayhan*, 19 Mordad 1377 [10 August 1998], p. 9.
3. Daniel Kurtzman, "Iranian's Testimony Reveals Plight of the Jews Left Behind," *JTA [Jewish Telegraphic Agency] Daily News Bulletin* 74, 19 March 1996, pp. 1–2.
4. US Department of State, *Country Reports on Human Rights Practices for 1994* (Washington, DC: Government Printing Office, 1995), p. 1077; see also Susan Birnbaum, "Elderly Jew Executed in Tehran for Associating with Zionism," *JTA [Jewish Telegraphic Agency] Daily News Bulletin* 72, 10 March

1994, pp. 1–2. Both reports indicate that the victim was tortured and his body was mutilated.

5. US Department of State, *Country Reports on Human Rights Practices for 1997* (Washington, DC: Government Printing Office, 1998), p. 1445.

6. FBIS, 24 March 1992, p. 15.

7. *Ibid.*, 21 June 1993, p. 2.

8. *Ibid.*, 18 February 1997, pp. 13–14.

9. Under the guise of a book review, one author wrote that Jews had plans for the whole world and, like a cancer, were out to destroy all nations; see Mohammad Reza Alvand, "Israil Bayad Beravad," *Kayhan*, 10 Day 1371 [31 December 1992], p. 16; for the response of the Association of Iranian Jewish Intellectuals, see *Kayhan*, 14 Day 1371 [4 January 1993], p. 18.

10. A copy of the letter appears in *Chashm Andaaz* 57, September 1997, pp. 81–82.

11. *Cheesta*, 12th year, no. 10, Tir 1374 [August 1995], p. 877.

12. FBIS, 22 November 1994, p. 1.

13. *Ibid.*, 17 March 1993, p. 53; 18 March 1994, p. 30.

14. In two short pieces, which try not to criticize the event directly, some of the problems were ambiguously pointed out; see *Cheesta*, 13th year, nos. 8–9, Ordibehesht–Khordad 1375 [May–June 1996], p. 768, and 14th year, no. 1, Mehr 1375 [October 1996], pp. 126–28. For an official account of the Congress, see *Ettela'at International*, 24 June 1996, p. 10; 27 June 1996, p. 10.

15. *Iran Times*, 13 November 1998, p. 1, in English; *Ettela'at International*, 4 November 1998, p. 10; 6 November 1998, p. 3.

16. FBIS, 18 December 1992, p. 50.

17. For one example, see the article from the *Salam* newspaper in Iran, published in *Iran Times*, 10 September 1993, p. 7. The article argues that the Iranian government has an obligation to support Muslims everywhere, particularly the Azeris who share the same religion, denomination (Shii), culture, and history with Iran.

18. See ch. 4, n. 82.

19. *Asbarez*, 20 February 1993, p. 11; (in English) 2 January 1993, p. 3.

20. *Ettela'at International*, 23 July 1997, p. 10.

21. FBIS, 8 August 1994, p 22. One of the priests, Tateos Mikaelian, had been a vocal supporter of the Armenian educational rights and legal equality for non-Muslims. This copycat statement (whether forced on the Armenian deputy or made on his own initiative) magnifies the tragedy of marginality.

22. FBIS, 2 June 1995, p. 27.

23. Fred Halliday, "What Does Mohammed Khatami Think?: Mohammed and Mill," *New Republic*, 5 October 1998, 30.

24. Menashri, *Iran*, p. 218 (the quote is taken from *Kayhan*, 24 November 1982); see also pp. 293, 368.

25. *Cheesta*, 2nd year, no. 1, Shahrivar 1361 [September 1982], pp. 70–71.

26. *Iran Times*, 23 January 1998, p. 3.

27. *Ibid.*, 28 August 1998, p. 6.

28. *Ettela'at International*, 20 December 1995, p. 8.

29. FBIS-NES-97–148, 28 May 1997.
30. *Ettela'at International*, 30 October 1998, p. 10.
31. FBIS-NES-98–044, 13 February 1998.
32. A partial text appears in *Iran Times* (in English), 3 October 1997, p. 15.
33. For a detailed description of erfan (not its distortion), see Roy Mottahedeh, *The Mantle of the Prophet: Religion and Politics in Iran* (New York: Pantheon Books, 1985), pp. 135, 138–44.
34. Telex Tehran, IRNA, 13 Aban 1377 [4 November 1998]; one copy provided to the author.
35. FBIS, 6 February 1989, p. 69.
36. Hossein Mehrpoor, *Hoquq-e Bashar dar Asnad-e Baenolmalali va Mozeeh Jomhuri-ye Islami-ye Iran* (Tehran: Ettela'at, 1374 [1995/96]), p. 153. This work is a masterful twisted explanation of human rights in Iran. The author suggests that enemies have presented an "unappealing" picture of the legal system of the republic, and presents a set of recommendations in order to improve the image rather than the substance of the law; see p. 80.
37. Soroudi, "Jews in Islamic Iran," 110. Also, the author has heard several stories to this effect.
38. All the above cases were conveyed to or witnessed by the author.
39. Stagner, "Foreword," p. 9.
40. Mahatma Gandhi, *The Essential Gandhi: An Anthology of His Writings on His Life, Work and Ideas*, ed. Louis Fischer (New York: Vintage Books, 1962), p. 80.

Bibliography

Abrahamian, Ervand, "Communism and Communalism in Iran: The Tudeh and the Firqah-i Dimukrat," *International Journal of Middle East Studies* 1, no. 4, October 1970, 291–316.

Iran Between Two Revolutions, Princeton: Princeton University Press, 1982.

Adhami, Davoud, *Besooye Kemal* [Toward Perfection], New York: Parkway Printing, 1996.

Afary, Janet, "Enqelab-e Mashruteh" [The Constitutional Revolution], in Sarshar, *Yahudian-e Irani dar Tarikh-e Moaser*, vol. II.

The Iranian Constitutional Revolution, 1906–1911: Grassroots Democracy, Social Democracy, and the Origins of Feminism, New York: Columbia University Press, 1996.

Afshar (Sistani), Iraj, *Moqadamehi bar Shenakht-e Ilha, Chadorneshinan va Tavayef-e Ashaeri-e Iran* [A Preliminary Understanding of Tribal Confederacies, Tent-Dwellers, and Nomadic Tribes in Iran], vol. I, Tehran: Homa, 1366 [1987].

Ahmed, Leila, *Women and Gender in Islam: Historical Roots of a Modern Debate*, New Haven: Yale University Press, 1992.

Akhavi, Shahrough, *Religion and Politics in Contemporary Iran: Clergy–State Relations in the Pahlavi Period*, Albany: State University of New York Press, 1980.

Amanat, Abbas, *Resurrection and Renewal: The Making of the Babi Movement in Iran, 1844–1850*, Ithaca: Cornell University Press, 1989.

Amanolahi (Baharvand), Sekandar, *Kuchneshini dar Iran: Pazhuheshi Darbarehye Ashaer va Ilat* [Migration in Iran: An Investigation of Nomads and Tribes], Tehran: Bongah-e Tarjomeh va Nashr-e Ketab, 1360 [1981].

"The Lurs of Iran," *Cultural Survival Quarterly* 9, February 1985, 65–69.

Amirahmadi, Hooshang, "A Theory of Ethnic Collective Movements and Its Application to Iran," *Ethnic and Racial Studies* 10, no. 4, October 1987, 364–91.

Arberry, A. J. (ed.), *Religion in the Middle East*, 2 vols., Cambridge: Cambridge University Press, 1969.

Arfa, Hassan, *Under Five Shahs*, London: William Morrow, 1964.

Arkun, Aram, "Armenians and the Jangalis," *Iranian Studies* 30, nos. 1–2, Winter–Spring 1997, 25–52.

"Dashnak," in *Encyclopaedia Iranica*, vol. VII.

Armajani, Yahya, "Christians – Christian Missions in Persia," in *Encyclopaedia Iranica*, vol. V.

"Armenia and Iran," in *Encyclopaedia Iranica*, vol. II.

Ashideri, Jahangir, *Tarikh-e Pahlavi va Zarthoshtian* [The History of the Pahlavi and the Zoroastrians], Tehran: Mahnameye Hokht, 2535 [1976].

Avanessian, Aida, "Armenian Community in Iran: Social and Legal Status," paper presented at the Middle East Studies Association Annual Meeting, 1996.

Awang, Abd al-Rahman, "The Status of the Dhimmi in Islamic Law," Ph.D. thesis, University of Edinburgh, 1988.

The Bahai Question: Iran's Secret Blueprint for the Destruction of a Religious Community, New York: Bahai International Community Publications, 1993.

Bakhash, Shaul, "Center–Periphery Relations in Nineteenth-Century Iran," *Iranian Studies* 14, nos. 1–2, Winter–Spring 1981, 29–51.

The Reign of the Ayatollahs, New York: Basic Books, 1984.

Bani Sadr, Abol-Hasan, *Moqeiyyat-e Iran va Naqsh-e Modarres* [The Condition of Iran and the Role of Modarres], vol. I, n.p.: Entesharat-e Modarres, 1356 [1977].

Barakat, Halim, "Liberation or Terrorism: Refuting the Language of the Oppressor," *Arab Studies Quarterly* 9, no. 2, Spring 1987, 133–38.

Barker, Paul, "Tent Schools of the Qashqa'i: A Paradox of Local Initiative and State Control," in Bonine and Keddie, *Continuity and Change in Modern Iran*.

Barth, Fredrik, "Introduction," in Barth (ed.), *Ethnic Groups and Boundaries: The Social Organization of Culture Difference*, London: George Allen & Unwin, 1969.

Bashiriyeh, Hossein, *The State and Revolution in Iran, 1962–1982*, New York: St. Martin's Press, 1984.

Bates, Daniel G., "Kurd," in Weekes, *Muslim Peoples*, vol. I.

Bayat, Mangol, *Iran's First Revolution: Shi'ism and the Constitutional Revolution of 1905–1909*, New York: Oxford University Press, 1991.

"Mahmud Taleqani and the Iranian Revolution," in Kramer, Martin (ed.), *Shi'ism, Resistance, and Revolution*, Boulder: Westview Press, 1987.

Bazargan, Abdol-Ali, *Masael va Moshkelat-e Nokhostin Sal-e Enqelab az Zaban-e Reis-e Dovlat-e Movaqat* [Issues and Problems in the First Year of the Revolution from the Leader of the Provisional Government], 2nd edn., n.p.: author publication, 1362 [1983/84].

Beck, Lois, "Nomads and Urbanites, Involuntary Hosts and Uninvited Guests," *Journal of Middle Eastern Studies* 18, no. 4, 1982, 426–44.

The Qashqa'i of Iran, New Haven: Yale University Press, 1986.

"Revolutionary Iran and Its Tribal Peoples," *Middle East Research and Information Project*, May 1980, 14–20.

"Tribes and State in Nineteenth- and Twentieth-Century Iran," in Khoury, Philip and Kostiner, Joseph (eds.), *Tribes and State Formation in the Middle East*, Berkeley: University of California Press, 1990.

Behnam, M. Reza, *Cultural Foundations of Iranian Politics*, Salt Lake City: University of Utah Press, 1986.

Bekhradnia, Shahin, "Decline of the Iranian Zoroastrian Priesthood: Its Effect on the Iranian Zoroastrian Community in the Twentieth Century," *BRISMES [British Society for Middle Eastern Studies] Proceedings 1991*, Exeter: Brismes, 1991, pp. 449–57.

Ben-Menashe, Ari, *Profits of War: Inside the US–Israel Arms Network*, New York: Sheridan Square Press, 1992.

Benard, Cheryl and Khalilzad, Zalmay, *The Government of God: Iran's Islamic Republic*, New York: Columbia University Press, 1984.

Berberian, Houri, "The Dashnaktsutiun and the Iranian Constitutional Revolution, 1905–1911," *Iranian Studies* 29, nos. 1–2, Winter–Spring 1996, 7–33.

Berg, Herbert, "Tabari's Exegesis of the Qur'anic Term 'Al-Kitab,'" *Journal of the American Academy of Religion* 63, Winter 1995, 761–74.

Bialer, Uri, "The Iranian Connection in Israel's Foreign Policy: 1948–1951," *Middle East Journal* 39, Spring 1985, 292–315.

Bill, James A., *The Eagle and the Lion: The Tragedy of American–Iranian Relations*, New Haven: Yale University Press, 1988.

"The Patterns of Elite Politics in Iran," in Lenczowski, George (ed.), *Political Elites in the Middle East*, Washington, DC: American Enterprise Institute, 1975.

Bill, James A. and Leiden, Carl, *Politics in the Middle East*, 2nd edn., Boston: Little, Brown & Co., 1984.

Binder, Leonard, "National Integration and Political Development," *American Political Science Review* 58, September 1964, 622–31.

Birnbaum, Susan, "Elderly Jew Executed in Tehran for Associating with Zionism," *JTA [Jewish Telegraphic Agency] Daily News Bulletin* 72, 10 March 1994, pp. 1–2.

Bonine, Michael E. and Keddie, Nikki R. (eds.), *Continuity and Change in Modern Iran*, Albany: State University of New York, 1981.

Borden, Morton, *Jews, Turks, and Infidels*, Chapel Hill: University of North Carolina, 1984.

Bournoutian, George A., *Eastern Armenia in the Last Decades of Persian Rule, 1807–1828*, Malibu, CA: Undena Publications, 1982.

A History of the Armenian People: Pre-History to 1500 AD, Costa Mesa, CA: Mazda Publishers, 1994.

Boyce, Ann, *Textual Sources for the Study of Zoroastrianism*, Manchester: Manchester University Press, 1984.

Zoroastrians: Their Religious Beliefs and Practices, London: Routledge & Kegan Paul, 1979.

Bram, Joseph, "Change and Choice in Ethnic Identification," *Transactions of the New York Academy of Sciences* 28, ser. 2, no. 2, December 1965, 242–48.

Brass, Paul R., "Ethnic Groups and the State," in Brass (ed.), *Ethnic Groups and the State*, Totowa, NJ: Barnes & Noble, 1985.

Brooks, David, "The Enemy Within: Limitations on Leadership in the Bakhtiari," in Tapper, *Conflict of Tribe and State*.

Brown, Daniel W., *Rethinking Tradition in Modern Islamic Thought*, Cambridge: Cambridge University Press, 1996.

Burkey, Richard M., *Ethnic and Racial Groups: The Dynamics of Dominance*, Reading, MA: Cummings, 1978.

Chaliand, Gerard (ed.), *People Without a Country*, London: Zed Press, 1979.

Chaqueri, Cosroe, "The Role and Impact of Armenian Intellectuals in Iranian Politics, 1905–1911," *Armenian Review* 41, no. 2, Summer 1988, 1–51.

"Sultanzade. The Forgotten Revolutionary Theoretician of Iran: A Biographical Sketch," *Iranian Studies* 17, nos. 2–3, Spring–Summer 1984, 215–35.

Charlton, Sue Ellen M., Everett, Jana and Staudt, Kathleen (eds.), *Women, the State, and Development*, Albany: State University of New York Press, 1989.

Chehabi, Houchang E., "Ardabil Becomes a Province: Center–Periphery Relations in Iran," *International Journal of Middle East Studies* 29, no. 2, May 1997, 235–53.

Iranian Politics and Religious Modernism, Ithaca: Cornell University Press, 1990.

"Staging the Emperor's New Clothes: Dress Codes and Nation-Building Under Reza Shah," *Iranian Studies* 26, nos. 3–4, Summer–Fall 1993, 209–29.

Choksy, Jamsheed K., *Purity and Pollution in Zoroastrianism: Triumph over Evil*, Austin: University of Texas Press, 1989.

"Zoroastrians in Muslim Iran: Selected Problems of Coexistence and Interaction During the Early Medieval Period," *Iranian Studies* 20, no. 1, 1987, 17–30.

"Christians Protest in Iran," *Iran Liberation* 103, 6 January 1984, p. 1.

Cohen, Avraham, "Iranian Jewry and the Educational Endeavors of the Alliance Israelite Universelle," *Jewish Social Studies* 48, no. 1, Winter 1986, 15–44.

Cohen, Yousef, *Gozaresh va Khaterat-e Faaliethaye Siasi va Ejtemai* [Reports and Memoirs of Political and Social Activities], Los Angeles: International Printing–Yousef Cohen Foundation, 1993.

Cole, Juan, "Baha-Allah," in *Encyclopaedia Iranica*, vol. III.

"Bahai Faith or Bahaism," in *Encyclopaedia Iranica*, vol. III.

"Conversions: V. To Babism and Bahai Faith," in *Encyclopaedia Iranica*, vol. VI.

Modernity and the Millennium: The Genesis of the Baha'i Faith in the Nineteenth-Century Middle East, New York: Columbia University Press, 1998.

Coleman, James S. and Rosberg, Carl G. Jr. (eds.), *Political Parties and National Integration in Tropical Africa*, Berkeley: University of California Press, 1964.

Connor, Walker, "Ethnonationalism in the First World: The Present Historical Perspective," in Esman, Milton J. (ed.), *Ethnic Conflict in the Western World*, Ithaca: Cornell University Press, 1977.

"Nation-Building or Nation-Destroying?," *World Politics* 24, no. 3, April 1972, 319–55.

The National Question in Marxist-Leninist Theory and Strategy, Princeton: Princeton University Press, 1984.

Cooper, Roger, *The Bahais of Iran*, London: Minority Rights Group, Report 51, 1982.

Cottam, Richard W., *Nationalism in Iran*, Pittsburgh: University of Pittsburgh Press, 1979.

Dabashi, Hamid, *Theology of Discontent: The Ideological Foundation of the Islamic Revolution in Iran*, New York: New York University Press, 1993.

Deshen, Shlomo and Zenner, Walter P. (eds.), *Jewish Societies in the Middle East: Community, Culture and Authority*, Washington, DC: University Press of America, 1982.

Deutsch, Karl W., *Nationalism and Social Communication*, Cambridge, MA: MIT Press, 1953.

Deutsch, Karl W. and Foltz, William J. (eds.), *Nation Building*, New York: Atherton Press, 1963.

Eagleton, W., *The Kurdish Republic of 1946*, London: Oxford University Press, 1963.

Ebadi, Shirin, *Tarikhche va Asnad-e Hoquq-e Bashar dar Iran* [The History and Documents of Human Rights in Iran], Tehran: Roshangaran, 1373 [1994/95].

Elliot, R. S. P. and Hickie, John, *Ulster: A Case Study in Conflict Theory*, New York: St. Martin's Press, 1971.

Enayat, Hamid, *Modern Islamic Political Thought*, Austin: University of Texas Press, 1982.

Encyclopaedia Iranica, ed. Ehsan Yarshater, vols. I–IV, Boston: Routledge & Kegan Paul, 1985–90; vols. V–VIII, Costa Mesa, CA: Mazda Press, 1992–98.

English, Paul Ward, "Nationalism, Secularism, and the Zoroastrians of Kerman: The Impact of Modern Forces on an Ancient Middle Eastern Minority," in Dohrs, Fred E. and Sommers, Lawrence M. (eds.), *Cultural Geography: Selected Readings*, New York: Thomas Y. Crowell, 1967.

Enloe, Cynthia, *Ethnic Conflict and Political Development*, Boston: Little, Brown, 1973.

   Ethnic Soldiers: State Security in Divided Societies, Athens: University of Georgia Press, 1980.

Entessar, Nader, "The Kurds in Post-Revolutionary Iran and Iraq," *Third World Quarterly* 6, October 1984, 911–33.

Esman, Milton J., *Ethnic Politics*, Ithaca: Cornell University Press, 1994.

   "The Management of Communal Conflict," *Public Policy* 21, Winter 1973, 49–78.

Esposito, John L., *Islam: The Straight Path*, Oxford: Oxford University Press, 1988.

Fadel, Muhammad, "Two Women, One Man: Knowledge, Power and Gender in Medieval Sunni Legal Thought," *International Journal of Middle East Studies* 29, May 1997, 185–204.

Faghfoory, Mohammad H., "The Ulama–State Relations in Iran: 1921–1941," *International Journal of Middle East Studies* 19, no. 4, November 1987, 413–32.

Farmayan, Hafez Farman, "Turkoman Identity and Presence in Iran," *Journal of South Asian and Middle Eastern Studies* 4, Summer 1981, 45–62.

Fazel, Golamreza, "Lur," in Weekes, *Muslim Peoples*, vol. I.

Fazel, Muhammad, "The Politics of Passion: Growing Up Shia," *Iranian Studies* 21, nos. 3–4, 1988, 37–51.

Fischel, Walter J., "The Bahai Movement and Persian Jewry," *Jewish Review* 7, 1934, 47–55.

   "The Jews in Medieval Iran from the Sixteenth to the Eighteenth Centuries: Political, Economic, and Communal Aspects," in Shaked, Shaul (ed.), *Irano-Judaica: Studies Relating to Jewish Contacts with Persian Culture*, Jerusalem: Ben-Zvi Institute for the Study of Jewish Communities in the East, 1982, 265–91.

   "The Jews of Persia, 1795–1940," *Jewish Social Studies* 12, no. 2, April 1950, 119–60.

   "Secret Jews of Persia: A Century-Old Marrano Community," *Commentary*, January 1949, 28–33.

Fisher, Sydney N., *The Middle East: A History*, 3rd edn., New York: Knopf, 1979.

Forand, Paul G., "Accounts of Western Travelers Concerning the Role of Armenians and Georgians in Sixteenth-Century Iran," *Muslim World* 65, no. 4, October 1975, 264–78.

Gandhi, Mahatma, *The Essential Gandhi: An Anthology of His Writings on His Life, Work and Ideas*, ed. Louis Fischer, New York: Vintage Books, 1962.

Garthwaite, Gene R., "Bakhtiari," in Weekes, *Muslim Peoples*, vol. I.

"Khans and Kings: The Dialectics of Power in Bakhtiyari History," in Bonine and Keddie, *Continuity and Change*.

Gelfand, Donald E. and Lee, Russell D. (compils.), *Ethnic Conflicts and Power: A Cross-National Perspective*, New York: John Wiley & Sons, 1973.

Gellner, Ernest, *Nations and Nationalism*, Oxford: Blackwell, 1983.

Gerth, H. H. and Mills, C. Wright (eds.), *From Max Weber: Essays in Sociology*, New York: Oxford University Press, 1958.

Gibb, H. A. R. and Kramers, J. H. (eds.), *Shorter Encyclopaedia of Islam*, Ithaca: Cornell University Press, 1953.

Goodell, Grace E., *The Elementary Structure of Political Life: Rural Development in Pahlavi Iran*, New York: Oxford University Press, 1986.

Gregorian, Vartan, "Minorities of Isfahan: The Armenian Community of Isfahan, 1587–1722," *Iranian Studies* 7, nos. 3–4, Summer–Autumn 1974, 652–80.

Gulpaygani, Mirza Abu'l-Fadl, *Miracles and Metaphors*, trans. Juan R. Cole, Los Angeles: Kalimat Press, 1981.

Haas, Michael, "Comparing Paradigms of Ethnic Politics in the United States: The Case of Hawaii," *Western Political Quarterly* 40, December 1987, 647–72.

Haddad, Heskel M., *Jews of Arab and Islamic Countries*, New York: Shengold Publishers, 1984.

Halliday, Fred, "What Does Mohammed Khatami Think?: Mohammed and Mill," *New Republic*, 5 October 1982, 30–34.

Harrison, Selig S., *In Afghanistan's Shadow: Baluch Nationalism and Soviet Temptations*, New York: Carnegie Endowment for International Peace, 1981.

Hasani, Ali-Akbar, *Nazari be Qavanin-e Jazai-ye Islam* [A Look at Islamic Criminal Laws], Tehran: Ettela'at-Iranchap, 1360 [1981/82].

Herzig, Edmund M., "The Deportation of the Armenians in 1604–1605 and Europe's Myth of Shah Abbas I," in Melville, Charles (ed.), *Persian and Islamic Studies in Honor of P. W. Avery*, Pembroke Papers I, Cambridge: Cambridge University Press, 1990.

Hodgson, Marshall G. S., *The Venture of Islam*, 3 vols., Chicago: University of Chicago Press, 1974.

Hoffer, Eric, *The True Believer: Thoughts on the Nature of Mass Movements*, New York: Harper Perennial, 1989.

"Hojjatieh Society, Past and Present – Conclusion," *Iran Press Digest*, 16 April 1985, pp. 5–8.

Horowitz, Dan, "Communal Armed Organizations," *Archives Européennes de Sociologie* 27, 1986, 85–101.

Horowitz, Donald L., "Three Dimensions of Ethnic Politics," *World Politics* 23, no. 2, January 1971, 232–44.

Hourani, Albert, *Arabic Thought in the Liberal Age: 1798–1939*, Cambridge: Cambridge University Press, 1983.

Minorities in the Arab World, London: Oxford University Press, 1947.

Hovannisian, Richard G., *Armenia on the Road to Independence, 1918*, Berkeley: University of California Press, 1967.

The Republic of Armenia, Vol. I: The First Year, 1918–1919, Berkeley: University of California Press, 1971.

Hunter, Shireen T., "Soviet Approach to Iran Outruns Complacent West," *Los Angeles Times*, 17 July 1989, Part II, p. 11.

Husry, Khaldun S., "The Assyrian Affair of 1933 (I)," *International Journal of Middle East Studies* 5, no. 2, April 1974, 161–76.

"The Assyrian Affair of 1933 (II)," *International Journal of Middle East Studies* 5, no. 3, June 1974, 344–60.

Irons, William G., "Turkmen," in Weekes, *Muslim Peoples*, vol. II.

Ishaya, Arian, "Family and Household Composition Among the Assyrians of Iran: The Past and the Present," in Fathi, A. (ed.), *Women and the Family in Iran*, Leiden: E. J. Brill, 1985.

The Role of Minorities in the State: History of the Assyrian Experience, Winnipeg: University of Manitoba Anthropology Papers 19, 1977.

Jacob, Philip E. and Teune, Henry, "The Integrative Process: Guidelines for Analysis of the Bases of Political Community," in Jacob and Toscano, James V. (eds.), *The Integration of Political Communities*, Philadelphia: J. B. Lippincott, 1964.

"Jews Are Our Brothers: Down with Zionism," *Review of Iranian Political Economy and History* 3, no. 2, Fall 1979, 52–54.

Joseph, John, *Muslim–Christian Relations and Inter-Christian Rivalries in the Middle East: The Case of the Jacobites in an Age of Transition*, Albany: State University of New York Press, 1983.

The Nestorians and Their Muslim Neighbors: A Study of Western Influence on Their Relations, Princeton: Princeton University Press, 1961.

Kasfir, Nelson, "Explaining Ethnic Political Participation," *World Politics* 31, no. 3, April 1979, 365–88.

Kazemi, Farhad, "Iran, Israel, and the Arab–Israeli Balance," in Rosen, *Iran Since the Revolution*.

Kazemzadeh, Firuz, "For Bahais in Iran, A Threat of Extinction," *Congressional Record* 127: no. 127–E4201, 97th Congress, 1st session, 15 September 1981.

Keddie, Nikki R., "Islamic Revivalism Past and Present, with Emphasis on Iran," in Rosen, *Iran Since the Revolution*.

Khomeini, Ayatollah Ruhollah (Imam), *Esteftaat az Mahzar-e Imam Khomeini* [Receiving Legal Opinions/Consultations in the Presence of Imam Khomeini], vol. I, Qom: Entesharat-e Islami, 1366 [1987/88].

Imam dar Barabar-e Sayhonism: Majmueh-ye Didgahha va Sokhanan-e Imam Darbareh-ye Regim-e Eshqalgar-e Qods [Imam Confronting Zionism: Collection of Views and Speeches of Imam About the Occupier Regime of Jerusalem], Tehran: Daftar-e Siasi-ye Sepah-e Pasdaran-e Enqelab-e Islami, 1361 [1982].

The Imam Versus Zionism, Tehran: Ministry of Islamic Guidance, 1984.

Majmuehi az Maktoobat, Sokhanraniha, Payamha va Fatavi-ye Imam Khomeini az Nimeye Dovom 1341 ta Hejrat be Paris (14 Mehr 1357) [A Collection of Writings, Lectures, Messages, and Decrees of Imam Khomeini from the Second Half of 1962/63 to His Move to Paris 6 October 1978], Tehran: Chanchesh, 1360 [1981/82].

Resaleh-ye Ahkam [Treatise on Judicial Orders] (includes *Towzih al-Masael* and *New Questions to Imam Khomeini*), Tehran: Ismailian Publishers, n.d.

Towzih al-Masael [Treatise on the Explanation of Problems], n.p., n.d.

Velayat-e Faqih va Jehad-e Akbar [The Rule of the Supreme Jurist and the Greater Warfare], Tehran: Nasr Publishers, n.d.

Kurtzman, Daniel, "Iranian's Testimony Reveals Plight of the Jews Left Behind," *JTA [Jewish Telegraphic Agency] Daily News Bulletin* 74, 19 March 1996, pp. 1–2.

Lang, David Marshall and Walker, Christopher J., *The Armenians*, London: Minority Rights Group, Report 32, 1982.

Laskier, Michael M., "Aspects of the Activities of the Alliance Israelite Universelle in the Jewish Communities of the Middle East and North Africa: 1860–1918," *Modern Judaism* 3, no. 3, October 1983, 147–71.

Lassner, J., "Abu Isa Esfahani," in *Encyclopaedia Iranica*, vol. I.

Leane, Edwin, "The Second Renaissance," *Armenian Review* 22, no. 2, Summer 1969, 48–50.

Levy, Habib, *Tarikh-e Yahood-e Iran* [History of the Jews of Iran], 3 vols. in 2, 2nd edn., Beverly Hills, CA: Iranian Jewish Cultural Organization of California, 1984.

Lewis, Bernard, "The Decline and Fall of Islamic Jewry," *Commentary*, June 1984, 44–54.

The Jews of Islam, Princeton: Princeton University Press, 1984.

Semites and Anti-Semites: An Inquiry into Conflict and Prejudice, New York: W. W. Norton & Company, 1986.

Loeb, Laurence D., "Dhimmi Status and Jewish Roles in Iranian Society," *Ethnic Groups*, December 1976, 89–105.

Outcaste: Jewish Life in Southern Iran, New York: Gordon & Breach Publishers, 1977.

Lustick, Ian, "Stability in Deeply Divided Societies: Consociationalism Versus Control," *World Politics* 31, no. 3, April 1979, 325–44.

MacEoin, D. M., "Bab, Sayyed Ali Mohammad," in *Encyclopaedia Iranica*, vol. III.

"Babism," in *Encyclopaedia Iranica*, vol. III.

"Bahai Faith: Bahai Persecutions," in *Encyclopaedia Iranica*, vol. III.

McLachlan, Keith, "The Iranian Economy, 1960–1976," in Amirsadeghi, Hossein (ed.), *Twentieth-Century Iran*, New York: Holmes & Meier Publishers, 1977.

Macuch, R., "Assyrians in Iran: The Assyrian Community (Asurian) in Iran," in *Encyclopaedia Iranica*, vol. II.

Majlesi, Mohammad Baqer, *Hilliyat al-Mottaqin* [The Countenance of the God-fearing/Pious], n.p.: Elmieh-e Islamieh, n.d.

Malandra, William W. (ed. and transl.), *An Introduction to Ancient Iranian Religion: Readings from the Avesta and Achaemenid Inscriptions*, Minneapolis: University of Minnesota Press, 1983.

Malekpoor, Parviz, "Payam-e Imam" [Imam's Message], *Cheesta*, 2nd year, no. 6, Bahman 1361 [February 1983], pp. 641–44.

Martin, Douglas, *The Persecution of the Bahais of Iran, 1844–1984*, Ottawa: Association of Bahai Studies, 1984.

"The Martyrdom of Seven Iranian Jews," *Israel Horizons*, March–April 1981, 9 and 13.

Mayer, Ann Elizabeth, *Islam and Human Rights: Tradition and Politics*, Boulder: Westview Press, 1991.

Mehr, Farhang, "The Impact of Religion on Contemporary Politics: The Case of Iran," in Rubenstein, Richard L. (ed.), *Spirit Matters: The Worldwide Impact of Religion on Contemporary Politics*, New York: Paragon House Publishers, 1987.

Mehran, Golnar, "Socialization of Schoolchildren in the Islamic Republic of Iran," *Iranian Studies* 22, no. 1, 1989, 35–50.

Mehrpoor, Hossein, *Hoquq-e Bashar dar Asnad-e Baenolmalali va Mozeeh Jomhuri-ye Islami-ye Iran* [Human Rights in International Instruments and the Position of the Islamic Republic of Iran], Tehran: Ettela'at, 1374 [1995/96].

Menashri, David, "Iran," in Ayalon, Ami (ed.), *Middle East Contemporary Survey*, vol. XVI, Boulder: Westview Press, 1992.

Iran: A Decade of War and Revolution, New York: Holmes & Meier, 1990.

Migdal, Joel S., "The State in Society: An Approach to Struggle for Domination," in Migdal, Kohli, Atul and Shue, Vivienne (eds.), *State Power and Social Forces: Domination and Transformation in the Third World*, Cambridge: Cambridge University Press, 1994.

Strong Societies and Weak States: State–Society Relations and State Capabilities in the Third World, Princeton: Princeton University Press, 1988.

Momen, Moojan, *The Babi and Bahai Religions, 1844–1944: Some Contemporary Western Accounts*, Oxford: Oxford University Press, 1981.

An Introduction to Shi'i Islam: The History and Doctrines of Twelver Shi'ism, New Haven: Yale University Press, 1985.

Montazeri, Shaykh Hossein-Ali, *Resaleh-ye Towzih al-Masael* [Treatise on Explanation of Problems], Tehran: Tabliqat-e Islami, 1362 [1983/84].

Moreen, Vera B., "The Downfall of Muhammad Ali Beg, Grand Vizier of Shah 'Abbas II (Reigned 1642–1666)," *Jewish Quarterly Review* 72, October 1981, 81–99.

Iranian Jewry's Hour of Peril and Heroism: A Study of Babai Ibn Lutf's Chronicle (1617–1662), Jerusalem: American Academy for Jewish Research, 1987.

"The Persecution of Iranian Jews During the Reign of Shah Abbas II (1642–1666)," *Hebrew Union College Annual* 52, 1981, 275–309.

"The Status of Religious Minorities in Safavid Iran 1617–1661," *Journal of Near Eastern Studies* 40, April 1981, 119–34.

Motahhari, Morteza, *Adl-e Elahi* [Divine Justice], Tehran: Hosseinieh-ye Ershad, 1349 [1970/71].

Mottahedeh, Roy, *The Mantle of the Prophet: Religion and Politics in Iran*, New York: Pantheon Books, 1985.

"Why Does Iran Kill Bahais?," *New York Times*, 22 June 1983, p. A27.

Naby, Eden, "The Assyrians of Iran: Reunification of a 'Millat,' 1906–1914," *International Journal of Middle East Studies* 8, no. 2, April 1977, 237–49.

"The Iranian Frontier Nationalities: The Kurds, the Assyrians, the Baluchis, and the Turkmens," in McCragg, William Jr. and Silver, Brian (eds.), *Soviet Asian Frontiers*, New York: Pergamon Press, 1979.

Netzer, Amnon, "Alliance Israelite Universelle," in *Encyclopaedia Iranica*, vol. I.

"Anjoman-e Kalimian" [The Society/Association of Jews], in *Encyclopaedia Iranica*, vol. II.

"The Fate of the Jewish Community of Tabriz," in Sharon, M. (ed.), *Studies in Islamic History and Civilization in Honour of Professor David Ayalon*, Leiden: E. J. Brill, 1986.

"Persian Jewry and Literature: A Sociocultural View," in Goldberg, Harvey E. (ed.), *Sephardi and Middle Eastern Jewries: History and Culture in the Modern Era*, Bloomington: Indiana University Press, 1996.

Nevitte, Neil and Kennedy, Charles H. (eds.), *Ethnic Preference and Public Policy in Developing States*, Boulder: Lynne Rienner, 1986.

Newbury, M. Catharine, "Colonialism, Ethnicity, and Rural Political Protest," *Comparative Politics* 15, 1983, 253–80.

Nikbakht, Fariar, "Barrasi-ye Tabliqat-e Barnamehrizishodeh va Tahrikat-e Khatarnak bar Alehye Yahudian dar Iran" [Analysis of the Organized Propaganda and Dangerous Incitement Against Jews in Iran], *Chashm Andaaz* 9, no. 66, February–March 1999, pp. 15–73 (condensed English-language version, pp. 3–10).

Niknam, Mehri, "A Jewish Childhood in Iran," *European Judaism* 28, no. 2, Autumn 1995, 99–101.

Nissman, David B., *The Soviet Union and Iranian Azerbaijan: The Use of Nationalism for Political Penetration*, Boulder: Westview Press, 1987.

Noori [Nuri], Ayatollah Yahya, "The Islamic Concept of the State," *Hamdard Islamicus* 3, no. 3, Autumn 1980, 71–92.

Nordlinger, Eric A., *Conflict Regulation in Divided Societies*, Cambridge: Harvard University Center for International Affairs, Occasional Paper 29, 1972.

Nuri, Ayatollah Allameh, *Hokumat-e Islami va Tahlili az Nehzat-e Hazer* [Islamic Government and an Analysis of the Present Movement], Tehran: Bonyad-e Elmi va Islami, 2nd edn., 1360 [1981/82].

Nyrop, Richard F. (ed.), *Iran: A Country Study*, Washington, DC: American University Press, 1978.

Pahlavanian, H. L., *Iranahay Hamaynk: 1941–1979* [Iranian–Armenian Community], Erevan, Armenia: Khach Ga Publishers, 1989.

Paidar, Parvin, *Women and the Political Process in Twentieth-Century Iran*, Cambridge: Cambridge University Press, 1995.

Pirnazar, Jaleh, "Jang-e Jahaniye Dovom va Jameeh-ye Yahud dar Iran" [The Second World War and the Jewish Community in Iran], in Sarshar, *Terua: Yahudian-e Irani dar Tarikh-e Moaser*, vol. I.

"The Place of Islam in the Persian Constitution," *Muslim World* 1, no. 3, July 1911, 341–42.

Potter, Simeon, *Language in the Modern World*, Baltimore: Penguin Books, 1960.

Pye, Lucian, *Politics, Personality and Nation-Building*, New Haven: Yale University Press, 1962.

Rabushka, Alvin and Shepsle, Kenneth A., *Politics in Plural Societies: A Theory of Democratic Instability*, Columbus, OH: Charles E. Merrill, 1972.

Rahman, Fazlur, *Islam*, 2nd edn., Chicago: University of Chicago Press, 1969.

Rain, Ismail, *Iranian-e Armani* [Iranian Armenians], Tehran: Tehran Publishers, 1949.

Ramakrishna, Sri, *The Gospel of Sri Ramakrishna*, New York: Swami Nikhilananda, 1942; 8th edn., 1992.

Ramazani, Rouhollah K., *Revolutionary Iran*, Baltimore: Johns Hopkins University Press, 1986.

Rasooli, Jay M. and Allen, Cady H., *The Life Story of Dr. Sa'eed of Iran: Kurdish Physician to Princes and Peasants, Nobles and Nomads*, Pasadena, CA: William Carey Library, 1983.

Rodinson, Maxime, "The Notion of Minority in Islam," in Chaliand, Gerard (ed.), *Minority Peoples in the Age of Nation-States*, London: Pluto Press, 1989.

Ronen, Dov, *The Quest for Self-Determination*, New Haven: Yale University Press, 1979.

Rosen, Barry M. (ed.), *Iran Since the Revolution: Internal Dynamics, Regional Conflicts and the Superpowers*, New York: Brooklyn College Studies on Society in Change, Social Science Monographs 47, Boulder, distributed by Columbia University Press, 1985.

Rothchild, Donald, "Ethnicity and Conflict Resolution," *World Politics* 22, no. 4, July 1970, 597–616.

Rothschild, Joseph, *Ethnopolitics: A Conceptual Framework*, New York: Columbia University Press, 1981.

Russell, James R., "Christianity in Pre-Islamic Persia: Literary Sources," in *Encyclopaedia Iranica*, vol. V.

Zoroastrianism in Armenia, Cambridge, MA: Harvard University Press, 1987.

Saidian, Abdol-Hossein, *Sarzamin va Mardom-e Iran* [The Land and the People of Iran], Tehran: Ilm va Zendegi, 1369 [1990/91].

Salzman, Philip Carl, "The Proto-State in Iranian Baluchistan," in Cohen, Ronald and Service, Elman R. (eds.), *Origins of the State: An Anthropology of Political Evolution*, Philadelphia: Institute for the Study of Human Issues, 1978.

"Why Tribes Have Chiefs: A Case from Baluchistan," in Tapper, *Conflict of Tribe and State*.

Sanasarian, Eliz, "The Islamic Republican Party," in *Oxford Encyclopedia of the Modern Islamic World*, New York: Oxford University Press, 1995, 312–15.

"Review Essay: Iran and the Revolution," *Iranian Studies* 19, nos. 3–4, Summer–Autumn 1986, 283–89.

"State Dominance and Communal Perseverance: The Armenian Diaspora in the Islamic Republic of Iran, 1979–1989," *Diaspora* 4, no. 3, Winter 1995, 243–65.

Sarshar, Homa (ed.), *Terua: Yahudian-e Irani dar Tarikh-e Moaser* [Terua: The History of Contemporary Iranian Jews], vol. I, Beverly Hills: Center for Iranian Jewish Oral History, 1996.

Yahudian-e Irani dar Tarikh-e Moaser [The History of Contemporary Iranian Jews], vol. II, Beverly Hills: Center for Iranian Jewish Oral History, 1997.

Savory, Roger, *Iran Under the Safavids*, Cambridge: Cambridge University Press, 1980.

Schahgaldian, Nikola B., *The Clerical Establishment in Iran*, Santa Monica, CA: Rand Corporation, 1989.

The Iranian Military Under the Islamic Republic, Santa Monica, CA: Rand Corporation, 1987.

Schermerhorn, R. A., *Comparative Ethnic Relations: A Framework for Theory and Research*, New York: Random House, 1970.

Schwartz, Richard Merrill, "Missionaries on the Rezaiyeh Plain, Iran," *Muslim World* 69, no. 2, April 1979, 77–100.

The Structure of Christian–Muslim Relations in Contemporary Iran, Occasional Papers in Anthropology 13, Halifax, Nova Scotia, Canada: Saint Mary's University, 1985.

Sears, William, *A Cry from the Heart: The Bahais in Iran*, Oxford: George Ronald, 1982.

Segev, Sammy, *The Iranian Triangle: The Untold Story of Israel's Role in the Iran–Contra Affair*, New York: Free Press, 1988.

Sethna, T. R., *Amoozeshhaye Zarthosht: Payambar-e Iran* [Teachings of Zoroaster: The Prophet of Iran], transl. and commentary by Rostam Mobed Shahzadi, Karachi, Pakistan: Farhangarayi, 1975.

Shahrokh, Shakrokh and Writer, Rashna (eds. and transls.), *The Memoirs of Keikhosrow Shahrokh*, Lewiston, NY: Edwin Mellen Press, 1994.

Shahzadi, Mobed Bahram, *Message of Zarathushtra*, Religious Instruction, vol. I, Westminster: California Zoroastrian Center, 1986.

Short, Martin and McDermott, Anthony (ed.), *The Kurds*, 4th rev. edn., London: Minority Rights Group, Report 23, 1981.

Simpson, George Eaton and Yinger, J. Milton, *Racial and Cultural Minorities: An Analysis of Prejudice and Discrimination*, 3rd edn., New York: Harper & Row Publishers, 1965.

Simpson, John, "Along the Streets of Tehran: Life Under Khomeini," *Harper's Magazine*, January 1988, 36–45.

Inside Iran: Life Under Khomeini's Regime, New York: St. Martin's Press, 1988.

Sitton, David, *Sephardi Communities Today*, Jerusalem: Council of Sephardi and Oriental Communities, 1985.

Smith, Anthony D., *The Ethnic Revival*, Cambridge: Cambridge University Press, 1981.

Smith, Peter, *The Babi and Baha'i Religions: From Messianic Shi'ism to a World Religion*, New York: Cambridge University Press, 1987.

"A Note on Babi and Baha'i Numbers in Iran," *Iranian Studies* 13, nos. 2–3, Spring–Summer 1984, 295–302.

Smith, Peter (ed.), *Studies in Babi and Baha'i History*, vol. III, Los Angeles: Kalimat Press, 1986.

Soroudi, Sorour, "The Concept of Jewish Impurity and Its Reflection in Persian and Judeo-Persian Traditions," in Shaked, Shaul and Netzer, Amnon (eds.), *Irano-Judaica III*, Jerusalem: Ben-Zvi Institute, 1994.

"Jews in Islamic Iran," *Jewish Quarterly* 21, Fall 1981, 98–114.

Stagner, Ross, "Foreword," in Boucher, Jerry, Landis, Dan and Arnold, Karen Clark (eds.), *Ethnic Conflict and International Perspectives*, Beverly Hills, CA: Sage Publishers, 1987.

Staudt, Kathleen A., "Sex, Ethnic and Class Consciousness in Western Kenya," *Comparative Politics* 14, 1982, 147–67.

Stiles, Susan, "Early Zoroastrian Conversions to the Bahai Faith in Yazd, Iran," in Cole, Juan R. and Momen, Moojan (eds.), *From Iran East and West*, Los Angeles: Kalimat Press, 1984.

Sundermann, Werner, "Christ in Manicheism," in *Encyclopaedia Iranica*, vol. V.

Suny, Ronald Grigor, *Looking Toward Ararat: Armenia in Modern History*, Bloomington: Indiana University Press, 1993.

Tabandeh, Sultanhussein, *A Muslim Commentary on the Universal Declaration of Human Rights*, London: Goulding & Co., 1970.

Tafti, H. B. Dehqani, *Moshkel-e Eshq* [The Problem of Love], Newport Beach, CA: Gutenberg Press, 1364 [1985/86].

Taheri, Amir, "Deep Roots in the Land," *Armenian Review* 22, no. 2, Summer 1969, 45–48.

Taleqani, Seyyed Mahmud, *Partovi az Quran* [A Ray from the Quran], vol. I, Tehran: Sahami-ye Enteshar, 1358 [1979].

Tapper, Richard (ed.), *The Conflict of Tribe and State in Iran and Afghanistan*, London: Croom Helm, 1983.

Frontier Nomads of Iran: A Political and Social History of the Shahsevan, Cambridge: Cambridge University Press, 1997.

"History and Identity Among the Shahsevan," *Iranian Studies* 21, nos. 3–4, 1988, 84–108.

"Shahsevan," in Weekes, *Muslim Peoples*, vol. II.

Ter Hovhanyants, Harutiun T. (compil.), *Patmutiwn Nor Jughayi* [History of the New Julfa], Isfahan: New Julfa Vank, vol. I, 1980, vol. II, 1981.

Van Bruinessen, Martin, "Kurdish Tribes and the State of Iran: The Case of Simko's Revolt," in Tapper, *Conflict of Tribe and State*.

Wallerstein, Immanuel, "The Two Modes of Ethnic Consciousness," in Allworth, Edward (ed.), *The Nationality Question in Soviet Central Asia*, New York: Praeger, 1973.

Walsh, Harry W., "Azeri," in Weekes, *Muslim Peoples*, vol. I.

Waterfield, Robin E., *Christians in Persia: Assyrians, Armenians, Roman Catholics and Protestants*, London: George Allen & Unwin Ltd., 1973.

Weekes, Richard V. (rev. and ed.), *Muslim Peoples: A World Ethnographic Survey*, 2 vols., 2nd edn., Westport, CT: Greenwood Press, 1984.

Wirsing, Robert G., *The Baluchis and Pathans*, London: Minority Rights Group, Report 48, 1981.

Wirth, Louis, "The Problem of Minority Groups," in Kurokawa, Minako (ed.), *Minority Responses: Comparative Views of Reactions to Subordination*, New York: Random House, 1970.

Yacoub, Joseph, *The Assyrian Question*, Chicago: Alpha Graphics, 1986.

Yarshater, Ehsan, "Communication," *Iranian Studies* 22, no. 1, 1989, 62–65.

Ye'or, Bat, *The Dhimmi: Jews and Christians Under Islam*, transl. David Maisel, Paul Fenton, and David Littman, Toronto: Fairleigh Dickinson University Press, 1985.

Young, Crawford, *The Politics of Cultural Pluralism*, Madison: University of Wisconsin Press, 1976.

Zanjani, Ayatollah Abbas-Ali Amid, *Hoquq-e Aqaliatha* [Legal Rights of Minorities], Tehran: Nashr-e Farhang-e Islami, 1362 [1983/84].

Zenian, David, "The Islamic Revolution: A Blessing in Disguise for Iranian-Armenians," *AGBU [Armenian General Benevolent Union] News*, September 1991, 8–11.

Zenner, Walter P., "Middleman Minorities and Genocide," in Walliman, Isidor and Dobkowski, Michael N. (eds.), *Genocide and the Modern Age: Etiology and Case Studies of Mass Death*, New York: Greenwood Press, 1987.

Zonis, Marvin, *The Political Elite of Iran*, Princeton: Princeton University Press, 1971.

Zubaida, Sami, "An Islamic State?: The Case of Iran," *Middle East Report* 153, July–August 1988, 3–7.

DOCUMENTS AND OTHER SOURCES

Aghayan, Felix, interview recorded by Habib Ladjevardi, 5 March 1986, Paris, France, tape 1, Iranian Oral History Collection, Harvard University.

Amnesty International, *Iran Briefing*, London: Amnesty International Publications, 1987.

  Iran: Violations of Human Rights 1987–1990, New York: AI USA, December 1990.

Asnad-e Mohajerat-e Yahudian-e Iran be Felestin: 1300–1330 Hejrieh Shamsi [Immigration Documents of Iranian Jewry to Palestine, 1921–1951], compil. Marzieh Yazdani, Tehran: Entesharat-e Sazeman-e Asnad-e Melli-ye Iran, 1374 [1995/96].

Dar Maktab-e Jomeh: Majmueh-ye Khotbehhaye Namaz-e Jomeh-ye Tehran [In Friday Congregration: Collection of Tehran Friday Prayer Sermons], vol. I, 1st to 25th week, Tehran: Vezarat-e Ershad-e Islami, Tir 1364 [July 1985]; vol. II, 26th to 70th week, Tehran: Vezarat-e Ershad-e Islami, Day 1364 [January 1986].

Human Rights Watch, *Human Rights Watch World Report 1995*, New York: Human Rights Watch, 1995.

  Human Rights Watch World Report 1996, New York: Human Rights Watch, 1996.

  Iran: Religious and Ethnic Minorities, Discrimination in Law and Practice, vol. 9, no. 7, New York, September 1997.

International Solidarity Front for the Defense of the Iranian People's Democratic Rights (ISF-Iran), *The Crimes of Khomeini's Regime*, n.p.: ISF-Iran, May 1982.

Iran Almanac 1977, Tehran: Echo of Iran, 16th edn., 1977.

Iran Yearbook '88, 1st edn., Bonn: Moini-Biontino Verlagsgesellschaft, 1988.

Majmueh-ye Qavanin-e Avalin Dorehye Majlis-e Shoraye Islami 7 Khordad 1359 to 6 Khordad 1363 [Collection of Laws of the First Islamic Consultative Assembly, 28 May 1980–27 May 1984], Tehran: Edareh-ye Kol-e Omur-e Farhangi va Ravabet-e Omumi, Majlis-e Shoraye Islami, 1st printing 1363 [1984/85], 2nd printing 1366 [1987/88].

Mashruh-e Mozakerat-e Majlis-e Shoraye Islami [Proceedings of the Discussions of the Islamic Consultative Assembly] or (later) *Ruznameye Rasmi:*

Mozakerat-e Jalaseye Alani-ye Shoraye Islami, Tehran: Majlis-e Shoraye Islami.

Middle East Watch, *Guardians of Thought: Limits on Freedom of Expression in Iran*, New York: Human Rights Watch, August 1993.

Moarefi-ye Nemayandegan-e Dovomin Dorehye Majlis-e Shoraye Islami [Introduction of Deputies in the Second Islamic Consultative Assembly], Tehran: Ravabet-e Omumi-ye Majlis, Mehr 1364 [September/October 1985], 2nd ed. 1366 [1987/88].

Nategh, Homa, interview recorded by Zia Sedghi, 1 April 1984, Paris, France, tapes 1 and 3, Iranian Oral History Collection, Harvard University.

National Spiritual Assembly of the Bahais of Iran, *The Banning of Bahai Religious Institutions in Iran: An Open Letter* (transl. from Persian), 12 Shahrivar 1362 [3 September 1983].

Negareshi be Avalin Dorehye Majlis-e Shoraye Islami [A Look at the First Islamic Consultative Assembly], Tehran: Ravabet-e Omumi-ye Majlis, 1364 [1985/86].

The Random House Dictionary of the English Language, unabridged edn., New York: Random House, 1983.

Surat-e Mashruh-e Mozakerat-e Majlis-e Barrasi-ye Nahaiye Qanun-e Asasiye Jomhuri-ye Islami-ye Iran [Proceedings of the Final Review of Majlis Discussions on the Constitution of the Islamic Republic of Iran], Tehran: Department of Cultural and Public Affairs of the Majlis, Azar 1364 [November/December 1985].

"Tarh-e Sarshomari-ye Ejtemai – Eqtesadi-ye Ashayer-e Koochandeh – Marhaleye Aval 1364" [Plan for the Socioeconomic Census of Migrant Tribes – First Period 1985/86], in *Gozide-ye Mataleb-e Amari* [Selections from Statistical Items], 3rd year, no. 15.

United Nations, Economic and Social Council, Commission on Human Rights, 39th session, *Annex II: Note Verbale Dated 3 February 1983 from the Permanent Mission of the Islamic Republic of Iran, Annex III: Statement Submitted by the Bahai International Community*, E/CN.4/1983/19, 13 January–11 March 1983.

    47th session, Agenda Item 12, *Report on the Human Rights Situation in the Islamic Republic of Iran by the Special Representative of the Commission on Human Rights, Mr. Reynaldo Galindo Pohl, Pursuant to Commission Resolution 1990/79*, E/CN.4/1991/35, 13 February 1991.

    51st session, Agenda Item 12, *Question of the Violation of Human Rights and Fundamental Freedoms in Any Part of the World, with Particular Reference to Colonial and Other Dependent Countries and Territories*, E/CN.4/1995/55, 16 January 1995.

United Nations, General Assembly, 43rd Session, Agenda Item 12, *Situation of Human Rights in the Islamic Republic of Iran*, A/RES/43/137, 31 January 1989.

    45th Session, Agenda Item 12, *Report of the Economic and Social Council: Situation of Human Rights in the Islamic Republic of Iran – Note by the Secretary General*, Part III, A/45/697, 6 November 1990.

    51st session, Agenda Item 110 (c), *Human Rights Questions. Human Rights Situations and Reports of the Special Rapporteurs and Representatives: Situation of Human Rights in Iran*, A/51/479, 11 October 1996.

US Department of State, *Country Reports on Human Rights Practices for 1982, 1983, 1984, 1985, 1991, 1994, 1997* (all published Washington, DC: Government Printing Office).
The World Almanac and Book of Facts 1998, Mahwah, NJ: World Almanac Books, 1998.

PRINT AND BROADCAST MEDIA

Alik
Armenian International Magazine (AIM)
Asbarez
Chashm Andaaz
Cheesta
Christian Mission to the Communist World, Inc.
Christian Science Monitor
Economist
Ettela'at International
FBIS
Gardoon
Hye Giank Weekly
Iran Times
Iran Zamin
IRNA/BBC
Jewish Chronicle
Jewish Quarterly
JPRS
Kayhan
Kayhan International
Kayhan (London)
L'Express
Los Angeles Times
Mojdeh
Nehzat
New York Times
Newsweek
Resalat
Time
The Times (London)

Index

Abadan, 75
Abd-al-Baha, 51, 52, 183n.94
Abduh, Mohammad, 22
Aghayan, Felix, 185n.115
Ahl al-Dhimma, 19, 20–21, 155
Ahl al-Ketab, 19, 20–21, 24, 25, 26, 27, 30,
   83, 85, 89, 122, 128, 131, 134, 139,
   144, 147
Ahvaz, 41, 43, 50, 105, 124
ajam, 21
Al-e Ahmad, Jalal, 33
Alliance Israelite Universelle, 46
Anzali, 75
apostate, 20, 53, 122, 124, 129, 130, 134
   law of apostasy, 45, 131, 135, 155
   Tabandeh, 26
Arab, 8, 9, 10, 14, 21, 24, 32, 47, 48, 49, 63,
   64, 67
Arak, 40
Ararat club and sports stadium, 78, 89, 90,
   191
Ardebili, Abdol-Karim Musavi, 17
Armenia,
   Republic 1918–20, 35, 39
   Soviet Socialist, 35, 39
   post-Soviet, 108, 157, 158, 202n.82
Armenian Apostolic Church, 34, 39, 77,
   148
Askari, Mehdi, 110
Ataturk, Kemal, 35, 38, 148, 205n.36
Azerbaijan,
   Iranian, 38, 41, 42, 43, 61, 202n.82
   Republic, 157, 158, 202n.82
Azeri, 9, 10, 14, 16, 41, 58, 63, 158,
   167n.39, 207n.17

Bab (Seyyed Ali Mohammad Shirazi), 50,
   183n.93
Babism, 50
Baghoomian, Artavaz, 95, 97, 148, 158
Bahaullah (Mirza Hossein Ali Nuri), 50,
   52, 183n.93
Bahonar, Mohammad-Javad, 17, 76

Bait Ushana, Sergen, 62, 66, 69, 70, 95, 96,
   99, 138, 139
Bakhtiari, 9, 10, 16
Baluch, 9, 11, 14, 63, 64, 69, 168n.39
Bani Quraizeh, 28
Bani Sadr, Abol-Hasan, 17, 93, 110, 116
Bazargan, Mehdi, 17, 28, 32, 58, 76, 115
Beheshti, Ayatollah Mohammad, 17, 32, 58,
   60, 61, 62, 63, 64, 65, 66, 68, 71, 72,
   76, 93
Borujerdi, Ayatollah Mohammad Hossein,
   52

Chaldean Philosophical and Theological
   College, 178n.42
Constitution (Islamic),
   Article 12, 17
   Article 13, 65–68, 70, 80, 83, 144, 154
   Article 14, 63
   Article 15, 80
   Article 16, 71
   Article 19, 161
   Article 26, 64
   Article 28, 144
   Article 64 (originally 50), 68–69
Constitutional Revolution, 38, 42, 46, 49,
   51–52, 54, 175n.9
conversion, 90, 129
   to Bahaism, 51, 122, 184n.96
   to Christianity, 24, 44, 92, 99, 124, 125,
   130
   to Islam, 20, 38, 45, 48, 109, 130–31
   to Zoroastrianism, 24
Council of Guardians, 88, 93, 95,
   187n.22
Cyrus the Great, 45, 161

Daneshrad, Aziz, 62, 63, 67, 70, 101,
   197n.102
Dar al-Harb, 21
Dar al-Islam, 21, 22, 23, 134
Dashnak, 101, 176n.9, 197n.106 and
   n.107

225

Titles in Series

For EU product safety concerns, contact us at Calle de José Abascal, 56–1°,
28003 Madrid, Spain or eugpsr@cambridge.org.

www.ingramcontent.com/pod-product-compliance
Ingram Content Group UK Ltd.
Pitfield, Milton Keynes, MK11 3LW, UK
UKHW010041140625
459647UK00012BA/1520